THE GREAT UNLEARNING

AWAKENING TO LIVING AN
ALIGNED AND AUTHENTIC LIFE

THE GREAT UNLEARNING

PHI DANG

Ⓚ THE KIND PRESS

Copyright © Phi Dang 2023
First published by the kind press, 2023

The moral right of the author to be identified as the author of this work has been asserted.

All rights reserved. Without limiting the rights under copyright reserved above, no part of this publication may be reproduced, stored in or introduced into a retrieval system, or transmitted, in any form or by any means (electronic, mechanical, photocopying, recording or otherwise) without the prior written permission of the publisher of this book.

A catalogue record for this book is available from the National Library of Australia.

Trade Paperback ISBN: 978-0-6453444-9-3
eBook ISBN: 978-0-6487927-8-9

Author photo: Ash, Candid Chaser Photography

Print information available on the last page.

The kind press acknowledges Australia's First Nations peoples as the traditional owners and custodians of this country, and we pay our respects to their elders, past and present.

THE
KIND
PRESS

www.thekindpress.com

We advise that the information contained in this book does not negate personal responsibility on the part of the reader for their own health and safety. The intent of the author is only to offer informative material on the subjects addressed in the publication to help you in your quest for emotional, physical, and spiritual well-being. While the publisher and author have used their best efforts in preparing this book, the material in this book is of the nature of general comment only. It is sold with the understanding that the author and publisher are not engaged in rendering advice or any other kind of personal or professional service in the book. In the event that you use any of the information in this book for yourself, the author and the publisher assume no responsibility for your actions.

This book is dedicated to, and made in memory of, my dad,
Dzung Dang.
I love you forever and always.
Thank you—for all that you've taught me.
Thank you—for loving me fiercely, even when I didn't recognise it.
Thank you—for all the times we had together, even if they were only brief in this lifetime.

My dad passed away from bowel cancer without recognising the symptoms.

In his memory, I would like to dedicate this page to some signs to watch out for:

Blood in your stool.
Obvious change in your bowel habits.
Weight loss you can't explain.
Extreme tiredness for no reason.
Lump or swelling in your abdomen.

Not everyone experiences symptoms, particularly in the early stages of bowel cancer. The above symptoms may be suggestive of bowel cancer, but they can also be due to other medical conditions, some foods or medicines. Don't delay talking to your doctor if you are experiencing any of the described symptoms for two weeks or more. When diagnosed early, almost 99 per cent of cases can be successfully treated. Blood in the stool or rectal bleeding should never be ignored. When in doubt, be on the safe side and speak to your doctor.

A portion of the proceeds from this book will be donated to Bowel Cancer Australia.

Source: Bowel Cancer Australia

CONTENTS

Introduction xi

Part I
SUCCESS

1	Success	3
2	Timelines	13
3	Busy, Busy, Busy	23
4	Massive Action, Or Is It?	31
5	Money, Money, Money	40
6	You Can Have It All	55

Part 2
SELF

7	Self-Identity	65
8	Self-Worth	73
9	Self-Love	83
10	Self-Care	93
11	Self-Body	103
12	Self-Pleasure	117
13	Self-Made	131

Part 3
INNER BEING

14	Thought Work	147
15	Happiness Is Everything	155
16	The Feels	162
17	Mental Health	172
18	Grief And Heartbreak	181
19	Light And Dark	193

Part 4
RELATIONSHIPS

20	Alonely	203
21	Ugh, Dating	212
22	Love Story	221
23	After The Love Story: Pleasure, Power & Liberation	235
24	We Are Family	249

Part 5
SPIRITUALITY

25	Spirituality Is Religion?	267
26	Time	274
27	Spiritual Breakthroughs	282
28	Gotta See It To Believe It	289
29	Life, Death And Beyond	301

The End...Of These Chapters	308
Acknowledgements	310
About The Author	313

INTRODUCTION

Dear beautiful soul, this book is not a guide or your stock-standard self-help (ahem: personal-development) book. If you're looking for that, there's a tonne of them—look at another shelf. Intrigued? Read on, I dare you.

This is *The Great Unlearning*.

From a young age, learning is indoctrinated within us. We are given an 'identity'—a name, an understanding of where we fit into our family, a religious status, a nationality and a race. At an early stage in life, we are told we have a great deal to learn as a child entering the 'real' world to become a 'proper' adult. That, in itself, instils us with the belief that we can't trust ourselves and that the truth comes from authority, people and places outside of ourselves.

As children, we're like sponges, soaking in and absorbing the world around us both consciously and unconsciously. From the moment we are born, we are perceptive to everything that is going on around us. Particularly, we are susceptible to what people are saying either to us or to another, such as 'that's not realistic', 'money doesn't grow on trees' and 'don't be like that. Why can't you be more…' These all go on to play a pivotal role in forming our beliefs. Maybe you were told to 'tone it down' or that 'you're too much', which has led you to shrink yourself and dim your light. Perhaps you believed that being a good person meant sacrificing yourself and that you had to put everyone else first.

Society and culture give us ideas of who we are meant to be and how we are meant to approach life, love, work, health and happiness. We are expected to follow a traditional path and timeline, which goes along the lines of attending school, receiving an education, getting a job, getting married and having kids, and all this supposedly leads to 'happy ever after'. Speaking of which, fairytales and what we see on TV and in the movies has led to this beautiful, idealised vision of what being in a relationship looks like. Social media leads us to believe success is being at the top of the career ladder, married with kids, living in a white-picket-fence home and that everyone else, except us, is always happy. Many of us will go on our whole lives without ever questioning these beliefs, falling deeply into the illusion that if we believe it—if it looks a certain way, because it's all we've ever known—then it must be true and it is how life is meant to be.

As a life coach who works with women and men around the world of all ages, I've come to realise that it's not that you need to learn more in life as you progress. You already know a lot. In fact, you already know too much that probably doesn't serve you (flashback to maths class: tan is sin/cos). The truth distilled from my experience is that there's a great deal to *unlearn*. My intention for this book is for it to be an awakening—medicine for your soul, a homecoming. Let me start by affirming that there's nothing wrong with you and that you're not broken. You don't need fixing or saving in any form, especially that of a knight in shining armour or Prince Charming. Your metaphorical cup has been filled to the brim with beliefs and conditioning and I'm here to help you empty it all out, not to fill it again but enable you to live with lightness, to just be. If you've learned a whole lot of shit that doesn't serve you… you can absolutely unlearn it and reclaim your power.

Unlearning is not a process but rather a journey, and in many ways it's a reckoning. It's like finding out Santa Claus isn't real, even though you held onto that belief for so long. It's like finding out that it wasn't the Tooth Fairy putting money underneath your pillow in exchange for your teeth but your mum instead. Unlearning isn't your typical hero's story of becoming anything or someone. This is *unbecoming* who the world taught you to be and dissolving everything that isn't you. This journey isn't for the faint-hearted. It can be uncomfortable and downright messy. It's burning down and shattering everything you thought you knew about yourself, others—including your loved ones—and the world around you. It's pouring on the gasoline and watching everything go down in flames. It's lifting the veil that has been covering and shielding your eyes. It's letting go with love and grace. It's swallowing your pride and dismantling your ego in what you thought was so true and real.

Unlearning is peeling back the layers of your belief system and conditioning. It's cracking open and shedding your skin like a snake. It's questioning everything you think you know and believe. It's placing a magnifying glass over your thoughts and examining them meticulously. It's untangling sticky stories and self-talk that play out in your head. It's being curious about your emotions and how you feel. It's the clearing of what you know so that you can rise from the ashes like a phoenix to who you really are and your inner truth. I know this sounds tricky, taxing and somewhat ironic, given that learning is easier, but it is my intention to show you that it is well worth it!

The beauty of unlearning is firstly that it's for you, but also, it's not *just* for you (we love a win-win situation). You're unlearning generations of thoughts and beliefs passed down your ancestral lines and cultural roots. You're unlearning for your family and future generations, which could mean your children, your grandchildren, your grandchildren's children, your grandchildren's children's children… (you get the point). You're unlearning for your friends and the greater good of the collective—everyone cohabiting Earth with you on this journey of life together.

You're in for a potent, powerful and life-changing ride. I'm so excited that you're here and, if I'm honest, a little nervous. As a first-generation Australian-Asian woman, growing up I was taught to keep things to myself. I was struck with the fear that if I shared things about myself then I would be perceived as weak, open to being attacked or taken advantage of, or that it may reflect poorly on my family/culture/gender (really, the list went on). Acknowledging and setting that aside, it's scary as a human to share because it makes us feel so vulnerable—I definitely feel that. Bless my mum… when I told her I was writing this book, first of all she was so proud and secondly, she told me that people only wanted positive stories to feel good. However, in honouring myself, you and the nature of being human, I'm actually going to share it all—the so-called good, bad and ugly, the light and the dark, the highs and the lows.

Before we dive in, there are a couple of things to note. All names in this book have been changed for the privacy of these real people in my world and life. All stories I share are from my own perspective and I acknowledge that these characters, who are actually people in my reality, may see or perceive events differently. I write this book as a heterosexual female with an Asian (Vietnamese and Chinese)-Australian cultural background. I consider myself a modern woman and share my experiences through this perspective. As a Woman of Colour, I'm passionate about being a voice in the personal-development space and an avid-embracing supporter of all people, irrespective of gender, labels and culture. I welcome anyone and all to read this book and hope that if you don't identify or relate directly with what I share or the language I use, you can still get something out of what I write. As with all things, please use your discernment: take what resonates and discard what doesn't.

Now, let's get into it and burn it all down…

Here's to *The Great Unlearning*…

Your Great Unlearning.

Part I
SUCCESS

The old status symbols for success were a fast car, a big house and millions… billions of dollars. The ultimate new flex is freedom, joy and inner peace—to live a life where your soul is pure love and happiness; where your highest self is realised; where your inner child is seen, heard and loved; where you find security in yourself and not others or things. It's a life that your ancestors would be proud of; a life that's a dream. Unlearn what you think you know is success and redefine what it means to you.

SUCCESS

THE LEARNING
Success means having money, being in a relationship and at the peak of your career.

You want success. I want success. We want success. Everyone wants success! We crave success because we believe the most successful people are the happiest. For many of us, it is dictated and defined by the people around us and what we see in others—especially our parents. We want to live up to what we believe are their expectations and to make them proud. This was definitely the case for me as a child of refugees who fled a war-torn country and left everything behind for a better life.

When we throw society into the mix, it gets confusing. We're told mixed messages that success means being nice, selfless and content in life, yet this is contrasted by undertones of feeling like it's all one big competition where you need to be the 'best'—the ultimate winner takes all. This inevitably cascades into comparison such as being triggered by someone who is younger than you. *They're only 20 years old! When I was 20 years old, I could barely figure out my university timetable, yet she's managed to achieve all of this already!?*

By societal terms, on a surface level, the greatest marker of success appears to be money, which is propelled by what we see on social media. We see those with money able to enhance their appearance, live in fancy homes and drive nice cars. We see money as the gateway to opportunity, freedom and security. However, this can be all smoke and mirrors to manufacture the illusion of the dream, of success.

You hear it thrown around casually and in all the self-development books that money doesn't buy you happiness. I would always roll my eyes and think deep down *well, maybe not, but I'd rather cry in a mansion and Ferrari, that's for sure.* However, have you ever *actually* stopped for a moment to consider what your definition of success is and why?

If you haven't, life has a funny way of getting you to do so—to reconsider and re-evaluate your success. When I first started to write this chapter, I struggled to put words to paper because I was going through a huge life transition that had shaken up the meaning of success to me. But now, I'm on the other side.

I'm writing this after having resigned from the corporate world as part of the 'Great Resignation'. The Great Resignation is a trend that has seen many people leave their corporate jobs after the COVID-19 pandemic longing for more fulfilment, freedom and flexibility in life. I am now a full-time life coach in my own business and my definition of success has changed multiple times.

Just before I quit my job to become a full-time life coach, on paper I 'had it all'. In a similar way to when you date someone, they might seem 'perfect' on paper, but something feels off. I lived in a beautiful two-bedroom apartment by the beach with my long-term boyfriend. I finally hit six figures in my salary (every refugee child's dream). I had incredible and supportive friends. But deep down, there was an emptiness exacerbated by the fact that I seemingly had it all, but I didn't feel happy.

Let's explore why this was the case. I barely had time to go to the beach and spend time with my boyfriend because I was either working or too stressed from work to appreciate the time we spent together. I had all this money, but I was using said money to recover from burnout at work with massages and wellness retreats to retail therapy and actual therapy. My friends weren't a priority as I was focusing on my career—my corporate job and building my business as a side hustle.

THE UNLEARNING
Success isn't clear-cut or one size fits all, it's something you define on your own.

On the surface, my corporate career was a consistent and fast rise up the ladder (not without its obstacles and hiccups). However, behind the scenes, there was turmoil, panic attacks and dark nights of the soul. A dark night of the soul is where you experience an existential crisis. You question yourself and life because you are achingly miserable. When it happened, I blamed work. Now as I write this, I hold no anger, sadness or hate because I don't identify as a victim anymore. For a while I did though because I was dejected and dispirited. In hindsight, I take responsibility for staying in a situation which depleted my soul. Many of us do the same thing. If you're reading this and are experiencing something similar, I send you all my love and compassion; I see you.

Before I'd resigned, I knew for a long time that I wanted to quit. I craved freedom on so many levels—physically, mentally and emotionally. Whether it was online or in my day-to-day life, I would see people working from cafes all over the world with envy for the freedom they had. They seemed to be mythical humans. That's when I questioned, *could that be me one day too? That maybe they weren't any more special than me.*

My career had been tumultuous because a majority of my bosses made my life hell. As a result, I had an unhealthy and untrue belief that older single female bosses were awful. I thought that they weren't as compassionate and understanding as their happily-married-with-children counterparts, but ruthless robots who wanted you to churn out work at all costs. They would double down on you because their personal life dissatisfaction and unhappiness spread like a disease into the workplace and, as a result, your life.

Under their management, I worked incredibly long hours, was criticised, micromanaged and encouraged to compete with colleagues. This was all under the guise of, 'I'm doing this to help you!' One time I walked out on one who told me I couldn't leave work at 7pm despite working weeks and weeks from 8am–8pm. When I told the senior leadership team, their response was, 'She's just jealous and new to being a manager.' Another example was another that told me I wasn't allowed to wear skirts above my knees in the workplace, yet she did exactly that. The worst one piled on my workload to the point where I had regular mental health breakdowns. Over the years it started as panic attacks and reached its crescendo when I developed high blood pressure despite being in my early twenties (more on that in the 'Mental Health' chapter). As a result, my doctor got involved and I was allowed stress leave. The day of my return I told said boss that my psychologist requested a check in with me at 3pm. She flew into a rage and told me that I had to take 'personal' appointments in my own time not during work hours.

Whilst I wanted to attribute it all to her, upon reflection I take responsibility for co-creating that experience by giving my power away. I was the last one standing on her team despite everyone else quitting due to her tyrannical behaviour. I wanted to be the 'good girl'. The good girl that said, 'everything's fine and I can handle anything'. The good girl that said yes to any request because she wanted to advance in her career quickly. The good girl that didn't speak her truth because she was scared to disappoint and make a 'fuss' or cause drama. The good girl that naively always saw the best in people and hoped that it would somehow change without any shred of evidence.

To this day, I am grateful for this traumatic yet truly transformational experience. If it didn't happen, who knows who I would be and where I would be? In the aftermath of this experience, new management came in and finally got rid of said boss. Temporarily, life became so much sweeter, *la dolce vita*, however, the underlying workload and pressure did not.

I experienced an avalanche of burnouts, with each one getting worse. I was alive but my soul was clinging on for dear life. I was so miserable. I could barely get out of bed because I was shaking nonstop. I spent a lot of time throwing up from crippling anxiety.

I wanted to retreat from the world. I hated when people asked how work was going because I would lie through my teeth and say everything was great. On social media, it looked like I was living the dream, but the reality was far from it.

Hearing email notifications would send me into overdrive. I would dream about work and then wake up to go to work. This vicious repetitive cycle made me realise that I could no longer keep it up and one day it may get to the point of no return. I was the metaphorical bird sitting on a branch scared to leave but it was time to fly (this coincidentally aligns with the Vietnamese meaning of my name, which means flying high).

It was time for me to actually do something about my unhappiness— to take the leap of faith and go all in making my side hustle life coaching into a full-time business. This leap of faith represented something huge not only for me but for my parents, my ancestors before me and for generations to come. It was about breaking free from the learned conditioning of success and safety in order to connect with my own version of success and happiness.

I had to trust that no matter what happened after I quit my job, I would be able to handle it. I ran through all the scenarios in my head, such as working jobs I never considered or thought I was 'above', such as moving back home and living off instant noodles. Thinking about every possibility gave me a sense of control when my life felt completely out of control. I was at the mercy of my body, which was understandably protesting the immense stress I was putting it under. I was at the mercy of my conditioned self who couldn't possibly leave a safe job and take a risk after making countless sacrifices to get to where I was today.

From the thought of resigning to actioning it, I felt such a mixture of emotions. It felt like constant rolling waves going from high highs to low lows, ebbs and flows. Two emotions in particular kept coming up to the surface.

The first emotion was guilt. The root of my guilt stems from the conditioning and programming I had as a first-generation child of refugee parents. My parents fled the Vietnam War for a better life in Australia. The life I was living was everything they had desired for me. In fact, even my mum admitted candidly to me that she was jealous I had so many opportunities and freedom that she never had at my age. Here I was 'throwing' that away for my dream.

Here's the thing about guilt... it's not just from one thing. Often, guilt piles on and weighs heavily. I felt guilty for being 'ungrateful'. Sure, I was miserable but at least I had a stable income, a roof over my head and food to eat. I had guilt because at this point in my life, not only did I have to take care of myself, but I was also supporting my mum financially. This guilt has been and will always remain on my shoulders as an only child and the only family left for my mum. I had guilt at work because we were drowning under a sea of work and everyone on the team was already stressed... *what would they do without me? Will they be okay?* Whilst they were my colleagues, they were also my friends that I deeply cared about.

The second emotion was fear—fear of whether it was all going to work out. I went into all the scenarios: *I'm going to end up homeless, I'm not going to have any money, I'm going to be the laughingstock of everyone I know.* A part of me had doubt... *Can I really do this? Who am I? I'm just some cute unassuming Asian-Australian girl, people aren't going to take me seriously...* These thought loops were useful in one aspect because eventually I came to a turning point. Throughout our lives, we're conditioned to believe that failure is a bad thing. I had to unlearn that one real quick. I asked myself, *what's the worst thing about failure? Nothing.* Failure, like many things, is what we make it.

I realised that the worst thing isn't failure, but not even trying at all! Avoiding failure is also avoiding success. When you make mistakes and fail, you learn faster and quicker ... so the decision was made. When I decided to resign, I finally not only felt but also embodied the mantra that money doesn't make you happy. I could've been offered any salary, but nothing was going to sway my mind.

My hands trembled as I wrote the letter, called my boss and hit the send button to make it official. Even though I was firm in my decision, I still felt scared, anxious and uncertain. However, deep down, there was a knowing that everything would be okay and I'd be supported. Many people have since told me that I made a big, bold move. Many said it was crazy in a post-pandemic world where jobs are scarce and the competition is fierce, yet here I am. I happily and willingly gave my job to somebody else.

Now, I'm my own boss full-time. I used to think success was money and my job title. Now, I feel truly successful because I make enough money to live a comfortable life without sacrificing my mental and physical health. I truly love what I do so it doesn't feel like a job. I wake up excited to work and start every day with a beautiful ocean swim. I feel so incredibly happy. Initially it was a foreign feeling not to be stressing out all the time but now it's the norm for me! I am at peace and appreciate everything I have in life and everyone I know. I have the space and freedom to see friends and volunteer at my local soup kitchen more regularly.

Reflecting on life, I realise that success is being happy and content in life and that money doesn't buy happiness. Syed Balkhi said, 'Happiness is the new rich, inner peace is the new success, health is the new wealth and kindness is the new cool.' Success isn't clear-cut or one size fits all. *You* get to define what success means on your own terms and in your own time. In fact, success isn't a precursor to happiness. Sometimes you chase it at the cost of your happiness, becoming overwhelmed and overworked (just as I shared in my story). Just because you have money, the car, the house or the relationship, it doesn't mean you'll be happy.

Success could be the tingle and butterflies you feel doing your job. For others, success *is* money, fame and power. What matters is that you make it your own. When you distil it down, success is a mindset *and* a feeling. You might like to ask yourself these questions: Are you truly successful if you're not happy? Is your success more important than your physical and mental health? Is it success if it's not sustainable?

Remember, contrary to popular belief, success isn't linear. It can look like four steps forwards and three steps backwards. It doesn't have a defined state, timing or age. Your definition of success will be different to someone else's, and that's okay! Here's to your success… whatever that may be!

YOUR GREAT UNLEARNING

1. WHEEL OF LIFE

The Wheel of Life gives you a holistic snapshot and satisfaction measure of different areas of your life that are important to you. This gives you a foundation for you to redefine what success means to you. Using the template to the right, rank each category out of 1 to 10, feel free to amend the categories as you see fit.

Create your scale of measurement of what constitutes being the worst (1) and the best (10). For example of health, (1) could be eating very poorly and not exercising at all whereas (10) is exercising three times a week and sticking to your meal plan.

WHEEL OF LIFE

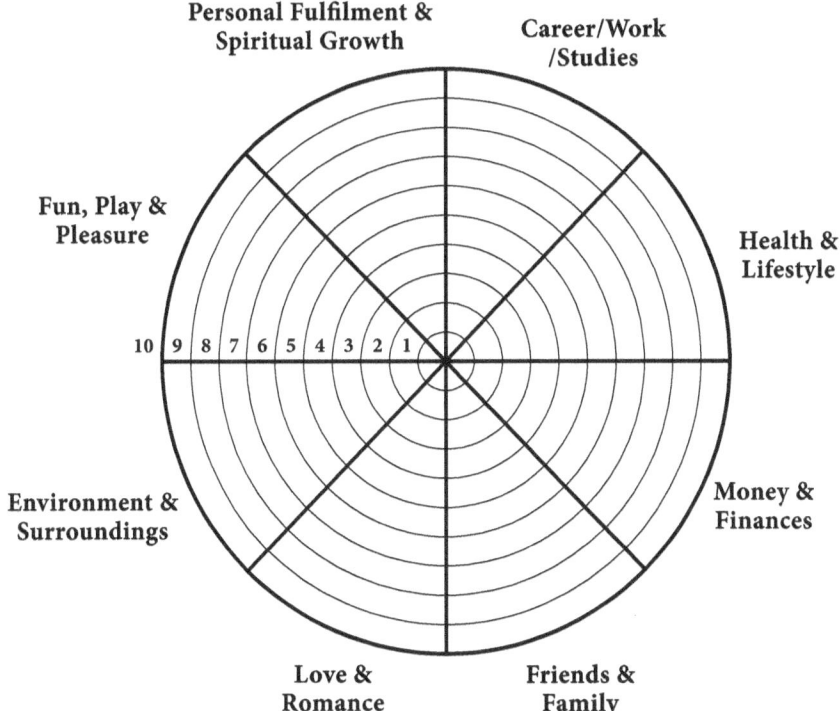

2. YOUR SUCCESS VALUES

Answer the following questions and based on those you're going to be able to identify your core values when it comes to success. Please note these may change over time and you can always come back to this exercise to refresh your success values.

- What helps you make big decisions in life?
  List the top 5 influences.
- Identify 5 times you were the happiest. What were you doing? Why were you so happy?
- What do you spend most of your free time doing?
  List 5 activities.

- Where do you spend most of your money? List 5 investments/expenses.
- Where does your mind spend most of its time? What are the majority of your thoughts about? What can't you stop thinking about? List 5.

After answering these questions, pay attention to common themes that emerge and group them to distil an important success value for you. For example, one may be freedom because you've identified when it comes to big decisions in life you don't want to be tied down so you can move countries some day and most of your thoughts are spent daydreaming about your next holiday. These values act as foundational cornerstones and a map in your definition of success.

3. REDEFINE SUCCESS

Based on the insights from your answers above, create a definition of success accordingly. Does it reflect your current beliefs about what you thought success was? How can you take tangible steps towards embodying your definition of success? Take into account not only what success looks like but also how you want it to make you *feel*.

TIMELINES

THE LEARNING
There's a set timeline of key milestones in life you need to achieve in order to be happy and fulfilled.

Do you feel behind in life? Maybe your career isn't as advanced as you'd like or you're struggling to pull together a house deposit. Maybe it feels like you haven't travelled enough or that your money is hanging in the closet instead of sitting in shares. Maybe you're the single one while everyone around you is getting engaged, married or popping out babies (who knows how many times you've tried to meet someone by swiping for hours). As you look around, it appears that everyone is living their best life and embodying their soul's purpose, except you. It seems like everyone around you has their shit together, and you missed the memo.

Here's the thing… you've unconsciously drunk the Kool Aid of the societal construct that life has set key milestones that you need to achieve to be happy, successful and fulfilled. It sounds like, '*I have to…*' and '*I should …*' by a certain time or age. It smells like success and status. It's the belief that life is linear—do this and then this happens, or if 'a' doesn't happen then 'b' and 'c' won't. It's the hope that a magical formula exists to make life perfect. So, when you haven't hit said milestones, you feel hungover on your huge expectations and comparisons to others and may have thoughts such as, '*I should be *insert achievement* at this age*' or '*everyone else is except me!*' You're not alone. Many of us experience this because of *timelines*.

From a young age, we're taught to think of life in terms of timelines and numbers. You start school at age five, you get your learner's licence at age sixteen, you go to university at age eighteen and you graduate at twenty-one. Then the timelines start to reference your career, love life, children, home, possessions and achievements, the list goes on. These are all the things you're *supposed* to be doing... I mean, can you even imagine a life where *there is no timeline?*

This is all exacerbated by the fact that we are suffering from 'comparisonitis', which is again conditioned as a young child at school (see a pattern emerging?). As children, we're constantly assessing ourselves based on others, whether it's grades, sport results or even house points. From there, we become stuck in the benchmark of the people around us, which is where I was once stuck too.

Click. Clack. Click Clack. The echoing sounds of my high heels were highly audible on the marbled floor as I made my way back up to the office. I'd just popped downstairs to get the standard 3pm pick-me-up-and-please-give-me-more-energy-and-focus liquid lifesaver (aka coffee).

I was wearing a big gold Michael Kors watch with champagne tones. To me, it was an elegant and stylish fashion accessory that carried a great weight of significance. My dad bought it for my nineteenth birthday before he passed away. I remember begging him for a watch like this—a strong statement piece. It was a status symbol for me. The watch screamed, 'Look at me! I have a fancy watch vibe! I'm special. I'm successful (at a young age, too!). Yes, I'm a #bossbabe!'

I was pushing to get it for my nineteenth birthday because I wanted something special after the milestone eighteenth birthday. I'd just started law school and all my new friends had nice new watches and attended private schools (my whole education was in the public system). I wanted to fit in so desperately and prove myself not to be a poor public school pleb. Comparing myself to them, at the age of nineteen they already seemed successful. They lived in huge houses with manicured lawns and perfect pools. They had fancy watches, designer bags, glamorous clothes, parties with unlimited bar tabs and nice cars.

Admittedly, my watch purchase was also inspired by the ever-so-chic character Rachel Zane in the TV series *Suits* played by Meghan Markle. In fact, I had googled what watch Rachel wore and copied her. Rachel was who you aspired to be in law school: she had big brains *and* big beauty. She was always so stylish and sophisticated in her crisp white shirts, pencil skirts and sky-high stilettos, which instantly imprinted in my mind that after law school, I needed to be just like Rachel! Meghan was so chic, successful and put together that she went on to marry a prince in real life (just saying).

Back to my story in the office… I was alone in the lift and checking myself out in the mirror (as you do). It's human nature to compare ourselves, whether it's to what we see or who is around us. The mirror covered the whole wall of the lift so the first thing you saw as you entered was your reflection staring back at you. I was impressed by what I saw. I was rocking my power outfit: a grey and baby blue striped blazer dress. This dress was my favourite, a classic menswear staple with a feminine and flirty twist. To match, I had brand new nude Tony Bianco heels (stunning beauties, but absolutely painful considering I hadn't broken them in). I'd just refreshed the roots of my hair and had a blow-dry. My make-up was on point—a natural polished look for work, of course. *This was the epitome of success and having it all together…. right?*

THE UNLEARNING
There are no set timelines in life.

One of my goals was to be a manager at age twenty-five. Technically I didn't achieve that, as I got promoted just as I turned twenty-six. It actually took me a while to reconcile with the fact that I was so close, but I'd missed it. I felt disappointed because I was meant to be aged twenty-five… this was not part of the plan!

I really had to push for this promotion. I felt I was behind schedule for that goal and career milestone. It was even impacting on my personal life, as I didn't receive a pay rise in time to secure a one-bedroom apartment to rent near the beach that I was yearning for (funnily enough, I now live in an apartment on that street, even closer to the beach, three years later). Instead, being in between places, I had to live with my mum an hour away from the city in the suburbs surrounded by families and married couples. Looking at the silhouette before me, even though on the outside it looked like I had it all together and I was successful, a twinge of sadness seeped within me.

I'd recently ended a 'situationship', feeling reluctantly heartbroken with my self-worth intact but bruised. A situationship is somewhere between a relationship and situation, although, let's be honest, more a situation. You're not officially together but you're doing all the things two people in a relationship would do without the commitment. Sound familiar? This was the second time I'd ended things with this guy after I gave him another chance—I thought he'd matured given he had just turned thirty. I had this belief that when he entered a new decade that he would magically mature overnight, finally be over his ex-girlfriend and be ready to commit to being in a serious relationship with me. Contrary to what dating columns and gurus had me believe, this experience taught me that commitment isn't an age thing, it's about being mentally, physically and emotionally ready.

Up until this point, I'd been single for eight years. My first and only boyfriend was my primary-school-turned-high-school sweetheart who cheated on me on a night out. It felt like salt to the wounds given earlier in the morning I'd been to a client meeting and vividly remember the advertising screen in the elevator promoting egg freezing (*great targeting work there from someone who worked in advertising herself at the time!*).

As the mind does, it flowed to another fleeting moment from my past: holding my grandpa's frail, leathery hand in hospital. It was such a sterile place—white, grey and clinical. I felt quite awkward because unlike many people I know, I'm not very close to my grandparents. In fact, I can't even speak to them because of language barriers. You see, I'm in the first generation of my family to be born in Australia. I'm the only child of divorced refugees. My parents fled the Vietnam War on a rickety boat and met serendipitously on the way to Australia. Truly a story of fate, my dad initially wanted to flee to America but there was no more room on the boat, so he ended up on the one to Australia which my mum was on. Honestly, it's wild to think I wouldn't be here without a war happening.

Growing up, there was always a conflict of values between the Australian way and the old-school, traditional Vietnamese way. I dreamed of being an artist, but my parents told me I needed a stable and well-paying job. My grandpa was the latter; he grew up strictly Roman Catholic, married my grandma at eighteen and had seven children (yes, seven children).

Being the first-born-in-Australia generation for my family, I wanted to fit in and didn't want to speak a foreign language. I wanted to be Australian, a true-blue Aussie however it was all stacked up against me. I didn't look like everyone else. There were no dolls or Disney Princesses, except Mulan, that looked like me. I wanted to have long, blonde hair and blue eyes instead I had short, black bowl-cut hair and dark brown eyes. Given all this, the last thing I wanted was funny sounding words coming out of my mouth.

My dad had told me I spoke fluent Vietnamese up until I went to primary school. Then, I completely forgot how to speak Vietnamese and struggled getting it back. Admittedly, at the time I was one of the only Asian-Australians at my school and my family would make fun of my Australian accent, which completely scarred me. I've since been told it was out of love for my 'cuteness' but as a child who didn't understand, it was traumatic. The memory of them laughing at me as I tried to speak Vietnamese to receive red packets of money during Lunar New Year is still etched in my mind. Growing up between two cultures was hard as I didn't feel like I was fully accepted and belonged in either worlds. At the best of times, I can still somewhat understand bits of Vietnamese and in this very moment with my grandpa, I did.

My aunt and uncle decided to leave me alone with him, which I dreaded because we can't communicate smoothly. It was awkward and disjointed. My grandpa, ông nội (as I called him in Vietnamese), asked me to hold his hand. He was in a sentimental mood. I learned later from my family that he didn't think he was going to make a full recovery, however he did.

He clenched my hand with as firm of a grip he could manage and said, 'Phi, when are you going to stop travelling the world, spending all your money and actually settle down? You know, find a husband? Have a family? Get a mortgage and buy a house? You're twenty-five years old; enough is enough. No more playing around. You're not getting any younger. In fact, you're getting older. Compared to your cousins, who all have partners, it makes me sad to see you alone and doing this. This is what your dad would have wanted for you if he was still alive…'

As he said this to me, I thought, *Yeah, I know Grandpa, I also thought this would all happen by twenty-five too…* Another vivid memory started playing in my mind: I'm sixteen years old scrapbooking, cutting out pictures from magazines and gluing them into a scrapbook. I'm thinking that I'll be married by age twenty-five, living in a white-picket-fence home with a big backyard in Sydney at twenty-six, a mother at twenty-seven, a CEO by thirty, retired by forty-five (the kids will be eighteen and independent by then, so Hubby and I can drive around Australia seeing the red dirt of the Northern Territory in a cute but chic campervan).

I can't pinpoint how I got this timeline in my head; however, I suspect it was from all the Disney movies I watched and what I saw on TV. I'll have you know that this is in contrast to what I would call the great stereotypical 'Vietnamese dream'. This one would first and foremost focus on having *the* career, graduating from university around age twenty-three with an undergraduate of medicine or law and somehow also have the time to be married at twenty-five, buy a home and fund your parents' retirement (you wouldn't dare let your parents live in a retirement home; it's still considered the ultimate insult and act of disrespect).

Back to the present day… I'd never considered getting my eggs frozen, but here I was at twenty-six, eight years single and not for lack of trying. I'd been on hundreds of dates and swiped thousands of online dating profiles… (*this may be a tad dramatic, but you get the point, the numbers were high!*). I really felt and believed that I'd missed the timeline and that there was a high probability of being single in my thirties. The hopeless romantic in me was just becoming hopeless. I pulled out my phone and added to my ever-growing makeshift to-do list in my notes: look up fertility options. But as they always say, 'When you aren't looking, you find it.' Funnily enough, once I accepted being single, I met Malcolm who I'd end up being in a relationship with for three years (more on that in the 'Love Story' chapter).

Timelines have been mostly imprinted subconsciously on our minds. We seem to be always working towards a timeframe, often speeding towards it. In fact, it's made us feel like we're always rushing to hit our next life milestone, whether it's love, money or career. I've since questioned where I got the idea that I *had* to be a manager at twenty-five with kids at twenty-seven, or my grandpa's belief that I should be in a serious relationship, considering marriage and buying a home at twenty-five.

The problem is that when we don't hit these timelines, we feel like failures. We feel like we're moving slower than those around us and it quickly turns into a crippling game of comparison. It's important to remember that life isn't a race and it isn't a competition. You may have had thoughts such as:

> 'Well, Sarah's my age, she's already married and owns her own property.'

> 'Well, Mandy and I started our jobs at the same time and she's already an associate director.'

> 'When my mum was my age, she already had kids!'

Have you ever questioned your thoughts and beliefs around timelines in life? Why do you have to get married by a certain age? Why do you have to be at the top of your career ladder by a particular age?

Do you have to live based on a timeline? Life is a string of moments, and each moment counts. Where you are right now is where you're meant to be. Life is a divine miracle unfolding in real time. At any moment, at any chance, life can change.

Lawyer Amal Clooney (née Alamuddin) met actor George Clooney when she was thirty-five, went on to marry him and have twins. Vera Wang entered the fashion industry at age forty and is now a household name. It's now even possible for women to have children at the age of fifty with the help of medical advancements.

Nothing in life is set in stone. You aren't getting on a bus with a set timetable (*we all know how reliable bus timetables are anyway...*). Think about it, more than seven billion people in this world can't hit every supposed life milestone at the same pace and order. Everything's right on time because it's *your* time. I'm reminding and reassuring you that you're exactly where you're meant to be. You're not too old, you're not too young, you're just here right now.

Maybe you're worried about going back to university and starting a new course aged twenty-nine that takes three years. By the time you finish, you'll be thirty-two. Whether or not you do the course, in three years, you'll still be thirty-two. You're nervous about never meeting 'the one' and you meet them aged thirty-seven. Are you upset you're aged thirty-seven or are you happily in love aged thirty-seven? The only thing that's keeping you behind is being fixed on a specific timeline. You can't be falling behind because *who* set the pace and tone anyway? You're allowed to move at your own pace. You're allowed to take your time. Life isn't linear but an open and organic canvas.

YOUR GREAT UNLEARNING

1. TIMELINE

On a piece of paper, draw out a horizontal line and insert particular milestones you believe you need to hit and at what age. For example:

- Married by thirty.
- Owning a property by thirty-three.
- Having kids by thirty-five.

Then, reflect on each milestone and ask yourself, *Where did I get this timeline from?* This is where you find out where you've learned timelines from in your life.

For example, perhaps you think you need to be married by thirty because when you were younger your Uncle Garry told your Aunt Barbara that the dating pool dwindles after thirty.

Next, grab a pen and destroy the timeline. Go on! Scribble on it. Crumple the paper. Set it on fire.

On another piece of paper, let's create a mind map. In the centre are your 'life intentions'. From there, branch it out with all the things you'd like to achieve and experience in your life. Before you jot down the societally typical norms such as marriage, mortgage and kids, ask yourself, *Do I really want this*?

That's better! A life designed according to your heart and soul, rather than a fixed timeline.

2. PERMISSION SLIP

Write yourself a permission slip and recite it out loud to yourself.

Here's an example, but I encourage you to tweak it and make it your own.

> Dear _____.
> I want to let you know that it's never too late.
> You're not behind.
> Everything's unfolding perfectly right now.
> I give you permission to live life on your own terms.
> I give you permission to take your time.
> I'm so proud of you.
> I love you.
> All my love, _____.

3. CELEBRATION JOURNAL

Keep a log of all your proudest moments and experiences in life. Ideally you would have something to celebrate everyday no matter how 'small' of an achievement or feeling it is.

It's important to keep comparisonitis at bay during this exercise. As psychologist Dr Rick Hanson says, 'The mind is like velcro for negative experiences and teflon for positive ones.' Drawing from neuroscience, we need to overcome the brain's natural negativity bias by rewiring our minds to be more conscious of the positives in life.

Return to your journal whenever you feel behind to remind yourself of all that you've already achieved and will continue to achieve.

BUSY, BUSY, BUSY

THE LEARNING
Being busy is a good thing and if you aren't busy, you're lazy and unproductive.

Forget the standard and basic 'good, thanks' when someone asks, 'how are you?' these days. The new norm is 'busy'. Forget expressing your feelings and your humanness, it's as if we're robots programmed to reply with what we're doing. Society has an obsession with the 'doing' mentality; it's an addiction to productivity. There's no better high than finding a way to multitask that while doing this or saving precious minutes to use on something else that also needs to be done. This societal programming has you conditioned to believe that in order to get what you want, you need to push, force and hustle. It doesn't feel safe to rest, otherwise you'll miss out and there's always something to do.

It can be hard to chill out because you might believe that everything you do should contribute towards something, whether it's dollars, likes or your life purpose. Accordingly, you can forget about doing passive things such as watching a movie because that won't help you get to the top of your career ladder. However, if you come up for air and realise that relaxing is important, that in itself can become a new wave of busy. You may feel inclined to squeeze in multiple meditations throughout your day, or cram in a gym class between your meetings. The pressure heats up because everyone on social media is always doing something. Given that, you can't possibly come home from work and enjoy microwaved leftovers while binging on Netflix. Instead, you should be dining at the new restaurant that just opened in the city (the bonus is that it'll be so social-media-worthy too).

Let's face it, being busy is a badge of honour in society, especially in the workplace. The metric of keeping your job is working hard or you can expect to be put out the door. Being busy means that you're important and responsible because you're always doing something. Being busy means being an overachiever, which is validated and praised by management. Being busy is the delectable carrot dangled over your head to run faster on the treadmill towards a promotion. Being busy means that you're making money, and if you're making money then you're a somebody, a champion, the people's people! No wonder we've equated busyness with our self-worth.

As a result, you take on more than you can handle, ignoring the whispers from your body. You'll smile and say yes to all the demands and requests while your soul screams NO! The word 'no' feels incomplete—you've always got to justify why you can't. The thought of that two-letter word in your mouth feels dirty and weak. As a result, your shoulders ache from the heaviness of all the 'shoulds' and 'musts'. Your eyes are always on the verge of tears from the overwhelm of life. You're far too busy to put yourself first.

We're told that it's not enough to be just as you are. As women especially, we're expected to be superwomen and juggle everything in balance. You've got to be the perfect woman, the perfect professional, the perfect partner, the perfect yogi, the perfect friend, the perfect sister, the perfect mum, the perfect housekeeper, the perfect chef, the perfect sexy siren… the never-ending list goes on.

To take the edge off stress and your discombobulated nervous system, you'll down a glass of wine, or two, or the whole damn bottle, and end up wretchedly hungover. You'll take something that elevates you into euphoria and come crashing down into reality. You'll sacrifice your sleep to try and get on top of your never-ending to-do list but end up exhausting yourself to the ground. You'll escape by fantasising about buying a one-way ticket to Europe instead of facing the real world. You'll try to justify everything as 'healthy stress', lifting heavy weights and running marathon distances, which leads to greater depletion of your wellbeing. You'll feast on all the food to numb the pain, only to throw it all back up. It's either that or you'll not eat at all, just to feel like you're in control. I know, because I've been there.

When my dad died, I was so scared to feel the emotions that came with grief that I'd keep myself busy. I was studying a double degree and attending all the lectures and tutorials in person, while also working four days a week in retail at Apple and two days tutoring English and Economics. At the same time, I was marketing executive of the Economics, Commerce and Finance Society as well as a member of a TedX Community at my university. I look back shocked because even though I was able to do it—it wasn't sustainable. This led to the demise of my health in the form of mental breakdowns, sleepless nights and heart palpations. I became a shell of who I was.

I'd try to recover, but the world kept screaming at me that busy was so much better. I went down the rabbit hole of 'busy' in the workplace. I'd clock late nights so often that the free dinner and cab home on work became a weekly ritual. I'd chug down countless coffees to keep going. I'd eat lunch at my desk to make the most of the time I had. I'd hold in my pee so I wouldn't waste time going to the bathroom. I was so worried about what other people would think if I didn't say yes to a project. I wanted to stay back later than everyone else to advance my career, being the 'hardest worker' in the room and the one my boss could rely on. There were such high expectations placed on me to get projects done, otherwise I'd be letting down my team.

I was made to feel 'over-sensitive' or 'a poor performer who didn't care' for needing time out to properly rest. It felt like I worked 24/7, if you count the obsessive need to check my emails first thing in the morning and just before bed to make sure I didn't miss anything. Even when I left the relentless hamster wheel of the corporate world to go full time in my own business, being busy was so deeply ingrained in my blood and bones. It was a shock to the system not to be working at least five days a week. I felt as if I had to still always be working in my business, which led to wobbly boundaries, speaking to clients around the clock with no regard for my own wellbeing. If I wasn't busy, I felt deeply guilty and as if I was doing something wrong.

THE UNLEARNING

You're a human being, not a human doing. Stop living by 'shoulds' and start listening to your soul.

I've learned what it's like to simply 'be' and truly live through my travels. A pivotal point was in Bali where I attended a silent retreat near Ubud. Silence isn't common in society these days. Supposedly, women speak an average of 20,000 words a day. In fact, silence can be scary and uncomfortable because it's foreign and unfamiliar. At this retreat, I practised the art of *nothing*. I also did a digital detox while I was at it. The retreat itself was so beautiful, large luscious green fields of rice nestled at the base of the holy Batukaru Mountain. A serene silence fell over the land, so much so you could hear the gentle swaying of the paddy stalks. At first, the silence was strange. I felt anxious hearing my own thoughts, panicking about whether I'd survive not talking.

Everything at the retreat was done from a place of stillness and presence: lying down on the grass watching the clouds go by. Meditating to the sound of running water trickling down hollowed bamboo shoots. Crunching on cassava chips and slowly sipping steaming hot turmeric tea. Savouring the salty sweetness of sweet potato 'bacon'. Fire gazing on a full moon. Meandering back and forth on the grassy labyrinth. By the end, silence was truly my friend and greatest teacher. I found peace in just being—there was no sense of time or anything to do but exist. I learned to intentionally quiet my mind and tune into my body. I could feel the energy within me circulating. I was so in tune and alert to my sensations. I could hear my soul because all the noise and clutter finally came to a still. When you lean into the silence you come to realise that presence is inner peace.

Travelling can unlock a different perspective on life. The most important thing we can do is take our key learnings from the experience and integrate them into our everyday lives. What this experience taught me was to let hustle give way to flow. I discovered that the voice in your head that says *you're not doing enough* isn't even you. It's been programmed by a society that justifies your existence by means of your output and what you achieve. There's nothing wrong with getting things done, but not at the expense of your health and it doesn't define who you are. Your calendar and days may be full, but what are they full of? Do these things fill you up or leave you feeling empty?

Sometimes the most productive and brave thing you can do is to take things off your plate and rest. In a society that values being productive to the detriment of your health, it takes courage to defy it by acknowledging you can't live up to extremely high expectations. It takes courage to admit that you don't have the energy for everything, especially for tasks and situations that drain you. It takes courage to simplify your life and make it more comfortable to get tasks done based on your mental, physical and energetic capacity. There's nothing to be ashamed of by staying in bed and recovering when you're exhausted or ill. You aren't doing 'nothing' because you're resting, recovering and healing. Remember, you are human. You're still lovable and 'worthy', even if you aren't working. You're allowed to be sick and you're allowed to rest. You're allowed to switch off your mind and body.

It's mad and sad that we see our health and body as an inconvenience to getting work done. Our poor bodies do everything to keep us alive and we tend to scorn them when they want a break, as this keeps us from being productive. It's terrifying that we worry about people thinking we're faking burnout or not really ill when we take a sick day. When you haven't allowed yourself to not be busy, it feels weird at first. It may even feel boring to recover, rest and recharge. Even if it feels this way, it doesn't take away from the importance of doing so. Rest at your own pace, because everyone's needs and bodies are different. Be gentle and patient, especially if you've pushed yourself to the depths of burnout. Please don't fall into the toxic trap of a mindset that believes you have to *earn* a break or rest, such as when you've ticked off everything on your to-do list. It's a human right. Don't just rest to be 'more productive', you can just rest for the sake of it, and it feels soul-nourishing to do so. I'll repeat this over and over again, resting is not quitting. Resting is a given.

The world may never stop reminding you to do more, work harder and put more effort in, but that doesn't mean you have to listen. Doing your best shouldn't mean pushing so hard that there are serious impacts on your wellbeing. Doing your best should be sustainable and in alignment with your health. You don't need permission to rest. Take time for yourself to replenish and refill your cup. Moving forward doesn't mean to charge at the speed of light. You're allowed to pause along the way and continue moving forward. The hustling and go-go-go mentality is the old paradigm. The new paradigm is being—trusting how your body feels in this moment, going at your own pace. This is how we unlearn glorifying being busy all the time.

YOUR GREAT UNLEARNING

1. THE NOT-TO-DO LIST

Forget your typical to-do list. Make a not-to-do list.
You could have examples such as:

- I don't need to take on more work.
- I don't need to prioritise other people before myself.
- I don't need to feel guilty for having a break.

2. DECLUTTER BUSYNESS

When we get caught up in being busy, we go into autopilot mode instead of being mindful and intentional. This exercise will help you determine what you need to do to alleviate your busyness in life.

Your current intentions in life.
Your current values in life.
Sort out everything you need to do in the columns below:

	#1	#2	#3
What are my top priorities and why?			
What would be nice to do but isn't necessarily a priority right now?			
What would I like done but can outsource or delegate?			

3. SOULFUL SILENCE

Start integrating intentional moments of silence and pause into your everyday life.

Silence can have many definitions, but if you're looking to recreate that of what I did at the silent retreat, it will involve:

- No technology or screens.
- No listening to music or podcasts.

No talking or making noises (you're allowed to read and write though!).

You may like to start your Soulful Silence practice with the following plan:

>Week 1: 5 minutes of silence a day.
>Week 2: 10 minutes of silence a day.
>Week 3: 15 minutes of silence a day.
>Week 4: 20 minutes of silence a day.

You may work up to even having your own silent retreat at home over a weekend!

MASSIVE ACTION, OR IS IT?

THE LEARNING
Go hard or go home. Success is all about big, bold moments and quantum leaps that result in instant success.

The seduction of instant success is so alluring. All over social media, we're plastered with examples of overnight successes that make it look so easy and, in comparison, you feel shitty. Examples range from bitcoin billionaire bros touting how easy it is to make millions to that girl from high school who now drives a swish Mercedes after she went #girlboss selling essential oils to that ad on social media about the single mum who's made a fortune off Airbnb. All of this? You can have it too—there's plenty of fast overnight success to go around! All you have to do is take massive action, because it equals massive results. It's simple: quit your job and go all in. Use your savings, or take out a loan, and take the chance! Push, push and push, more than the average person, because you're so committed!

All of a sudden, you're on the 'bigger, better, harder' rollercoaster. If you're taking those massive actions, which are 'risky', and you're not achieving the desired results, then you need to take more massive action—this is according to society through the plethora of entrepreneur teachings and self-help books. The mantra is big, bold, breathtaking moves. This may look like waking up at 4am every day (because all successful people do), giving it your all in a HIIT workout, changing your diet to include probiotic water and chaga mushrooms (or whatever the latest superfood is), swapping downtime spent mindlessly watching TV for reading educational books and listening to podcasts, working on weekends, maximising every minute of your day, being consistently out of your comfort zone (flight or fight 24/7, baby!)... it's exhausting. I'm tired just writing and reading that sentence! Based on all of this, your belief comes down to this one learning: success and everything you've ever dreamed of will happen from one massive action or consistent massive actions quickly. You've got to be a relentless action taker, all day, every day.

But on the other hand, this is what you may be thinking and feeling: *It's so damn exhausting... There must be something wrong with me... Why aren't I motivated all the time... I feel scared, but these successful people clearly don't... I'm trying, but I'm a failure because I'm working really hard and it hasn't happened for me... I'm overwhelmed... My goal seems so far away, even with supposed 'massive actions'...* So based on these programmed learnings, you're supposedly a lazy, weak, failure of a person with an obsession on the end destination: success. Let's explore this. From the outside, it could look like I'm an 'overnight' success. I started my side hustle during COVID-19 in April 2020 and by July 2020 I'd organically amassed more than 10,000 followers on Instagram (thanks to a post going viral on men's mental health). I started coaching by demand in October 2020 as a side hustle while working full-time in advertising strategy. Less than a year later in September 2021, I resigned from my corporate job to go all in on my own business and dream. Since then, I've been mostly booked out in 1:1 coaching. I've made six figures in my business and, at the time of writing this, I have 37,000 Instagram followers. Depending on your beliefs, you may think this is quick success or you may think this is slow—it's all relative.

Here's the thing... I went against the grain and never expected to be an overnight success. That's because my parents came to Australia with nothing, knowing no one and it took time for them to rebuild a life over here. My dad was a qualified teacher, but his university qualifications weren't recognised and therefore he had to work in a factory with my mum. I hoped I'd have 1,000 followers by the end of the year and quit my job in three to five years—how differently that turned out! When I quit my corporate job, my colleagues were so impressed as the majority of them had no idea I even had a side hustle. I was praised with compliments about how quickly I achieved my goals. However the truth is, it wasn't quickly or through massive action. Sure, I definitely attribute my achievement to some massive actions: I quit my secure, high-paying job in a post-pandemic world despite then being offered a promotion and pay rise, which was risky. I also invested $7,000 in my first business coach, followed by $20,000 in a life coach and $10,000 in courses. The investment in my own life coach truly did catapult my growth, because I believe it represented putting money where my mouth was. These massive forms of action activated me, but it didn't stop there. I invested, but I also had to do the work behind the scenes, which goes the same for the clients I work with today as a life coach.

It wasn't *only* massive action, because so many things in my life had led up to that moment. Sure, when it was time to make a move, I moved. Having a following and posting content about mental health doesn't make you a life coach. Zooming out and gaining perspective on this all, I realised that throughout my whole life, I'd been preparing to become a life coach—not that I consciously knew it. Even from a young age, my friends would confide in me, and I was known as the one in the friendship group to go to for advice on anything, be it what to wear for a date or how to ask for a raise at work. When I was cleaning up my home recently, I found a diary which showed that I had the intention to create an Instagram account in August 2019, seven months before I actually did it! I always had the excuse of no time, but the pandemic certainly gave me some.

I attribute my achievement to consistent, imperfect action. When I started, while I worked in offline media advertising (TV, movies and radio), not online media. I really didn't know a thing about Instagram when I started. When it came to creating graphics, I had a dusty skill set! When I was eleven, I used to play around a lot in Adobe Photoshop, which again was an action I did a long time ago that aligned to help me. When it came to life coaching, I did a certification that taught the basics of how to run a life coaching session, but other than being coached myself for a few months, I didn't know. I figured it out and the training I had for being able to help other people is the eternal school of life. My whole life had been preparing me for this moment, through all the struggles I faced and the dark times I overcame, as well as all the incredible moments of joy and love.

When it came to building my business, it wasn't always big, bold moves. Instead, it was a commitment—a devotion to helping people—that kept me going. I mean, how else would you have the mental, physical and energetic capacity to sustain your efforts? Yes, I did have to wake up early to coach clients before work and stay up late to do so after work. It was hard, but I loved and still do love it so much. For me, coaching wasn't just a side hustle or career change, it was a vehicle for my life purpose to make a difference in people's lives for the better. I wouldn't glamorise it, though. It was tough and I hit points of burnout before having to strengthen my boundaries and take time off to rest in between. So, from the outside, perhaps it might look like a quick overnight success, but as you can see now, it took time, a mixture of massive action and dedicated actions throughout the years. To add some spiritual sprinkle to the mix, I truly believe when you're in alignment with your heart and soul, the universe conspires to support and help you in every way it can. It certainly did with me, and you'll hear more about that in the Self-Made chapter.

THE UNLEARNING

Big, bold moves are great, but they won't instantly equal success. There's nothing wrong with achieving goals over time with imperfect action.

Rome wasn't built in one day, and neither are you or your dreams. An age-old saying attributed to Desmond Tutu goes, 'There is only one way to eat an elephant: a bite at a time.' Every little bit counts because it all adds up. It doesn't always have to be fast and ferocious growth.

I hope you remember the beauty in slow growth. I hope you know it's okay to go slowly. Slow, in the way that the sea erodes the rocks to make way for majestic cliffs. Slow, in the way that a drop in the ocean becomes tidal waves. Slow, in the way that a caterpillar spins its cocoon to eventually emerge as a beautiful butterfly. Slow, in the way a seedling becomes a mighty tree and, in turn, a grand forest. Slow, in the way that you're changing and growing. Slow growth is still growth. On the journey to success, at times the growth may be silent and subtle. But just because no one else knows or has acknowledged your achievements out loud, that doesn't mean progress isn't being made. Further to that, the concept of 'massive action' is relative. To one person, massive action is going all in and quitting their job to start their own business. To another person, massive action is allowing herself to contemplate leaving her job to travel the world.

You're going to blossom and bloom, beautiful soul, and there's no rush. We don't reap the rewards of the seeds we plant on day one. *(What fun would that be anyway?)* The beauty is in your growth, expansion and transformation. Allow yourself the space and freedom to grow. Every mistake is a seed. Every wound is a seed. Every heartache is a seed. Every fall is a seed. Every tear is a seed. Every seed starts small and then grows beyond comprehension. The end result is beautiful, whether it's lovely flowers or mighty trees. But what's more beautiful? The journey of the seed. I love taking inspiration from nature. Growing a pineapple takes longer than growing a human baby. From a pineapple top, it takes at least two years to flower and then another six–twelve months before we see the pineapples that we do in the shops. A persimmon tree takes three–four years to flower, but then only seven days for the fruit to ripen. In the small island of Seychelles, the native Coco de Mer tree takes twenty–forty years to start flowering!

Don't fall for the illusion that success will always be quick and easy. It can be, but it won't always be necessarily. The most important thing is to just start—plant the seed. Start, and you'll figure out the 'how', 'what' and the rest of the path later. As you get going, it may feel like your days are the same, over and over again, where nothing is changing. But just because it feels that way, it doesn't mean that you aren't making progress. You aren't wasting time or your life. Maybe it's just that you can't see any changes yet. You're making waves in oceans that cannot be seen yet. You're making tremors in earthquakes that cannot be felt yet. You're making sparks in lightning that hasn't struck yet. You're making heat in blazes that haven't burned yet. You're the catalyst. You're the power. Just because it's not here yet, it doesn't mean that it's not happening... It's simply in the making. You don't have to feel guilty or ashamed as if something's wrong with however long it's taking—everyone's path is different.

You're allowed to take your time. You can have success without exhausting all your energy and depleting your health. Go at your own pace, despite what conditioned anxiety and fear says to you. It's okay to take a break, it's okay to rest and it's okay to take time. You don't have to be an overnight success if you don't want to be. From what I've witnessed, it often isn't sustainable in the long term.

Don't get lost in the search for success by focusing on your end goal and concentrating on grand moments such as 'massive action'. Don't forget *why* you're doing what you're doing to get there. Enjoy the journey *and* the destination. Maybe you'll think of an incredible idea in the shower randomly one day (*seriously... why do all the best ideas happen there?*). Maybe you'll think of a solution to a challenge while watching the clouds go by. Maybe you'll get a direction-changing epiphany while hanging up your washing. If you're so focused on the grandiosity of it all, you might miss those special little moments in between. Success and achievement aren't only found in big moments. Appreciate the full spectrum of it all. I often think about my life and of course there's been grand gestures that have taken my breath away. However more often than not, it's the small details that I truly cherish, such as my first ever client Stacey or when I'm feeling down and a friend texts me, *I haven't heard from you in a while.*

To distil this unlearning to the finest degree, I'd say that action *isn't* the be-all and end-all. Action is one part of the equation of success. There are so many other factors externally out of your control, let alone internally. Internally, your thoughts, beliefs, energy and intentions are examples. When I think of successful athletes, their skill and practice are one thing, but I'd argue that mindset is equally as, if not more, important. If we look at Olympic athletes, they have the mindset of devotion to continually show up and train for years and years for just one moment that occurs every four years. They have the mindset of a winner; when they participate, they believe that they're capable and will walk away with a gold medal. Action is important, but it isn't the only factor for success.

You don't have to have everything all figured out at once. I see success as a masterpiece. We start with a blank canvas. Over time, we introduce the vision and blueprint through sketching with pencil. Next comes the colours onto the canvas. Layer by layer, it builds. Then, we add textures. We work with all of this until we're happy with what we see. There may be a time when you decide to pivot destinations, and that's okay. It isn't because you can't achieve your goal or reach a certain target. I haven't achieved every single goal or dream that I've set. I prefer the word 'intentions', as there's less pressure involved. Sometimes it might not happen for you and that doesn't mean you're a failure or something is wrong with you. You just need to recalibrate and reassess. One goal not being met doesn't invalidate all the other things you've achieved, and it doesn't define who you are. Here's to action—not only massive action, but to all the actions you take, because they all add up.

YOUR GREAT UNLEARNING

1. CHUNKING

Looking at what you want to achieve can be overwhelming and daunting. My favourite activity to address this is breaking it up into smaller, manageable parts, which also relieves the self-doubt and fear in your mind.

For example, maybe it's your dream to buy a house.

You could break it up like this:

- Have enough money for a deposit. (That can be broken down even further with savings goals.)
- Take out a mortgage. (Again, break that down, researching lenders, researching brokers, researching options, etc.)
- Look at real estate listings.
- Attend real estate viewings.

If you're having difficulties, you can even reverse engineer from your end goal to figure out a potential path to take.

For example, you want to make $20,000.

What are the ways you could do that?

One lump sum of $20,000, or it could be four sums of $5,000, ten sums of $2,000 or making $54 every day for a year (365 days).

2. 1 PER CENT

How can you contribute or move forward by 1% towards your goals/desires/dreams right now?

3. THE SMALL THINGS

Think about all the small things in your life. Take a moment to pause, acknowledge and appreciate how they contribute to your joy and wellbeing. For example:

- Gratitude for your health—being appreciative for your body each morning when you get out of bed. Waking up means you're alive—what a gift.
- Gratitude for making tea every day—a moment of pause, appreciation and joy in your day.

- Gratitude for brushing your teeth—practising appreciation for your teeth, each and every single one. Teeth are essential to eating and we need teeth to enjoy a variety of different foods. What about when you have teeth or mouth nerve pain? It's excruciatingly painful.
- Gratitude for breathing and your beating heart—your body keeping you alive to live another moment in life.
- Gratitude for advances in modern technology—it has allowed us to connect with one another with ease and anywhere across the world.

MONEY, MONEY, MONEY

THE LEARNING
Money is hard to make but it will solve all my problems.

Let's talk about money. For so long it's been taboo and hush-hush, shrouded in secrecy. The thing is finances are the blood of life. Whether you like it or not, we need money to sustain ourselves. Yet many of us have a tricky and complicated relationship with money. As children, we're subconsciously soaking in so many things like a sponge that will go on to influence our money mindset. I didn't even realise that money mindset was a thing until I started life coaching. Money mindset has nothing to do with the figure in your bank account but rather what's going on in your mind—how you see money, how you feel about money. We don't pay attention to the subconscious because it's automatic. More often than not, we are aware of our surface-level conscious beliefs such as, *I want to have lots of money,* or *I believe one day I'll be really rich.*

Our subconscious largely makes our decisions on money—deep-rooted beliefs that start from childhood and are informed by our personal experiences with money. Statements that roll off the tongue in everyday vernacular contribute to this, such as, *money doesn't grow on trees, money is the root of all evil, people who make lots of money aren't good people* and *making money isn't easy.* Perhaps your mum spoke about not being able to reach the top of the career ladder because she needed to take a step back to parent you—that would create a subconscious belief that making money takes sacrifice. Further to that, it may form the subconscious belief that you can't be a good parent *and* make money. Perhaps your dad told you to never get into debt. Therefore, you equate money to trouble (*so it won't even feel safe to have money in the first place, ironically!*). Moreover, that's too simplistic at surface level because what about good debt, such as investing in your education and future?

Don't underestimate the impact of the people around you on your money mindset. For example, my ex-boyfriend constantly criticised and complained about wealthy people. He'd say *they're selfish, greedy, entitled, snobby and egoic.* How do you think I felt when I started making lots of money in my business, knowing that's what he thought about people with money? On nights out, I'd buy rounds of drinks for him and his friends, not expecting one in return. He'd pull me to the side and tell me to stop because I didn't have to. But I wanted to. What's the point of having lots of money if I couldn't enjoy it and spoil the people I love and care about? Not only that, he also constantly said no to going out because he said he was poor and travelling to Paris or Morocco was out of the question (even though I offered to pay for it!).

The situation felt toxic, and it was dragging me down. In fact, it was a contributing factor in my decision to break up with him because I realised I couldn't have a life partner with this mentality around money. When we did break up, I told him that if he kept having these thoughts about money, it'd be the exact reason why he'd stay 'poor'—not only in money but in mindset too. Sure, he didn't have lots of money at the time having quit his job and the investment of our relationship visa, but he had access to money in the forms of savings which he chose not to access. Ironically, he didn't grow up poor. His family home was substantial, and we enjoyed many delicious meals and outings with his generous parents in the UK. It just shows the power of conditioning on our thoughts around money.

As we get older, we pick up even more money beliefs that accumulate in our subconscious. At its core, money is a neutral resource and tool used to get what we want. However, money is also more than that and less than that. What do I mean? Money is used as a medium to represent value—it came in to replace bartering. For example, before money, you'd bake a loaf of bread for someone in exchange for helping to build your home. Now, money is a universal currency. It's an energetic exchange because money is a form of energy (as is everything in life). When you adopt this as your perspective, you can see that no one truly owns money. Money is in flow. Money needs to be circulated. We are temporary stewards of money.

Our minds like to complicate our relationship with money. Nowadays, money has been equated to a myriad of things. Self-worth—because as a human being, you only offer money, right? Success—sure, you can be very rich, but what if you're sad and lonely? Are you still truly successful? Evil—money isn't inherently evil, but people can desire money for power, control and manipulation. Stress—making money can be taxing (literally, physically and mentally), but it doesn't have to be. Controlling our emotions—or is it that you haven't resolved underlying issues that you project onto money?

For the first time in my life, I truly feel that I am in a place where I have overcome my scarcity money mindset. I've just had one of the biggest months in my business and money keeps flowing to me, even though I'm not heavily pushing coaching or human design readings online. I don't have to convince people to work with me; they come ready and willing to work with me (without paid advertising too). It's taken a long time to get here, and it's been far from easy. I've had to unlearn a lot of bullshit and assumptions I had about money. It hasn't always been this way. In fact, I've always had a rollercoaster relationship with money. I've had lots of money and I've also been in the reds and negative. Money is so important, yet I, like many of us, never got taught directly about it to a great depth.

What I've come to realise is how greatly our nervous system influences our capacity to hold and receive money. One of the most stressful incidents of my life was when I had saved up $10,000 to go to Europe for three months with one my best friends, Sonia. The trip was planned in advance and happened to fall around a year after my dad died. Unfortunately, I had delayed onset grief that largely occurred a week before I was meant to set off. I was unable to sleep as my nervous system was so activated—I couldn't switch off. I hadn't been officially diagnosed therefore I was unable to get any of the money I paid for flights, accommodation and tours back through travel insurance. I hoped that my tax return for the year would recoup some of that money but instead it went to my mum to support me.

This event embedded in my subconscious a fear that I couldn't handle money. I'd worked so hard to save that $10,000 and it all came crumbling down because of my anxiety and depression. Later on, I would go on to take a year off university and worked hard to go on that very trip a year later, alone and to the USA too. It was honestly a dream—the trip of a lifetime. I visited twenty-five countries and forty cities in three months. Even though I saved up the money for the trip, I ended up taking out a credit card. Now, I don't know how this happened, but at a young age I was able to borrow $20,000… Not a great idea when I wasn't properly financially educated. I didn't even realise I had to pay interest for using the credit card.

At age twenty-three, I was drowning in a mountain of debt but moved out of home for the first time anyway. I was barely keeping up with payments and was surviving on instant noodles and my mum delivering food to my place. As it goes, years later after my dad's passing, I unexpectedly received a large inheritance. So, what did I do with the money? Well, I did the responsible thing first and paid off the travel and life debt I had accumulated (yes, I maxed out that $20,000). Then, I blew the rest on shopping, eating, luxury and more travelling. I ended up back at $0 and that's because I didn't know how to handle having that much money in the first place, let alone after getting into deep debt. I didn't feel safe having a lot of money because I'd never had so much money before. I didn't know how to hold onto a lot of money because I didn't think I was worthy of it. I was way out of my financial comfort zone.

Generally speaking, a greater self-worth leads to a higher net worth. Taking these experiences into account, I fell into a shame spiral where I let my debt define my worthiness. You cannot be defined by money, let's be clear on that, you can't put a price to a human soul. I felt so guilty that my dad posthumously gave me all this money and if I could go back in time, I would have saved that money and used it to start my business. But here's the thing… you only know what you know! I didn't understand money back then. To give you some context, growing up I experienced two extremes of money, and they were very confusing. We always seemed to have money and, for the most part, I got everything I wanted.

When my mum's business was booming in high school, I remember feeling rich because we had pay TV at home and I'd get any consoles I wanted (yes, I used to be a mad gamer*)*. I was never really told 'no'. She would always pay, but I didn't understand or see all the hard work that was put into earning that money. Upon reflection I realise this was her way of appeasing the guilt of divorce and distracting me from her absence because she worked long hours. All I saw was the end result. So, in a way, earning money looked easy. However, when I entered the workforce at age fifteen by choice because I wanted independence, I realised I needed to apply effort and energy to make it.

My mum had lots of money, but she could never hold onto it. Her business ended up going under and she declared bankruptcy. Observing her spending habits, she spent money freely like a running tap. I didn't see her save, just spend. Growing up, I was stressed hearing about her owing debts to friends and family. She would ask me for money as soon as I started working which made me angry and resentful. I felt burdened by her financial problems which forced me to have 'adult' problems as a child. My dad's commentary also heavily conditioned my perception of her and money. He would say things like she was 'irresponsible with money' and it was 'her stupidity' that meant they sold my childhood home and ended up renting a small apartment in the suburbs. Despite this my dad would help her pay off debts that she'd get into and continue to financially support her even after they divorced.

Not only that, my mum would throw money at her problems. Up until recently, she's always told me if I can't do it, pay someone else to. I have compassion and sympathy for her because she obviously meant physical problems and jobs around the house because for the majority of my life, I didn't grow up with a full-time dad in my home where it's stereotypical for a man to change the lightbulbs, put together flat pack furniture and so forth.

If only it was that easy to throw money towards mental health problems. If you have money, you'll be happy, right? Clearly not, which I learned after my dad passed away. My family didn't understand mental health—it isn't commonly spoken about in Asian culture. Struggles with mental health are often kept invisible, to not burden or worry other family members yet mine became very visible when I was so depressed I couldn't function day to day anymore. At the peak of it, my aunt offered to fund a trip for me to New York so that I would feel better as she knew I loved travelling. I declined, because what was New York in comparison to a dead dad? Nothing. Looking back now, I have a lot of love for her because this was her way of trying to help me feel better based on her life experiences and values.

My dad was on the other extreme of the financial scale. He was conservative and traditional with money. He mostly spent money on necessities or occasional holidays, although I still have fond memories of him treating me to a Magnum ice cream every time we went to the petrol station together—it's a habit I still carry on to this day in memory of him. He was financially responsible and savvy. Not only that he always encouraged me to save for 'a rainy day.' The rigidity and tightness I experienced around money made me believe that money needs to be taken very seriously—hence the shame spirals. Sadly, my dad passed away not long after he'd retired. He had all the time in the world, saved a large sum of money and didn't end up using it because he wasn't here anymore. It crushed my heart to hear from my stepmum that my dad was waiting for me to finish university before going on his very own adventures to see the world. That very heartbreak has informed my mindset on money and encouraged me to be fully present with it. What's the point of saving if I randomly die and don't use it?

The biggest catalyst to changing my money mindset was having my own business. I remember being so conflicted to leave my job because I was so scared of working full-time in my business and making no money. I was even caught up in the self-limiting belief that I never had enough money (which was not true at all). Even though I knew dying was the worst thing that could happen to me, I was so petrified of not making any money in my business. No, I wouldn't die, but it felt like death if I had to move back home temporarily with my mum or stepmum (now, I can see how blessed I was that I had places to go!). It felt like death to my ego to have to get an additional job if it didn't work out. It felt like death if my friends and family found out that my business didn't succeed and would label me a 'loser' or 'failure' (not that they would—these were the stories I created in my mind).

Looking back, at the end of the day it came down to trust. I didn't trust myself to find a way to create or make money without the security and safety of being employed with a steady pay. After working on my money mindset with my coaches, I did figure it out. I realised all along it wasn't the job that made the money, it was me. My work ethic and my skills. Further to that, I started facing my money fears and not avoiding them. I would check my bank account every day and track expenses. I created a budget to determine how much money I needed to survive vs what I desired. I forgave myself for past spending habits when I wasn't money educated or conscious. I'm so glad I came to trust myself because it all worked out in the end.

THE UNLEARNING
Money doesn't have to be hard to make, but it won't solve all your problems either. Wealth is the consciousness of abundance and poverty is the consciousness of lack.

Abundance isn't the goal; it's the starting point. You aren't abundant because you have lots of money; when you're abundant, you get lots of money. Money is a by-product of your being. All abundance starts in your mind and energy. It's feeling the juiciness and richness of life, regardless of the reality right now. Sure, you desire feeling rich by travelling on a private jet, but could you tap into that energy by flying premium economy or paying for entry into a private lounge prior to your flight? Sure, you desire buying the house of your dreams, but could you tap into that energy by booking yourself a luxurious weekend at an Airbnb in the style of it? When you start there, you truly become a magnet for all the incredible things and experiences life has to offer. What's more, it translates into money in your physical reality.

Abundance isn't what you get paid, what's in your bank account or what you own. Abundance is the fullness of this moment. Why is it that we always associate abundance with money *only*? It's definitely a form, but it isn't just all about the money. You don't *need* anything to have abundance right now. Our mind often can't wrap its head around this, and to that I offer you this: If abundance is only about money, wealth and happiness, then why are there plenty of people who have no money or little money that feel so rich with hardly any material possessions? Yeah, money is great, but have you ever experienced true joy in just living? Can you put a price on that? Abundance is a state of being you consciously curate and cultivate.

You tap into abundance when you realise that nothing is missing and everything in this moment is complete. Time is irrelevant in the present moment, hence why you aren't taking stock of time when you're fully present in the moment. Money is just a channel and vehicle. We give it value through the energy we place on it. Our mind and world conditions us to believe that we need something or someone outside of ourselves, when really everything you already need is right here, right now.

When you're identified with the mind, you're closed off to receiving and embodying the abundance of this moment. When you're identified with the mind, you're running off programming and conditioning, instead of your conscious choices and decisions. If you want to change your money mindset, you've got to change your thoughts and beliefs about money. When you're identified with the mind, you feel lack and scarcity because something is missing, and this isn't enough.

When I was in Singapore in March 2022, I felt very scarce. Truth be told, I didn't want to be there. I was feeling constricted by my perceived lack of money. Singapore is the world's second-most expensive city in the world. I'd already been to Singapore twice in previous years for transit purposes and had an upcoming two-month Europe trip to budget for. I was happy to go for one reason only this time, which was to meet my dear friend and past client, Carrie, in person for the first time.

Knowing this, I wanted to dedicate all my time to being with her, so I didn't bring my laptop to work on. Carrie was meant to fly in from Canada but due to a series of unfortunate events, she was unable to enter Singapore. So, there I was in Singapore where there were hardly any other tourists around because they still had COVID-19 restrictions (that, in itself, was abundance: being able to travel when no one else was). Then, I realised the universe had conspired to get me there! It wanted me to be among luxury and the finer things in life. It wanted me to see how money gets to be light and pleasurable. So, I thought *screw it, I'm going to embrace my time here.*

I stayed in five-star hotels and got to truly enjoy it: lounging poolside, lazing in a king-size bed with silk sheets, being chauffeured around privately, room service, $50 cocktails. I had the abundance of time. Having an empty calendar made me feel like a millionaire! I didn't have to rush anywhere or work. When you're your own boss, you can have holidays whenever you want. No more waiting for leave approvals. Given all my hard work and the success of my business, I finally bought my first designer handbag: the Louis Vuitton Speedy 30. It'd been on my vision board for years. Even at the store, I was reluctant to buy it, but I decided to override my money story. I deserved the bag. The money I spent would come back to me (and indeed it did, later in the year I went on to have my biggest months in business).

For years, I kept telling myself that I couldn't afford the bag. However the reality was that I could with my corporate job. I had the money in the bank, but I chose not to spend it, because it wasn't a priority in comparison to other things. It's more financially empowering to say, 'I'm choosing not to buy this' versus 'I can't afford it'. Indulging in a purchase you really want is money magnetism at its finest and creating space for more abundance. In Singapore, I also splurged on a solo photoshoot at the Gardens by the Bay because I wanted a keepsake of my time to capture this luxurious moment in my life. That was priceless. Through these actions, I shifted from the belief that money was serious and painful to pleasurable and fun. I'd broken free from limiting money beliefs.

I also had to work through the belief that I couldn't be spiritual and rich at the same time. Being spiritual doesn't mean you to have to be poor. Being rich doesn't mean you can't have spiritual values at the same time. With this mentality of spirituality being akin to low wealth, you'd believe that you have to work for free to help people. That doesn't help people. You need money to cover your living expenses and general wellbeing so that you can be at your best to help others. By running an abundant business, you can show other people that this life is possible for them too.

Money is a powerful tool that can lead to greater consciousness. The capacity to create free resources. In early 2022, I had the privilege of running a free in-person women's circle for clients and friends because I had the wealth to do so. I hired out a beautiful space with glass-stained windows and put on a delicious spread of food and nibbles, including freshly made cacao by my assistant. It was wonderful. Not only that, through my online personal growth membership The Soul Sister Collective, for every soul that has joined I donate a menstrual cup that will give a woman in need up to ten years of access to a safe sanitary care through The Cova Project.

Choosing to see spending money as an investment was a huge game-changer for me when unravelling the shame and fear of debt. Whatever your past history is with money, it doesn't matter in the present moment because *you* get to decide how you approach money right now. If you're more aware and conscious of what you're spending money on and why you're spending money, you'll rewrite the story that you're 'bad' or 'frivolous' with money. One of the scariest things I've ever done was invest $30,000 into my personal development and business. My mind was telling me I was crazy and being irresponsible and that the money could've been put towards a property deposit. Yet, I had to trust the pull of my heart. I had to stop playing small and go big. I had to listen to the woman I wanted to become and not the chains of my money. I really wanted to work with coaches who were living the life I desired, in particular my coach Kristina. I shifted from saying it's 'expensive' to it's 'expansive'. I had to invest and hold the vision that this would be an investment that would change my life, and it did. Your thoughts are just as much an investment as money in your future. You're an investment.

Using the perspective of this amount as an investment and energetic exchange truly did catapult me into success. It was exhilarating to spend such an amount on myself—not a house, not a holiday, me. It was my signal to the universe to say, 'I'm serious about my personal growth and ready to fully back my business.' The mind only knows what it knows. Money isn't just logical, it's also emotional and can be irrational. Putting that $30,000 on my credit card, I thought I'd pay it off through my corporate job, but I ended up paying it off within months through my own business! By doing this, I rewrote my money story on debt. Previously, my mum and I had been rescued by my dad financially, but this time I did it on my own. I showed myself that I could be trusted with money, and I could create money. I chose to deliberately plug into a higher energetic frequency of money, which then became my reality. I trusted the highest version of myself, because she knows what she's doing.

Your internal beliefs reflect your external reality. I believed I could use money in a wise way, and so I did. I believe that investment quantum-leaped me into the success that I have now. Circling back to the example of my ex-boyfriend, if you believe you're poor and can't make money, your reality will reflect that. If you believe you're internally poor, you'll be externally poor. Being afraid to spend money blocks you off from the flow of money. It's vital in the game of money mindset to consciously curate your thoughts, beliefs, actions and energy in order to attract money. It can be helpful to think of money as a person. You might like to ask yourself, is money attracted to you through confidence or fear? Another perspective you could take is to imagine stepping outside of yourself and becoming the universe. As the universe, what relationship do you see yourself having with money? What are your actions and energy signalling? Your bank account is your belief account.

When you're unlearning thoughts and beliefs about money, you're getting out of your own way. Perhaps you're being the 'good girl' who's limiting her capacity to receive money. The glass ceiling is real, but so is the one you create for yourself. The good girl is afraid of being seen as greedy, selfish or uncaring. She's afraid to ask for money. She's afraid to desire money. The good girl assumes that if she works hard, she'll eventually be recognised and given more money. The good girl is afraid to lay out her value and output, so she ends up being unrecognised and underpaid. The good girl assumes that if she asks for more money, people will think she's only in it for money. There's no shame for wanting more in life. Were you born to live a practical, safe, mediocre life? Or were you born to fully enjoy the human experience and live life to the fullest? Having money isn't bad or evil. Having money can help you do so much good and change the world. Money can be an ally and friend. One of the best things I've ever done with money is retire my mum early, as a single mum she's worked her whole life to provide for me. Further to that I am able to consciously use my money to consistently purchase from small businesses and regularly donate to charitable causes dear to my heart.

A truly wealthy woman knows that she's not just abundant, she *is* abundance, and nothing can take that away from her—not even an empty or negative bank account. A truly powerful woman doesn't give her power to money, she steps up and rises above it all. True wealth and abundance start from within. You can elevate your money mindset to a money 'heartset'. You get to choose who you want to be with or without money. You get to feel juicy and expanded by money. You get to have fun with money (because women just wanna have funds, right!? I hope you get this reference to Cyndi Lauper's *Girls Just Want to Have Fun*.) You get to feel pleasure by your prosperity. You get to be turned on by money. You get to do incredible and meaningful things with money. You get to be supported by money and use money to support the people and causes you love. You get to evolve while your money does too.

YOUR GREAT UNLEARNING

1. MONEY MANTRAS

I love that entrepreneur Marie Forleo speaks about getting yourself an ATM. By 'ATM', she means an 'Automatic Transformative Mantra'. A mantra you repeat to yourself over and over, because repetition is powerful. I also love mantras because they're about deciding to consciously choose a thought that serves your highest self. Below are some of my favourite money mantras:

- Money is always attracted to me. I'm a money magnet.
- I choose wealth. I choose abundance.
- I'm a channel for money. I use money for good and to better this world.
- Money likes to be in my hands.
- Money wants to be in the hands of the good, and I volunteer.
- Beautiful things happen in the world because of money, and I want to be a part of that.
- Money is hot for me.
- I don't spend money; I help money flow freely.
- I love money and money loves me.
- Money is easily replenished for me.

- Money always finds its way to me.
- I get to enjoy a luxurious and abundant life.
- I was born to live an abundant life.
- I am meant for wealth.
- Money is always looking for me.
- Being abundant and wealthy is a natural state of being.
- I always have more than enough money.
- I'm always provided for by the universe.

2. MONEY MINDSET CHECK

Open your bank account and look at how much money is in your bank account. How do you feel? Be honest with yourself. I used to bury my head in the sand about money because I didn't want to see the truth. But the best way to improve your money mindset is facing it head-on. Make it a challenge to look at your bank account every day and stay grounded in your body as you do so—feel the discomfort, feel the joy, feel it all.

Secondly, get real about your finances. At the bare minimum, work out how much money you need to survive every week and how much money you desire to have every week.

Thirdly, start delving into your money mindset. The below questions provide a solid foundation to understanding your money mindset. (In the below questions, you can replace 'mum' or 'dad' with your main caretaker.)

- What was your dad like around money?
- What did your dad say about money?
- What was your mum like around money?
- What did your mum say about money?
- What do your friends say about money?

3. MONEY MAGNET

Money is flowing in and out constantly, yet we become scarce and tightly grip to it. This exercise will show you how much money fluctuates and how you're receiving more money than you think you are. I want you to track the movement of your money for a whole month. Every single thing—money that goes out, money that goes in—everything counts. Everyday examples include:

- Buying something on discount represents money. Give the 10 per cent a monetary value.
- Receiving a rebate.
- Receiving a cashback.
- Receiving something for free, such as friend buying you a coffee or shouting lunch.

Do this every day for a month, and you'll see that you're a money magnet! You can further amplify abundance energy by being appreciative and grateful for all the money flowing into your life. I like to do this by saying out loud how much I appreciate the money or writing it down in a gratitude diary.

YOU CAN HAVE IT ALL

THE LEARNING
You can't have it all.

We're conditioned to have things in life as 'good enough'—good enough sex, good enough money, good enough relationships, good enough jobs. But what about great? What about excellent? In fact, we're shamed for wanting more—more pleasure, more money, more appreciation. We've been conditioned to equate wanting more as superficial, dirty and to the detriment of others. We're told it's ridiculous to believe we can be an amazing partner, mother and career woman at the same time. Our culture celebrates sacrifice through these beliefs: If you want lots of money, you have to work lots. If you want to be successful at work, you have to spend less time with loved ones. If you want a passionate life, you'll have to pick between your career or hobbies. If you want a happy family, you'll work less and therefore be materially scarce. If you want to help people in this lifetime, you won't make much money unless you're in the corporate sector. If you want to own property, you can't travel, and you certainly can't eat avocado on toast. If you want to be healthy, you'll have to miss out on the meals you love. The fear of missing out has turned into joy of missing out. And what's the proposed solution? Wanting less.

To have it all is apparently an impossible standard and it's unattainable. Even with all the advancements society and women have made, it's still deemed not possible. The idea is that if you try, you'll end up anxious, burnt out and miserable. You'll end up stretching yourself thin in the pursuit of apparent perfection at the cost of your health and happiness. You'll probably have multiple nervous breakdowns along the way too. Therefore, you should dilute your dreams and expectations of life. You have to choose between things. Remind yourself of the limits and boundaries in place. Accept them. You can't balance everything. You can't excel and be great at everything. Life is full of sacrifices. Therefore, you'll desire and dream less. You ought to be okay with what you have, grateful even! It reminds me of being a little child when your hopes are crushed. You're told, 'Don't be silly! Be realistic!' If you continued to dare to dream, then as you got older, you'd be met with scepticism and contempt along the lines of, 'Who do you think you are?' With all the naysayers, I have to admit, I believed them. That is, until my life showed me otherwise...

For me, it seemed that life was like a seesaw. If my love life was great, then my career was terrible and vice versa. I was conditioned to believe things had to be this way, especially while crossing paths with various older women in the workplace. It felt like I could only have one or the other—like choosing between this or that. When I finally got promoted at work, I felt like my career was going great. But as time went on and the work and responsibilities started piling on, I was so stressed. The guy I was dating at the time said to me, 'You worry about work way too much. What happened to the fun, cheeky girl I met?' Eventually, the seesaw came to balance out. I ended up getting promoted as a manager (finally!) and the guy I dated after him would turn out to be my second love Malcolm. Things with Malcolm were going well, initially. Shortly after meeting him, I started my side hustle as a life coach. I was doing well at work, winning awards and to my delightful surprise, my side hustle grew extensively, and I ended up quitting my corporate job after nine months. My colleagues and friends told me I was living the dream.

I felt on top of the world, but the seesaw came back to haunt me. Yes, my career was at an all-time high, but my relationship began to feel stagnant. It felt safe and very comfortable. I know many people would've been happy in this situation. On the outside, it looked like all was well, you'd never suspect anything was wrong. It was a love story: I'd been single for eight years and here came Prince Charming

(I was actually told he looked like one on a few nights out). He said 'I love you' to me first and it was evident to everyone he was deeply in love with me. The icing on the cake? My family adored him. But deep down, something was niggling at me. Doubts started to brew, particularly in the lead-up to our breakup after being together for three years. Then the cracks started to appear. From my perspective, Malcolm was supportive initially with my business as a side hustle. However, as it grew and scaled into my full-time job, he began feeling resentful as my business was taking up the majority of my time. He wasn't as open and respectful to my spiritual beliefs as I'd hoped either.

I was very successful, which was hard for Malcolm to swallow. He even told me he was jealous because it seemed that everything I did worked out, despite all the odds, and that it was hard as a man to see me make much more money than him. From my perspective because of this, I felt that he didn't do 'gentlemanly' things for me. He expected me to kill bugs on my own, take out the trash, change the lightbulbs and always carry my own bags even if I struggled to do so... our energetic polarity of 'masculine' and 'feminine' was out of sync. We had so much love for each other, but our sex life and spark dwindled. It felt like we had a lack of chemistry and sex drive, mostly on my half. Logically, it didn't make sense and it was hard for me to wrap my head around because I found Malcolm very attractive. However truth be told, we were more companions and best friends than romantic lovers. So, I began to wonder... Could there be someone else out there for me? A partner who was more understanding of the nature of running my own business *and* having spiritual beliefs and gifts. A partner who was adventurous *and* had an insatiable thirst for enjoying life *and* money to the fullest, like me. A partner where there was deep love *and* a sizzling hot sex life.

THE UNLEARNING
You CAN have it all.

As I write this chapter, it's been a few months since I broke up with Malcolm. The innate part of me wishes that I could say since then, I've met 'the one'—the man that'll be my husband and the father of my children. Life isn't like that, though; that's often the stuff of fictional stories and instead, this book is my reality. In writing this chapter, I believed I had to have the above before going to print because then I'd really have it all, right? At this point in my life, everything's going well—my business is booming, I live in my dream place, and I have an incredible support network. The only thing missing is the love of my life. After days of going back and forth on this chapter, including many tears shed at the frustration of not 'having it all' in time for the completion of this chapter, I now realise that I *do* have it all. I'm embracing my new beginning, my latest adventure.

Sure, I'm not with the love of my life... *yet!* But that doesn't mean I don't have love in my life! I'm surrounded by it every day. I can feel it every day. I feel it when I read the testimonials of my beautiful clients. I feel it when my friends and family celebrate my achievements. I feel it when I see angel numbers and synchronicities, it's validation from my higher spiritual council that I'm on the right path. In fact, I am whole on my own and I don't need anyone to 'complete' me or to be 'my better half'. Writing this, the realisation has hit me that there will be two loves of my life. One, he's coming. But the most important one of all? Me. *I'm the love of my life.* I'm love. I didn't settle for a great love with a romantic partner because I want an amazing love. I chose myself, my growth and the vision I desired for my life over clinging to a relationship that had run its course and hit its expiry date. It's not even just about romance. I chose my heart, soul, true happiness and purpose when I left my corporate job to be a full-time life coach. I didn't settle for four weeks of annual leave and following the orders of someone else. I have the ultimate freedom to choose my work hours and travel the world while working as a by-product of doing what I love.

Beautiful soul, I'm here staking the claim and holding the space for you to remember that you *can* have it all. You can have *all* of whatever you want. What person has the right to tell you otherwise, based on what merit? (Are they the dream police?) Some people think there's danger in having 'too big dreams'. Those triggered will project on to you their disillusion based on their experiences or what they've seen in other people's lives. Funnily enough, I never hear of men being told to be more realistic about their dreams. Often when they dream big, it's an admired quality—he's got vision! What's important to define in your life is this: 'What's your all?' I never thought it was possible to enjoy doing what I love and make more than enough money to live from it. Yet here I am living that life! I'm glad I tried because if I didn't, then who knows what I could've missed out on?

The secret is that this didn't all happen by accident; it happened by living my life very intentionally by design, particularly in alignment. Whatever your 'all' is, (I love this quote by author Anna Sabino for inspiration) 'Wear your too large wings with confidence. You'll grow into them.' People and society will always have something to say. Some will say you can have it all, but not at the same time. Others will say having it all is being content with what you have. Maybe I'm a dreamer, but here are some powerful questions that I'd love you to contemplate about life: Why live a safe, standard and mediocre life? Do you just want average? What are you truly here for? If you never try, will you ever truly know?

I'm glad I didn't listen to my parents/society/friends/*insert whoever or whatever is an influence in my life* because it gave me the opportunity to learn and try for myself. I needed my own experiences and evaluation in order to come to my own conclusions. Wouldn't you like to do the same? As poet T.S. Eliot says, 'Only those who will risk going too far can possibly find out how far one can go.' Maybe having it all isn't the point. Maybe going after it all and believing you can have it is the point. I choose to believe that I can have everything I desire and maybe that's why I can, I will and I do. What do you choose to believe?

YOUR GREAT UNLEARNING

1. WHAT IS YOUR ALL?

What does having it all *actually* mean and look like for you? Consider the major areas of your life, such as health, career, relationships and money as examples. This should reflect what your dream life looks like. Imagine you're a keynote speaker in front of a large audience, sharing the story of having your dream life. How would you describe it?

Go into great depth and detail articulating this. If you can't, perhaps it's a sign that it isn't as important as you thought it was. This will help clarify where your energy and mindset should be focused. Translate these words into something you can read every day to inspire you. If you're a visual person, then make it into a vision board, as an example.

As a follow-up exercise, address *why* you believe you can't have it. Identify the limiting source. Perhaps it was something someone said to you or something you read in a book, for example.

2. THE PROOF IS IN THE PUDDING

Look for evidence that it's possible to have what your all looks like. Your mind only knows what it knows and by doing this you are showing your mind a new, possible reality. Instead of being jealous or resentful towards someone who has what you want, shift your perspective and energy to gratitude that if they can have it, you can have it too.

3. YOUR PLAN TO HAVE IT ALL

Create a plan to make this achievable in a way that you 110 per cent believe in it. For example, you may want to consider:

- How you measure having it all. Having it all may not mean 100 per cent all the time. Perhaps you're happy with a 75 per cent spread across your all.
- Your resources and how you can get help and support in certain areas.
- The organisation and scheduling of priorities.
- How you can work smarter, not harder.
- Taking consistent, inspired action towards your all (because it's not enough to only dream and manifest. You have to take action!).

Part 2
SELF

Self-identity, self-worth, self-love, self-care, self-body, self-pleasure, self-made… there's a reason they all start with 'self'; they can't be found in anyone but you.

SELF-IDENTITY

THE LEARNING

You are (insert name). You are (insert number) years old. You are a (insert job here).

Who are you? Who are you *really*? Are you *you* because of you or because the world made you this way? Do you know your place in this world? How do you answer those awkward ice breakers in a group environment? Fun fact about yourself? (Cue the anxiety racking your brain for one.) Two truths and a lie? What makes you, *you*? You are normal, right?

Many of us want to be 'normal' and fit in. We aren't born with an identity, we are taught an identity from those that surround us. This is then embedded in our minds and becomes the precedence of who we think we are.

You are told your age, which family you are a part of, what type of person you are. The list goes on. The older you get, the more this develops. If someone or something stated who or what you are, you must be that.

- An ex-boyfriend once mentioned you were selfish, so you must be selfish.
- That one aunt you see only at Christmas commented on your weight, so you must be fat.
- You're a Scorpio, so you must be crazy.

Don't get me started on the personality tests! ENFP-A anyone? Maybe you let social media assign your identity. Write a witty bio (but don't try too hard); upload photos of your life that create an ideal, perfect version of you (with just the right ratio of self to non-self); post thirst traps (you look amazing and he regrets breaking up with you); post travelling photos (because you're a cultured jet-setter); post photos with the girls (because you have friends and you're not self-obsessed); post a cute photo of your puppy (because everyone loves dogs); post a photo of the sunset (everyone has one); post a photo of a family gathering (because #lifevalues); write self-depreciating captions (because you don't want people to think you're too confident and therefore arrogant).

We have learned to attach our identities to so many things outside of ourselves: your relationship status (I'm Mrs… or my boyfriend is a surgeon); your achievements (I've won this award and that); your success (#femaleceo); your possessions (I own an apartment and have three Chanel bags).

It seems we don't have much of a choice as to who we are because of the conditioning we've received from those around us.

Then there are the labels!
One that I dislike is 'cute'.
'You're cute, Phi.'

'Cute' made me think of puppies and flowers. I wanted to be sexy because I thought that's what I needed to be in order to be loved and wanted. Men love 'sexy'! They don't want cute. That's what sexually-saturated Pop Culture had me believe.

Aah yes, being a woman… We're even taught that being a woman is hard. We're expected to be perfect, yet being a woman is messy, chaotic, raw and beautiful. We are conditioned to be ashamed of our desires (see 'Self-Pleasure' chapter for more), to be ashamed of our feelings (see 'The Feels' chapter for more). We bleed, burp, sweat, smell and… fart.

We are also judged by our appearance. Our body has to look a certain way. Showing off skin is slutty and if you wear knee high boots you're 'asking for it'. You hardly see Pop Culture discuss what men are wearing. Being a 'feminine woman' means wearing flowy dresses and having long hair. Historically, femininity has been associated with the colour pink, wearing high heels, having a lightness to your step, speaking softly and smelling of jasmine and roses. We feel the pressure to strip ourselves of our true nature and sanitise to become palatable for others. We filter our feelings and repress our thoughts and desires.

Do you identify as a 'high-achieving woman' who is good at everything and has their life together? You not only want to meet expectations, but you also want to exceed them.

I believe the 'high-achieving woman' stems from the 'good girl'. Being a good girl means behaving and achieving. Your accomplishments and productivity determine your worth. You put everyone before yourself. You walk on eggshells to keep the peace, no matter what. You're nice all the time and get along with everyone, even at the expense of your sanity. You're always busy and need more in your life. You're desperate to obtain approval, to be validated and, most of all, loved. Beneath the good girl is meticulous, painstakingly, forced control.

Beautiful soul, underneath it all you are a soul having a human experience. In actual fact, you *aren't* a lot of things. You are not your thoughts. You are not your emotions. You are not your parents. You are not your past. You are not your mistakes. You are not your bank account. You are not your job. You *are.*

Stories aren't just found in fairy tales, books and movies. We live inside stories that our mind creates and identifies with. Our brain pieces these stories together to create the ultimate story of 'me'.

The voice inside your head has created 'you' by weaving together pieces of your past experiences and what you believe to be true. It all then pieces together like a jigsaw puzzle. Only certain pieces make it into this jigsaw puzzle.

Have you noticed this storytelling? The stories you weave that begin with 'I'. I am the type of person who… I am not like that because… I am not worthy because… I believe that… I am right because… The stories make us feel a certain way, the stories make us act a certain way.

THE UNLEARNING

You are a soul having a human experience. Your identity is a costume you wear and you're the one that gets to decide what that looks like.

Your true self doesn't identify with the stories. Your true self is in your expression, being, essence and knowing. There's nothing to defend, assert, prove or cling to (that is what we call ego). The ego isn't necessarily as bad as it's made out to be. We need ego. Saying the ego is evil is like saying water or fire are evil. Water *can* drown you. Fire *can* burn you. The ego *can* distort your personality. However, all three are needed in life and only become hurtful when misused.

You haven't done this knowingly; it has instinctively happened through your experiences and conditioning. You aren't who you think you are, who you are is the presence underneath the layers. You awaken to your true self when you become conscious of this and free yourself from all the stories. You are. You are 'I am'. That's it. So freeing, so powerful.

You are the space between your thoughts. Pure consciousness, soul and presence.

In saying that, yes, you are here on Earth as a human for a reason. To live a human experience which involves this concept of 'identity'.

Many of us believe that we have to be and act a certain way so we can be liked. It's not your job to be likeable. It's your job to be *you*. There is no soul that has been through what you've been through. Not being you is a disservice to the world! You are the universe expressed in human form. You are divine. You are pure magic.

We spend our whole lives desperate to be seen, desperate to please, desperate to be heard and desperate to be loved. The question is, do you really like and respect yourself? Do you want to be loved for who you really are or the mask that you wear? You don't even like everybody so why does everybody have to like you? Your people are your people. Forget being liked and focus on being true to you!

You are here to live your life for *you*. Not your mum. Not your dad.

Not your friends. Not your family. Not your children. YOU.

You aren't here to live a sacrificial life or to be a martyr like the many women who have come before you. You don't have to appease the desires of others at the expense of your health and happiness. You don't have to abandon yourself to be loved or to get what you want in love, life, relationships, success and beyond. You aren't just a daughter, friend, sister, mum, aunty, colleague etc. You're not here to be everything to everyone.

As a human, you're allowed to take up space. You're allowed to be outrageous and bold. You're allowed to be emotional and sensitive. You're allowed to be 'slutty'. You're allowed to not desire sexual intimacy. You're allowed to hold high standards without being called a 'bitch'. You're allowed to demand for what you want. You're allowed to be messy. You're allowed to feel without being labelled 'crazy' or 'sensitive'. Most of all, you're allowed to have a voice.

Your voice and confidence are currency. They impact how you move in this world.

You are not here to just be a follower. You aren't here to be a slave to your mind. You aren't here to follow the same rules. You aren't here to do what has been done. You're here to rise. Rise above it all. To tune into the magnetic pull of the bliss in your heart, body and soul. You are here to break the mould. You are here to be unique and different. You are here to be a catalyst of change. You are here to be a leader. A visionary. A maverick. A wonder. A revolutionary.

Tell me, beautiful soul, are you exhausted from carrying all those labels and stories that have defined who you are? You are not your trauma. You are not your illness. What you've been through is valid. No matter how bad someone else has it, no matter what anyone else says, no matter what anyone else thinks, no matter who believes you, you are resilience beaming through. You are the bravery that roars. You are the wisdom books can't contain. You are the light that continues to shine. You are the power beyond measure.

In this lifetime, we will mourn and hold funerals for all the versions of ourselves that we've been. You aren't who you were in the past anymore. You are who are you are now, here, in this present moment. Thank your past self for helping you survive. Thank your past self for being strong and enduring pain. Thank your past self for doing her best and fighting hard. Thank your past self for being brave. Thank your past self for getting back up and continuing to try. Thank your past self for making you who you are today. Thank your past self for making mistakes which you've learned from. Thank your past self for letting you move forward. Thank your past self because even if she no longer resonates or aligns with who you are today… you couldn't have done it without her.

As you work on yourself and reach the next level in your growth, don't be surprised if you feel joy and sadness at the same time. As we evolve and let go of our past self, we mourn who we were. The past you that put up with bad behaviour, that gave so much without return, that always needed something or someone to feel complete, that was blind to what was unfolding before your eyes, that self-sabotaged and the past you that deserved better not only from yourself but those around you. It's normal to grieve over the past you and to love the past you, yet still grow into who you are now. You are allowed to change; your identity isn't fixed.

If you're reading this and don't know your 'identity', great, what an opportunity… Your identity isn't outside of you. It's not the money that makes you feel rich, it's you. It's not love that makes you feel worthy, it's you. It's not your career that makes you feel successful, it's you. It's not your body that makes you feel desirable, it's you. It's not your friends or partner that makes you feel loveable, it's you. It's not your appearance that makes you feel beautiful, it's you. It's not your home or bank account that makes you feel secure, it's you. It's not social media that makes you feel seen, it's you. It's not your clothes that makes you feel pretty, it's you. It's all you. Nothing can make you feel anything because it's all you. None of these things have any inherent value or meaning, you are the one that gives it meaning and puts your energy into it.

All in all, maybe it's not that you're changing… maybe it's that you're remembering and reawakening to who you really are through the process of unlearning. The visual process that comes to mind is that of the 7-stage transformation of the scorpion in astrology. Fun fact, based on this a scorpion starts as a spider. Through these stages, the scorpion dies in order to be reborn as the phoenix, transcending and rising from its own ashes to soar and shine. This is *The Great Unlearning* coming home to you.

YOUR GREAT UNLEARNING

1. MEDITATION

Meditation is an incredible tool used to connect with your present self. Meditation is not undertaken to achieve thoughtlessness, but rather to return to your true nature.

Ways to enter meditation:

- Focus on your breathing. Have you noticed that it's difficult to think whilst focusing on your breathing? Continue breathing, as long as your exhale is longer than your inhalation, you'll be sending signals to your nervous system to relax.
- You can meditate in various forms, but this is how I do it. Sit up in a position that supports your back if you can. Whilst lying down is an option, I tend to find I fall asleep! If you do fall asleep, don't feel bad—it clearly demonstrates how you need rest. Take a few deep breaths and relax into your body. Close your eyes and focus on the point in-between your eyebrows. Thoughts and feelings will come and that's okay. Observe them instead of going into them. At some point you will get lost in a thought and as soon as you realise, come back to the present moment. Breathe.

2. STORY SELF

Answering the below journal prompts can help you become aware of the mental narratives you identify with.

- What are the stories that make up your identity?
- Reach out to your network and ask their story of who you are.
- Observe and reflect on your social media presence. What story have you created there?
- How do you introduce yourself to someone?
- What are your go-to stories to tell others about yourself?
- What stories stem from your culture?
- What stories stem from the society you live in?

3. MIRROR MIRROR

Spend some time looking at yourself in the mirror. Focus on your reflection and look deep into your pupils. How does it feel to look directly into your own eyes?

- What do you see?
- What do you feel?
- What thoughts come up?
- What stories do your eyes tell?
- What have your eyes seen?
- How can you have peace with the person in the mirror?

Talk to yourself out loud. You can try phrases such as:

- I love you.
- I accept you.
- You're important to me.
- You got this.
- You can handle anything.
- I'm proud of you.
- I know you.

SELF-WORTH

THE LEARNING
Your self-worth wavers depending on what others think of you.

How much are you worth? Did you respond in terms of dollars? It seems society sees your worth in dollars.

Would you reply with your achievements and perhaps how they've contributed to the world in some shape or form? Would you freeze and not know what to say? Would you opt for the 'call a friend' option and ask them?

We don't often think about how we define our own worth because we look to others for the answer. Ultimately, we often care more about what someone else thinks of us, than what we think of ourselves. This stems from our natural desire to be accepted and to belong, which was essential for survival for our ancestors. Nowadays, we grow up with the core belief that if we are *something* enough, then we can have whatever we want. It could be pretty enough to have love. It could be smart enough to be successful. It could be successful enough to be powerful. The list goes on.

Maybe you've never known what it's like to have self-worth, because you have low self-esteem. You may think things like *no one will ever fall in love with me*, or *I'm not good enough*, or *it's impossible for me to be successful or pretty*. It's looking in the mirror with dread or repulsion and yearning to look like the people you see on social media or TV. You might feel like a failure. You might think you're broken. You might treat yourself like an incompetent fool because you believe you can't complete basic tasks.

We aren't born loathing ourselves. This is something that we've learned based on how other people have treated us. Maybe you were ignored as a child. Maybe your parents always compared you to your friends or siblings. Maybe that one thing that kid at school said about your appearance has stuck with you. Maybe your parents only showed you love when you had good grades at school or came first in sporting activity. Maybe you were bullied.

I've been in the ebb and flow of the self-worth circus my whole life. My first memory involving self-worth was when I lost my self-worth, not that I had memorable instances of having it in the first place. Growing up, I felt I was shy and ugly. I was quiet and during my schooling years, I pursued good marks because even if I tried to pursue boys, they weren't interested in me. When I took a break halfway through my degree, I honestly thought I was going to die, and I did… just not in the way I thought I would. My dramatic brain equated this with literal death when it was my ego and the construction of who I thought I was that would. I took a break in the middle of my double degree after losing my dad, which caused me to have a meltdown. I burst into tears at the doctor's office when she told me if I didn't have a break, my insomnia and mental health would be deadly. I couldn't even fathom who I would be without the piece of paper that would declare I had completed a Bachelor of Commerce and a Bachelor of Laws. My life was ruined. I was meant to become a high-achieving corporate lawyer. It honestly felt like my whole identity crumbled.

I guess you could say I was a late bloomer, because later on I became very invested in men, particularly after my first boyfriend cheated on me. That shredded my self-esteem. Where did I go to try and find my self-worth? To other men, of course. I needed to prove to myself that I was lovable, attractive and desirable. I got so high on the validation of men that I put them on a pedestal. The likes climbing up on my social media was euphoric. I loved getting friend requests, DMs and texts. I yearned to be lusted after. I would wear outfits that showed off my cleavage and legs. I wore high heels. I wore double-padded push up bras. I regularly went to the gym. I did everything I could to be appealing in the male gaze. When it came to sex, I did everything to please them: faked my orgasms, faked that I had no emotions and faked that I was the cool girl so detached and yet deep down I desperately wanted an emotional connection with them. Even with this all, I was still regularly ghosted and the idea of being someone's girlfriend seemed far out of reach.

I would find myself testing my validation and so called 'self-worth'. I would get into situations just to try and prove to myself that I had self-worth. I found myself dating fuckboys to prove to myself that I was amazing enough to tame them and become their girlfriend. I found myself flirting with old flings just to feel the high of them wanting me again when I was no longer interested in them. I would find myself dating men I deemed highly successful (like high-flying financiers, successful start-up entrepreneurs, doctors, lawyers and ex-football players), hoping their self-worth would rub off on me. It just seemed like my worth came down to being wanted by a man.

I'll never forget one of my lowest points. Molly, my Canadian friend, was in town and I decided to take her out, along with the guy I was seeing, and his friends. All seemed well until I came back from the bar to hear a woman accusing the guy I was seeing of trying to sexually assault her in the bathroom. The worst thing is, I had previously seen him get with other girls in front of my face. I wish I could tell you that it all got better from there, but it didn't. My self-worth would take a few more hits before I finally decided to do something about it.

I regularly pretended to be okay with not being in an official relationship even though I wanted commitment. One guy I was seeing got high on nangs (small canisters of laughing gas that give you a temporary high) and badly berated me, calling me every name under the sun because I wanted to be in a relationship with him. At one stage, I was even in a long-distance relationship (from my perspective at least) with an older globe-trotting banker who I would never live in the same city as because I didn't think anyone would truly want me in my own state, let alone country.

Even writing this now makes my heart so sad because I was in such a bad place back then in my early twenties, but I've gained so much wisdom from these experiences.

As a life coach, I've seen the cycle of self-worth play out in various ways with my clients. The most common one being imposter syndrome. Perhaps you've experienced it too? Doubting yourself and feeling like a fraud.

I still experience this. Especially when I've had huge opportunities, such as writing this book or walking the red carpet for the Cannes Film Festival. I work with a lot of high-achieving women who bind their self-worth to their work and how much they could get done in a day. I've seen them plagued with stress, too scared to take a sick day and being unable to say 'no' to any workplace request. Being seen as a failure is mortifying for them, they have to excel in everything they do.

You are worth more than a pay cheque and nothing is worth causing your health to deteriorate. More often than not, this notion also extends into perfectionism paralysis prodded on by self-pressure. It's as if they believe there's a constant spotlight on them and every single move of theirs is being watched (spoiler alert: it isn't). Most people tend to be consumed by their own lives and don't notice what you're doing.

I believe this hyper self-awareness stems from our endless social media scrolling and tapping. Our constant comparison cycle. We naturally do so with people in our circles, now we do so with anyone and everyone online.

In our modern-day society digital likes seem to mean that someone likes you. Being loved looks like someone commenting on your photo or sharing a photo of you on your birthday (*let's be honest, you always pick the pictures that you look good in!*). Being someone's friends means that you 'follow' each other. Quality time means exchanging DMs. Every notification is a buzz of validation.

Social media has become the modern day *Keeping Up with the Joneses* whereby we're striving to be like and to own as much as those around us. Working with clients that believe social media to be just as real as their immediate lives is astounding. Social media is not real. It's a carefully curated highlights reel for many.

You wouldn't let just anybody enter your house, right? Why would you let any stranger from the internet into your mind and influence what you think of yourself? It's also scary that filters and face/body tuning are the norm. We have normalized these to the point where we have forgotten that normal skin has texture and pores. At the tap of an app, you can lose a couple of kilograms or enhance your butt—if only it was that easy in real life!

THE UNLEARNING

You have no worth because you are truly priceless. You are beyond having a 'worth' like a product.

One thing I know for sure is that you cannot measure your soul.

If you were to try measuring *you*, how would you start? How could you encapsulate everything that is you? Instead of attempting this, remember the following points:

- You feel unworthy because you're basing your worth on how much you do in a day.
- You feel unworthy because you're basing your worth on how 'successful' you are.
- You feel unworthy because you're basing your worth on your relationship status.
- You feel unworthy because you're basing your worth on the negative self-talk in your head, which is a product of conditioning, your upbringing and your life experiences.
- You feel unworthy because you think you have worth in the first place.

You aren't a product or service for sale. You are a miracle. A divine soul. You can't put a price on that. You are beyond worth. You can't be measured in dollars, likes, followers, promotions, weight, lovability, grades, scores, status because you are the universe in human form. This is beyond science, scales and measurement. You are life in motion. Life has no limitations or boundaries. Life is magic. Life is poetry and prose. Life is clear skies and thunderstorms. Life is sunshine and shadows. Life is the inhale and exhale. Life is living.

Whilst you have no 'worth' it's important to recognise the importance of valuing yourself. What I mean by this is understanding that you are an irreplaceable one of a kind. We live in a world full of incredible people, like yourself, and I hope you never forget that. It's easy to feel tiny and insignificant when there's almost 7.8 billion of us. We do a great job of recognising how amazing and special other people are but forget our own strengths and specialities. The sun and moon are great, yet the sun is special in its own way and so is the moon. The sun can't be the moon or do its job and if it could we would lose out on the sun! Your existence is needed. You would be missed by so many people if you weren't here. Your life causes ripple effects throughout the world even if you don't think so. That drunk girl you spoke to in the bathroom is thanking her stars she met you on a night out and finally got around to dumping her toxic ex. Your local barista who remembers your order off by heart not only because you order regularly but also because they appreciate you. That donation you made to charity has changed someone's life and you'll never even know about it.

Drop the assumption that you aren't as valuable as somebody else. A life is a life. Everyone is so different and on a different journey that there isn't a plausible comparison to make. Even identical twins are completely different in their own ways. Each person experiences and views life in a different way. The only thing we all have in common is the fact we were born and will die. Can you imagine if you were born a year or two earlier or later. What if you had different parents? Lived somewhere different? Had different friends and/or family? Different thoughts? All these factors would completely change you and your life. You're not pretty like her, you're pretty like *you*. You're not smart like her, you're smart like *you*. You can't make everyone happy… If you want to compare yourself, compare yourself to a past version of you. Get hyper-focused on your own lane. As they say, the grass isn't green on the other side, the grass is greener where you water it. So, start watering yourself! Watch yourself flourish and bloom.

Be conscious of the way you talk to yourself. You are always listening.

Words have power. Don't overlook the weight and power of a single word. Be mindful of saying mistake instead of flaw, blunder, failure or error. Mistake could be seen as *'mis'* and *'take'* as in you missed a take. That's it, no more and no less. Imagine if all the mean things you said about yourself were rocks you'd thrown at yourself. Would you still throw them? Being hard on yourself won't make life easier. Life is already difficult enough without negative self-talk making it even more so.

Think of your self-talk as if it were the loving voice of your best friend. What would she say? I know at first being kind to yourself can be hard but the fact that you're willing to try will make a difference. When you stop using self-depreciating humour, you'll be surprised by the change within yourself. When you catch yourself being unkind, opt for more positive wording. Reframing is particularly useful. Instead of 'I could have done better,' try 'I did the best that I could at the time given circumstances'.

Don't search for validation outside of yourself, instead turn within. It's natural for us to search outside for validation as social beings and the sting of rejection is rooted in our evolutionary biology. Social acceptance was a necessity to being alive because rejection from others was death. If you were cast out it meant less chances of eating, sleeping and being protected by the community.

In the modern day we see this with dating (I have been rejected many, many times). In fact, a 2013 study by the University of Michigan Medical School team found that the human brain responds to social rejection the same way as it does to physical trauma: by releasing opioids (natural painkillers) to reduce pain.

I love to use this example with my clients: we all love dessert. Imagine you're a dessert. Maybe you're a gooey chocolate cake. Somebody else is a carrot cake and another tiramisu. They are all super tasty, but everyone has a different preference.

I believe we all have to be aware of what we bring to the table. This sentiment is inspired by one of my favourite quotes: '*A woman who knows what she brings to the table is not afraid to eat alone.*' Fall in love with yourself first. Date yourself first. Be the type of person you want to be with. It all starts with you. You don't have to wait to have a partner, to experience love.

When I started working on my self-love, the way I saw dating and sex completely changed. The people that entered my world changed. When you realise how special you are, you'll stop seeing people who don't. You're allowed to ask for what you want and you're allowed to have standards. The act of asking is different to begging or demanding. It's not unreasonable to ask that your love be reciprocated, especially when it comes to the context of looking for a partnership: that's exactly what it is, two people working together. You deserve to be loved, cherished and adored for all of you, not just parts of you. You deserve to know where you stand and not be in limbo questioning and getting annoyed at yourself for wanting to know. You deserve to be with someone who feels safe, someone you can rely on. You deserve the kind of love you give to others and envision for others.

The best thing you can do to value yourself is accept who you are right now. Be unapologetically you. Don't waste your precious time trying to be good enough for someone else. Don't waste your precious time with someone who doesn't want to or can't commit to the relationship you desire. This might be difficult because you've conditioned to believe otherwise. You've been told who to be and what attributes makes you worthy. I'm here to tell you that you are beautiful and incredible as you are. You can be yourself, whoever you want that to be. You don't have to be extraordinary, it's okay to just be… average… boring… fun… playful… bubbly. You don't have to be a completed masterpiece, you are a masterpiece in progress. You don't have to justify your existence, because you're already here. Be here right now and open to becoming a masterpiece. Live your life, enjoy it and forget about the ideas of self-worth that you've been conditioned to believe. You are beyond them.

YOUR GREAT UNLEARNING

1. SELF-TALK REALITY

In your journal, write down what the voice in your head says about you (your self-talk).

Now imagine that a stranger said these things to you. How do you feel?

2. SELF-VALIDATION

Below are some methods for self-validation that you can start with:

- When talking about gratitude, ensure you have saved a section for yourself. What attributes of yourself are you grateful for?
- When wanting something from someone else, how do you give it to yourself? Whether it's praise or a certain behaviour/action.
- Speak to your inner child as if a parent—your wiser older self.
- Check in with yourself. What do you need right now? What do you desire right now?
- Reaffirm your feelings. Whatever arises, say to yourself it's okay to feel this way. It's safe to feel this way.
- Pay attention to your body, particularly gut feelings and 'knowings'.
- Acknowledge your thoughts and feelings instead of pushing them away.
- Be compassionate when it comes to yourself. Embody love and kindness.
- Self-soothe: take a shower, drink a cup of tea or hug yourself.

3. SELF-ACCEPTANCE

Below are some ways to help you to accept yourself:

- Take a sceptical and discerning approach to your inner critic's voice.
- Acknowledge your strengths and gifts as well as the areas you are working on.
- Forgive yourself. This takes baby steps but it's important that you decide and intend to do so.
- Practice a compassionate and understanding dialogue with yourself.
- Reframe your thoughts, find different perspectives.

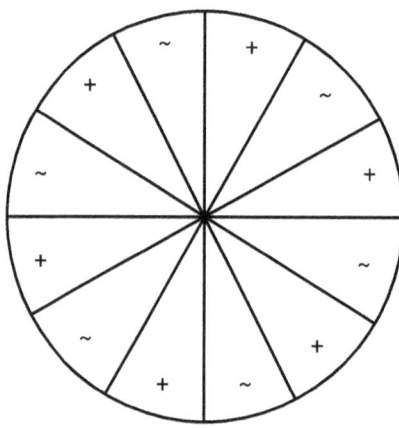

Have a balanced approach to who you are:
+ = a positive area of self
~ = an area you are working on

You may find speaking to loved ones can help you form a better understanding of yourself.

SELF-LOVE

THE LEARNING
It's easy to love others but hard to love yourself.

If I were to ask you to name all the places, things and people you love, I can almost guarantee that your name is last, if it is even on the list at all. We aren't taught how to love ourselves. Can you imagine if your school's curriculum included self-love? That would be a start. Although I understand this would be difficult as there is no standard, one size fits all of what self-love actually looks like. It depends on the individual.

On the other hand, we are taught how to love others. We are taught we must love our family because we are related to them, which can lead to difficulties later on in life where guilt, shame and expectations are concerned. *Forgive him because he's family. She didn't mean that, she's your sister.* If you grew up religious like me, you would have heard, 'love one another' and be expected to love God above anything and anyone else. It's even gotten to the point where we feel guilty for loving ourselves—we believe it means we are arrogant or self-obsessed.

We are taught that we aren't enough—we aren't 'good' enough, 'pretty' enough, 'palatable' enough and the list goes on. We believe that our flaws prevent people from loving us. We set unattainable standards for ourselves. We even try to buy self-love with shopping sprees to boost our happiness hormones for that small moment of intoxicating confidence. This ideology is promoted by businesses because they benefit financially from our lack of self-love. The rush you feel when you're wearing a new outfit or find parcels waiting at your door. If you're feeling down, Uber Eats has you covered—I love me a good comfort meal and nothing tastes better than overpriced sushi that you didn't have to leave the couch for. Heck, I've even tried to buy someone's love, thinking that they'd finally commit to me if I buy them tickets to that sold out gig they wanted to go. I tried to buy them but realised something was wrong when they cost $600 a ticket! I'm embarrassed to admit that I told him and he responded with, 'Why didn't you get them?' After working up the courage to reply, I sent him a long text (one of those essay ones) admitting that I wanted to be exclusive, since we had been dating for seven months. He replied, 'That's very sweet of you. I still want to sleep with other women, but you can be my top girl. That's pretty much like my girlfriend!'

Through all the conditioning and programming, we have come to believe that we have to meet certain criteria in order to be loved. You believe that you have to be perfect in order to be loved. You believe that you have to be successful in order to be loved. You believe that you have to be beautiful in order to be loved. You believe that you have to put others first in order to be loved. This notion becomes evident when you look in the mirror and all you see are flaws instead of what you love about yourself. It becomes all too evident when you look at the life choices you've made from a place of fear and scarcity instead of love and abundance. When you don't love yourself, you self-sabotage. You make choices that feel good in the short term but often lead to pain and destruction (anyone else ever drink too much alcohol and blackout?). You'll also turn to doing radical things. When I was younger, I made a fake male profile on Facebook and commented on one of my pictures because I thought no one was even remotely interested in me. Embarrassingly enough, in my early twenties, I even fantasised about anonymously sending flowers to my office to look desired.

So not loving yourself—yeah, I know all too well about this. Ironically, all I ever wanted was to be loved. I didn't even know I could love myself—it was a foreign concept. My parents wanted to me grow up independent as an only child. I remember when I was around eight my parents suddenly decided it was time to withhold their affection so that I wouldn't rely on it. No more goodnight kisses. No more saying I love you. I asked them later on why they did this, and they said they didn't want me to get too used to being loved or receiving validation, because I would only wind up getting hurt… however, their actions had the opposite effect. Through their actions, it was clear they loved me, but I never got to hear the words I so desperately wanted.

The only times I was validated verbally from them was when I was successful at school and so I was conditioned to believe I had to be successful to be loved. This was amplified by the fact that both worked very long and very hard hours. On a subconscious level, I know I thought I wasn't lovable enough because my parents separated and divorced (which had nothing to do with me). As a result, I also had abandonment issues which led to an anxious attachment style in dating. Cue the huge mess if someone took more than a day to reply to a text. Cue overthinking and overanalysing. Cue me becoming an obsessive private investigator to try and figure out who else they were dating.

I believed that I had to prove to myself and everyone else that I was lovable. I had to be very successful and the best way to show it to the world was to be in a relationship—look at me, I'm worthy of love—someone *chose* me!

As a result of all of the above, I became so hungry for love that I would binge on scrap—breadcrumbs. When it came to dating, I felt like I constantly had to prove I was the best person for men. I would go above and beyond for them even though we weren't in a committed relationship. I made sure to never ask for anything because that made me look needy. I treated dating like a job, constantly doing so many things to gain affection. I believed I had to earn love. Sex on tap? You got it. Constant blow jobs even though I didn't feel like it? You got it. Home cooked meals? You got it. Ironing your shirts? You got it. As I did this, I subconsciously started believing love was hard work, so much so that I became exhausted. All this work and still nothing to show for it. I became the woman who was never the girlfriend but always the side chick or the one only in it for fun. It seemed like the guys I dated would end up in a relationship, not with me, but after me.

When I look back at my dating history, I can see all the holes in my concept of self-love. My dad wasn't an emotional man. He was a 'classic Asian' dad. After his death I came to realise he loved me not in the outwardly way I craved for but through his actions. He provided me with food and a roof over my head. He helped me do my homework. He taught me how to speak and write. He taught me how to draw. His absence after the divorce amplified my desire for his affection. It then became exacerbated when I lost him forever. I unconsciously looked for what he represented—love, affection, strength and protection—in older men. When I was twenty-one, I was already dating twenty-eight-year-olds.

I even noticed that I dated men to borrow their self-love because I lacked it in myself. The men I dated were considered distinguished achievers with lots of money and status, particularly bankers. The men I dated were football players, and when they would walk into a room, heads would turn, and their presence would captivate everyone's attention. The men I dated were influential in their networks. People would gush about how amazing they were, but behind the scenes, I would be confused because, in reality, they weren't very nice at all. Doctors are stereotypically admired for their commitment and kindness, yet I dated one who led me on, only to tell me I was probably the eighth priority in his life. He would reappear in my life, a year later and even then, I was willing to give him another chance until I found out he had a girlfriend. So, how did I begin loving myself…?

THE UNLEARNING
*What if it's not about loving yourself but
loving being yourself?*

Even though you weren't taught self-love, it's never too late to begin. You are never too old for the love you deserve to give yourself. Notice how I said that this is something you have to learn. There is no on switch for self-love unfortunately. It won't happen overnight; you will have to practice it in every moment of your life. Self-love takes conscious work. Especially when you realise that it's an ongoing and dynamic journey. Change is constant. No one talks about how uncomfortable and scary it is to learn self-love in the beginning. It's a leap of faith into the unknown. It's a commitment and devotion you make to yourself in every moment. You have to try, even when facing challenging moments.

A huge part of this journey is learning to accept and allow all the parts of being you. The parts you try to hide in secrecy. The parts you deem undesirable and strange. The parts that have experienced trauma and pain. The parts that have been deemed difficult by others. All of it—the 'good,' the 'bad,' the 'beautiful' and the 'ugly,' through the highs and the lows. In the beginning, loving yourself may feel foreign but over time you will become accustomed to it—no one speaks about that. Self-love is consciously choosing the kind and loving voice within, despite the negativity and noise. Self-love is a vow you make to yourself to speak in the way you've always wanted to be spoken to.

Start a self-love revolution with yourself. Out of all the people you could fall in love with, you chose yourself—that is powerful. There's nothing more bold, brave and beautiful than doing this. Love being yourself for exactly who you are. Not buying into the limiting beliefs that you are broken and that something is missing. Stop neglecting your needs and desires. This doesn't make you more lovable. In fact, it makes it harder to love you because it isn't the truth. Moreover, it is inevitable that your resentment will internally build and spill over into others. Therefore, shift your attention from everyone else towards yourself. If you're anything like me, you will do well to take your energy away from living a life for romantic relationships.

We try to find a home in other people's arms and hearts yet become strangers with ourselves. Home isn't a physical place but a place within you. Within you there are so many answers you are afraid to acknowledge. Instead, shift your focus to living a life that revolves around your path and purpose. The purpose of your life is not to love yourself but to love being yourself. I saw it explained on social media this way, *'be the subject, not the object.'* Game changer. Go out on solo dates. Romance yourself. Forget love language with another, what's your own love language?

When it comes to dating, I know you're sick and tired of being alone. I know you're sick and tired of feeling like you will be single for the rest of your life. I know you're sick and tired of searching for the one. I know you're sick of going on dates and having your heart broken or being disappointed. I know you're sick and tired of waiting for the one to show up. I know you're sick and tired of trusting the universe. I know you're sick and tired because you're on the verge of giving up. If there is one thing I can share with you, it's this, from my heart and soul to yours: a relationship doesn't bring love into your life, love brings a relationship into your life. Fall in love with the person in the mirror. She is still here despite everything that has happened. You are strong. You are special. Learning to love yourself is not a necessity or prerequisite to receiving love like the toxic part of the self-development world has pushed but I truly believe loving yourself sets a good foundation for all forms of love. As Stephen Chbosky wrote in the Perks of Being a Wallflower, *'we accept the love, we think we deserve.'*

Don't wait to be chosen. Unlearn being validated from people who don't truly care for you. You deserve better than messages that are left unread or haven't been responded to. You deserve better than feeling like an option rather than a priority. You deserve better than last minute cancellations and made-up excuses. You deserve to be appreciated. You deserve to be treated well. You deserve to be adored for who you are. Don't be afraid to realise you deserve better. Therefore, choose yourself. Give yourself so much love that you don't have the capacity to accept anything less. You do that when you decide to stay home instead of going to the party you couldn't care less for. You do that when you decide not to reply to that person who broke your heart several times.

Exercise the ultimate act of self-love, honouring your inner truth even when it is painful. This means walking away from and letting go of what no longer serves you. Maybe it's a job, relationship or location. It's breaking free from what boxes you in—the pressure of society, the weight of what other people think and your own beliefs. When everything falls away, one thing will always remain: the truth. It cannot be ignored. You can live in ignorance, but the truth won't.

There will be days when loving being yourself will be tough. Sometimes all you can do is love a tiny bit more than yesterday and that is more than enough. Patience is a must, it's one of the greatest forms of self-love. It's beautiful to acknowledge there are things you'd like to work on and improve whilst simultaneously blooming at the same time. Reframe self-criticism into self-compassion. Try giving yourself credit for how much you try instead of being so critical of everything you do. Love looking at yourself in the mirror and not picking out all the flaws you see. Love getting up after you've been knocked down. Love eating what you crave for instead of the lower calorie option. Love that your triggers no longer have a hold over you after all your personal growth and development. Most of all, love yourself as you are here and now in the present moment. You deserve love right here, right now. Not when you achieve that goal looming over you. Not when you finally fit into that dress. Not when you have that specific amount of money. *Now*. So many people focus on who they will be in the future that they forget and neglect who they are right now. You deserve love now and always have.

As a life coach, I have noticed self-love as being one of the main areas of focus for my clients, and one of the most important aspects I have found is forgiveness. We tend to be able to forgive others but when it comes to forgiving ourselves, we seem to be harsh and stubborn critics. To not make mistakes and to be perfect has been ingrained in us from early childhood. You've learned that making mistakes means that you're a failure and something is wrong with you (not true). This fear of making mistakes holds you back, cradled by the safety of your comfort zone. You become afraid to try when trying is the most important thing. It's okay to make mistakes. You can't get it right every single time. Remember that time you got a low score in that test, does that really matter right now? Making a mistake is evidence of progress and tenacity. Making a mistake is an opportunity to learn and grow.

Therefore, whatever you've done, beautiful soul, forgive yourself. We have all made mistakes we aren't proud of. The past cannot be erased or changed but you can rescript the future. You now know better, and you're allowed to move forward with the gift of hindsight. As a result, you will be and will do better in the future. After all, who doesn't love a character redemption arc?

To love being yourself also requires self-respect. Self-respect is how you treat yourself and what you think of yourself. Holding yourself in alignment with your values. This means standing up for yourself and what you believe in. Having standards and upholding them. Acting from a place of integrity. The promises you make to yourself are very important. If you break them, you lose respect and trust for yourself—a huge price to pay. This happens from time to time, of course, however, try your best to stick to your promises, for everyone but especially for yourself. When you act with integrity your word is your word. What you say, you do. Take ownership and responsibility for what you put out in the world, whether it's your thoughts, feelings or actions. This doesn't mean you'll never put a foot wrong, but it helps keep you accountable. Self-respect also encompasses how you deal with situations particularly when things go wrong. You want to hold your head high and be proud of yourself. Self-respect means being aware of and acknowledging all the incredible strengths you have. In fact, self-respect is being you, in all your authenticity. The world doesn't want a copy of someone else or a diluted version of you. The world wants and needs you!

The self-love journey isn't easy. At times it feels easier to fall into old habits. This doesn't mean the journey isn't worth it. How you speak to yourself, how you meet your needs, how you honour yourself and how you enjoy the experience of being human are all important factors. Life is already hard, why make it harder by hating yourself? Self-love means appreciating yourself. Self-love means to be kind to yourself. Self-love will teach you how to care for yourself. Caterpillars deserve to be as loved and as appreciated as butterflies are. You deserve to be loved wherever you are in your self-love journey. I hope you are proud of yourself for every step of self-love you take despite the setbacks. I hope you appreciate how far you've come and will continue to go. On this self-love journey, I hope you take a moment here now to hug yourself and celebrate. You are so lovable and loved, beautiful soul.

YOUR GREAT UNLEARNING

1. LOVE LETTER

Write a love letter to yourself.
Some prompts to help you:

I am so grateful for you…
Your best qualities and traits are…
I love the way you…
Your favourite memories include…
I love how passionate you are about…
I am proud of you for…
You are beautiful because…
You are like no one else because…
I know you feel loved when…
The ultimate date I would have with you involves…

Now read your letter out loud to yourself in the mirror.

Mirror work can be hard, so I always advise to build up to it. A great way to start is to stick post it notes around the perimeter of your mirror with loving self-affirmations and reminders.

You may also want to record yourself reading the letter so you can listen to yourself talking to yourself (trippy I know, but so powerful).

2. SELF-RESPECT ANALYSIS

This exercise will help you understand and reflect on your self-respect. Score yourself out of ten for each area. You may find it useful to journal upon the reflection of your scores.

I uphold my values	1 2 3 4 5 6 7 8 9 10
I am accountable for my actions	1 2 3 4 5 6 7 8 9 10
I take care of myself	1 2 3 4 5 6 7 8 9 10
I keep my word and promises	1 2 3 4 5 6 7 8 9 10
I am mindful of the way I talk to myself	1 2 3 4 5 6 7 8 9 10
I speak my inner truth	1 2 3 4 5 6 7 8 9 10
I communicate my needs and desires	1 2 3 4 5 6 7 8 9 10
I make my own decisions	1 2 3 4 5 6 7 8 9 10

3. FORGIVENESS GROWTH ACCELERATOR

i) Acknowledge what you need to do to forgive yourself for *insert mistake here*

ii) Context Circle—Draw a large circle around the above. Within it in the spaces, note down different factors that may have played an influence. Consider:

- Feelings
- The Past/History/Memories
- Upbringing
- Mindset
- Intentions

iii) Write down at least three things you have learned from making that mistake.

iv) Empty Chair Technique: Imagine sitting in front of you is the younger version of yourself in the chair. Have an open discussion and dialogue on the above.

SELF-CARE

THE LEARNING
Self-care is nice to have. It comes with face masks…

Our lives are so busy. All hustle and bustle. Grind and shine. It can be easy to forget to look after yourself. Thankfully, in recent times, self-care is moving into the societal spotlight. However, it's become very glamourised. Bubble baths. Bath bombs. Boujee blowdrys. Massages. Coffee scrubs. Extra avocado. Scented candles. Self-care can be luxurious. In fact, the wellness industry is now worth trillions of dollars. Portions of the industry are what we know as traditional money makers that are disguised under the veil of wellness (such as diet and beauty). Splurging at the spa for the latest natural wrinkle remedy. Splashing out on a special water that detoxifies whilst boosting your immune system. The roll out of self-care journals, self-care facials, self-care tea, self-care crystals and so forth. Doing acts in the name of self-care has become a means to an end. You can't just enjoy a face mask anymore, nowadays it must brighten your skin! Self-care has been idolised, put on a pedestal. If you practice self-care, everything will turn out just fine…

In all the noise, the true meaning of self-care has become muddled and lost. At its core self-care is about taking care of yourself, so it should be simple, right? In the societal spotlight, self-care has blown out into long, tiring regimes of what we think it should look like. Ironically, this just creates stress. In fact, self-care has even become something performative to show off on social media. Taking up those new fitness fads—anyone for jumping on trampolines whilst wearing waist trainers? It could even look like splurging on a week's worth of organic and activated green juices (whilst you secretly starve and binge on pizza at night—been there, done that). The act of treating yourself has been taken too far. Personally, I would end up racking up debt. Spending money on the highly raved about facial oil that would set you back hundreds. In fact, it has a rebellious edge to it when you're beyond burnt out—just absolutely fucking depleted. What's the point of it all anyway? I might as well spend all my hard-earned money in a matter of minutes. In a way, this looks like a toddler throwing a tantrum.

Sometimes the true reality of self-care becomes a shadow unleashed. For me, self-care looked like a glass of wine. In the name and act of 'self-care' I would drink lots of wine on a Friday night after a stressful week at work. Self-care involved numbing my mind and shutting it off. Another glass of wine? Go on. Self-care.

In fact, work was where my lack of self-care really showed up. No matter how many face masks I did, I still felt burnt out. I naively believed that self-care meant doing what felt good without consideration for the long-term impacts and consequences. Quick fixes that temporarily helped were my go-to. Maybe you're like me and you also turned to escapism. Whatever I could do to take my mind off it all. Bingeing Bridgeton on repeat, wondering when Simon or Anthony was going to swan in and sweep me off my feet? Having rough sex so that you could forget about all the stress in your life. Fantasising and booking a holiday to literally get away from it all only to be disappointed it still lingers in your mind. But, hey, at least I was in Bali!

At times self-care can become a form of shame and self-loathing. Trying to meditate because you think that will cure your anxiety. Going on a diet and extreme amounts of exercise because you've been unhealthy. Putting on a tonne of make up because you've become a slob and lost yourself.

The lines between self-care and self-sabotage can blur. We use self-care as an excuse or loophole to justify certain behaviours that likely aren't beneficial for us in the long-term, but that short-term gratification feels so damn good—I know. It looks like 'I deserve this' or 'I earned it.' We then borrow on future time that is yet to happen,

'I'll put it off until tomorrow, next week, next month, next year…' Other times, it looks like relinquishing our power and being defeated by the cards dealt by life. 'There's nothing else I can do so I might as well…' The most common statement? 'This doesn't count…' Instead of addressing the root causes, we buy into self-care to alleviate it.

No matter how many massages I got, I was still burnt out. I was burning out because of the 'hustle culture'. I neglected my sleep because I would always go out after work to take the edge off things. A dinner with friends. A drinks date. I was burning the candle at both ends. There were times I forgot to eat until dinner or the opposite, I kept eating to find comfort in the name of self-care. I put everybody but myself first. I was a people pleaser. I would have sleepless nights stuck in endless loops of anxious thoughts jumbling around my mind like a washing machine. *Did I remember to do this? What if that person doesn't get back to me?* It went on and on. I would break out in sweats, waking up. Everything would get to be too much, and I would make it worse by procrastinating. I would reminisce about simpler and quieter times at work. I was under the conditioned belief that self-care was selfish (it's not, taking care of yourself is very important). I started to overcome this at work by taking a self-care day because, yes, being sick isn't just physical.

Ironically, even in my own business, I still experienced a lack of self-care. When my business was only in the side hustle stage, I worked so much that I had no energy left to be present in my relationship or spend time with friends. I lacked boundaries initially so I would reply to clients at all sorts of hours, like midnight. This led to me energetically taking on my clients' problems, which was a disaster as I did not have the capacity to take care of myself at the time.

As a result, one of my intentions was to create passive forms of income as a form of self-care for my energy. I also worked on my boundaries with my coaching, which resulted in me being happier and healthier. When I went full-time, I worked on this mindset: without you, there is no job, career, business, friendship, relationship, etc. Now, more than ever, I make my self-care a priority because when I'm at my best, I can give and do my best. This then creates those ripple effects I previously discussed. These ripple effects affect everyone

I encounter. After all, flight attendants give the best advice: in the event of an emergency, put your own oxygen mask on first. When you do, then you can help others.

THE UNLEARNING
Self-care is essential.

Self-care isn't just a nice thing to have or indulge in, it's a must. I love the analogy that compares recharging our personal batteries to that of our phone battery. You wouldn't let your phone run out of charge, so why would you let yourself?

Self-care is highly personal. It doesn't look a certain way. For one person it could be a luxury holiday to Paris and for another it could be wearing less make-up. One universal act I have found that benefits everyone is doing something for yourself first thing every morning, no matter what. Doing something for yourself before the rest of the world because messages, emails and notifications can wait. Let this be a flexible intention. For example, some mornings I like to start off with a swim in the sea and other mornings I'll meditate for at least thirty seconds.

Let's be real, self-care can be ridiculously unglamorous and unsexy. It's finally washing the bedsheets after months of use. It's washing the dishes that have been stacked up by the sink. It's making yourself get out of bed to take a shower and brush your teeth. We've all been there when we feel at rock bottom—in a slump and stuck in a rut. In times like this self-care can feel forced and as if it takes a lot of effort. Sure, it will take some energy and willpower but it's important because the things that seem trivial make a difference. It could look like eating when you're not in the mood. It could mean catching up with friends even though you'd rather continue being a hermit at home. It could be talking to a life coach or therapist about traumas that make you cower from healing. These practical things won't solve all your problems, but they will give you some breathing room and space to tackle the big tasks. When we neglect self-care, the little things add up.

Self-care has all the benefits. Funnily enough, do you want to know the best hack I've learned for productivity? It's self-care. Forget, stress and guilt. Self-care is win-win. Imagine if we lived in a society where measuring and increasing self-care were important aspects of life?

When you're happy you can do more. You can help more. You can give from an overwhelming stream not a depleted puddle. Though, don't just rest to be more productive. Rest because it is nourishing and replenishing. Rest isn't something you need to ask permission for, it is a given. Rest isn't something you earn from having a busy day or hitting all your goals. Rest is simply for when you want and need it. It's okay to be closed off and retreat from the world. You're just temporarily closed for mental and spiritual maintenance.

Self-care is also mental peace. We all know the feeling of having a million tabs open in your mind like your web browser. Take a digital detox. Go offline and get on~~line~~ life. Log out of social media and log into yourself. At times this may look like lots of unread messages and phone calls that you haven't replied to in days or weeks (for me to even write that is revolutionary, I used to feel bad if I didn't reply straight away, hours felt like a crime!). Especially if the messages are from people wanting something from you when you simply don't have the energy or resources to give. You're not a bad person for taking care of and putting yourself first. You are not a bad person for wanting to enjoy your free time instead of helping other people. You are not here to fix and help every single person (though it's admirable you'd like to). You're running on a low reserve which does not require you to pour every bit of fuel you have into others. Put yourself first because we are all responsible for our own wellbeing. I know that you may feel guilty but doesn't mean that you did something wrong. You aren't bad because you cancelled plans you don't feel up for. You aren't bad because you left early due to being tired. You aren't bad because you can't do what they asked as you don't have the capacity to (even if you do, doesn't mean you have to).

Energetic self-care is coming to the realisation that you don't have to give 100% all the damn time. That is exhausting. Some days 85% is good enough or even a 50%... 5% is also okay. If you think about it, if that's all you have to give, technically you did give it your all,

100% of what you capacity you have. You don't have to be obliged to complete that thought in your head that says, 'what's the point of doing it if I'm not giving 100%?'. Your efforts will eventuate, all that you give, whether its 1% or 100%, will add up. If you're feeling lost and disconnected, it's not about following your mind and thoughts. Forget about what you 'should do,' 'must do' and 'need to do.' Forget about what other people think because at the end of the day you're the one that lives with the impact and consequences of your actions and choices. It's about listening to your heart, body and soul. What is going to spark a fire in your soul again? Where does your body ache and yearn to be? Where is your heart drawn to? What fills you with overflowing joy? Follow this bliss and the path will reveal itself. Not just any path, *your* path.

I hope through the unlearning, we normalise not feeling okay and having days where we feel off. Let's normalise just feeling okay (because we aren't always going to be happy or sad—we can be in the space in between). Let's normalise the joy of missing out. Let's normalise cancelling plans for mental health. Let's normalise speaking about mental health. Let's normalise feeling our feelings. Let's normalise going offline. Let's normalise putting ourselves first. Let's normalise saying no to things. Let's normalise feeling negative. Let's normalise feeling lost. Let's normalise knowing that you're going through a hard time but knowing you'll be okay.

One of the most nourishing things to do is *nothing*, especially in a culture obsessed with hustling. Seriously! I mean it's really a privilege. How often do we truly do nothing? I mean nothing. Not lazily watching a show. Literally nothing. Lying down or sitting in meditation. To fully be wherever you are.

Being mindful of your self-care is important. This is the antidote to the avoiding, numbing and escaping we often do. Choosing what will benefit your soul over what your ego wants. Being mindful is being consciously aware and present with everything including your thoughts, actions and feelings. If you've ever played Sims before, you might remember the green diamonds that hover over their heads which gauges how they are feeling.

In the aftermath of a life-changing breakup, I was so grateful that my past-self had added a few days off to write on top of a work trip to Byron Bay. I stayed at a gorgeous organic farm on the outskirts of town. It was quiet, the sound of palm trees rustling in the wind and birds chirping. Whilst I wanted to write, some of the time I could not. All I could do to help myself was be in the present moment with the pain and emotions I had to process. People wanted to see me but I couldn't accommodate for all because I simply didn't have the energy and desire to socialize. This experience showed me how far I had come. Previous heartbreaks had seen me do anything to distract myself, like jumping on dating apps or being jam packed with work. The key here was that I knew what I used to do and wanted to do but in my conscious awareness I knew that the best form of self-care was to be present with the pain.

Sometimes we need moments of silence to truly hear what our soul wants. I'm creating my own perspective of self-care: quiet self-care. Quiet self-care looks like the things no one else will ever know about or see. That may be folding your clothes or emptying the toast crumb catcher. Quiet self-care looks like minimal noise. Going inwards instead of outwards. Journaling. Reflecting. Contemplating. Processing. Quiet self-care looks like having space to talk to yourself consciously. Quiet self-care looks like tuning inwards to your senses. Listening to the tap drip. Feeling the cool water running through your fingers. Sipping refreshing water. It looks like being unstimulated in a world that's full of things trying to grab and maintain your attention. Quiet self-care is time for yourself in solitude without devices. Quiet self-care looks like finding inner stillness and balance. One of my favourite yoga poses is Vrksasana (tree). Standing tall with your hands in prayer position, place one of your feet resting on the other leg's thigh. Quiet self-care looks like picking up on the subtle signs of your body. Feeling exhausted? Feeling thirsty? Pay attention.

Self-care is a beautiful journey to enjoy. There's no better feeling than consciously choosing to nurture your mind, body, heart and soul by taking care of you. From a place of self-care you can rest, recharge and recalibrate. It's an important aspect of self-love. Self-care is realising you are important, and you need to take care of yourself for not only your benefit but everyone else's. Take care of yourself now before it's too late, before you end up in a bad place or your health is affected. Don't let a health scare propel you into the arms of self-care. You owe it to yourself to figure out what self-care looks and feels like for you. Make self-care a consistent practice so that it becomes ingrained into your life as opposed to making it something you reach out for in moments of overwhelm and exhaustion. Here's to your own perspective and take on self-care!

YOUR GREAT UNLEARNING

1. ENERGY PIE

Out of a total possible 100%, check in with yourself to see where your energy is going and rate it as a percentage.

70% work
10% friends
10% volunteering
10% side hustle
= 100%

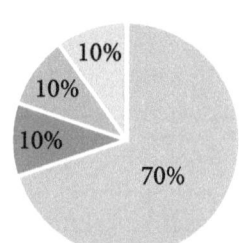

Rework it to:

50% work
10% friends
10% volunteering
10% side hustle
10% personal development
10% exercise
= 100%

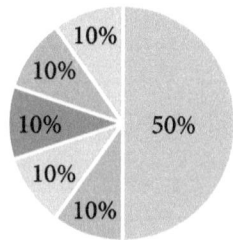

From here you can see where you want to put more of your energy. Put your energy into the things that fuel you and add to your self-care and nourishment.

2. SELF-CARE CALENDAR

The intention of this calendar is to ensure you do at least one thing for yourself each day. Personalise it for yourself!

For example, it could look like.

> Day 1–Meditate for at least 5 minutes
> Day 2–Cook a delicious meal from scratch
> Day 3–Clean up a room in the house
> Day 4–Call a friend for a catch up
> Day 5–Go for a walk by the beach

You may want to take inspiration from the 6 areas of self-care that have been defined in psychological terms.

> Physical Self-care–Your body
> Emotional Self-care–Your emotions
> Spiritual Self-care–Your soul (or religion)
> Intellectual Self-care–Your brain (stimulation)
> Social Self-care–Connecting with others
> Practical Self-care–To function (think safety, security–Maslow's hierarchy of needs pyramid)

3. SELF-CARE CIRCLE

This exercise has been created for you to gain perspectives on self-care, particularly when you're struggling to.

Big circle. What is written on the inside: What would an outsider think of my situation and thoughts right now? For example, someone who doesn't know you too well.

Medium circle. What is written on the inside: What would someone who loves me think of my situation and thoughts right now? For example, a best friend or family member.

Small circle. What is written on the inside: What would a younger version of myself think of my situation and thoughts right now? For example, yourself at age five or ten.

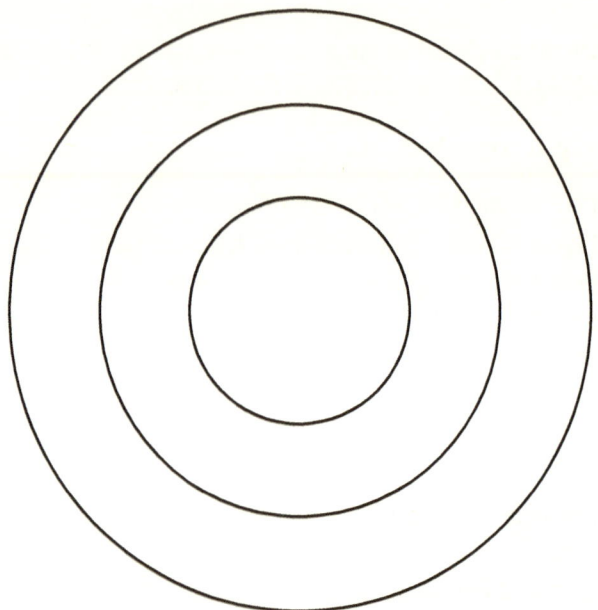

SELF-BODY

THE LEARNING
Your body is imperfect and beauty looks a certain way.

As women, we have complex relationships with our bodies. In fact, we haven't learned to love our bodies—no one taught us that at school. In fact, we've learned the opposite—why our bodies aren't perfect and what is wrong with them. You stand in front of a mirror critiquing and dissecting yourself—*Eugh, my fat rolls. Why am I not skinny enough? Why don't I look like her?* I feel you, we've all had those moments were looking at the reflection in the mirror is painful. We have been moulded to believe there is such a thing as a 'normal' body and that does not constitute a long list of features such as stretch marks, pimples, cellulite, touching thighs, tuckshop lady arms, hip dips, visible pores, under eye circles, laugh lines, a protruding stomach and the list goes on. These are all 'normal' because it's a human body—anything that occurs and stems from it is natural. However, you must understand that society benefits from the way we hate our bodies and think they look disgusting. Flaws sell products and services. Injectables. Surgeries. Diets. Exercise regimes. Ask yourself who taught you not to be satisfied with your body? Who benefited from it?

This very same vein of commerce leads us to believe that our body and beauty define us. We first have to acknowledge that these so-called body and beauty standards change depending on which culture they acknowledge. For example, it's interesting for me to note that in Australian culture having tanned skin is desirable. It makes us look slimmer and showcases the fact we spend a lot of time in the sun—a lady of leisure down at the beach or travelling around the world. It's quite the opposite in Asian culture, pale skin is desired because it mimics 'Western' skin. Tanned skin represents the working class because of their time working out in the sun.

Furthermore, the idea of the 'perfect' woman has never stayed consistent. From a Western perspective we know that the trend as of late is 'big'. Big butts. Big boobs. Big lips. Yet in the late 90s and early 2000s flat stomachs and thigh gaps were in. The early 90s was about being extremely skinny, disturbingly dubbed as 'heroin chic'. The 50s were all about having an hourglass figure.

It's all so difficult because if you're ethnic in anyway, like myself, you don't see anyone in the public sphere that looks like you or is even deemed beautiful. Except maybe for the one token character. Mulan was that token character in my childhood.

It's like our bodies aren't even ours. It's like our bodies are owned by people outside of us because we've become so self-conscious and aware of what other people think. One of the biggest hallmarks of being body conscious is the 'summer body' ideal that is based on aesthetic trends. It has led to many women feeling uncomfortable to be seen in their swimming costume. Another is that of the 'revenge body', a post-break-up achievement to make an ex regret breaking up and come crawling back. It often looks like losing a dramatic amount of weight. We've seen this play out in the public eye through the transformations of celebrities such as Khloe Kardashian and Adele. We believe these concepts to be positive and empowering when really, they aren't. They reinforce the narrative of how your body needs to look a certain way. This plays out in the lives of many through eating disorders. There are so many complexities and layers to this. An example is being fuelled by sayings such as 'nothing tastes as good as thin feels' and 'a minute on the lips, forever on the hips'.

Seeing this unfold in friends and clients is heartbreaking. Forms of eating disorders have sublimated into sneakier forms. Obsessions with calorie counting. Extreme exercising. Cheat meals. Laxatives. In fact, it's led to an attempt at different body movements such as #bodypositivity. That is met with controversy whether it's enabling behaviours or isn't inclusive of everyone.

However, let's acknowledge it doesn't have to be all doom and gloom for our bodies. Many are trying to shift the way we view our bodies. An example is Jameela Jamil's 'I weigh' movement which seeks to look beyond the flesh on our bones. The movement encourages one to share their 'weight' in terms of attributes such as 'being a good friend', 'making an honest living' and 'speaking out for women's rights'. Some celebrities have been vocal about being airbrushed and photoshopped. Sharing raw photos of cellulite and unfiltered images. Models speaking out about their rollercoaster rides in the industry. There's still long way to go but every step forward is important.

Social media plays a huge role in the way we perceive bodies. When I moved to the beaches, I found myself shockingly confused by all the different body types on the beach. I was so conditioned to perceive a beautiful body as looking a certain way based on social media. I saw women of all different shapes and sizes at the beach, with all sorts of marks: birth, stretch and scars. This was a huge wake-up call.

Nat, my past-colleague-turned-good-friend, is unapologetically herself and the queen of influencers. She's the friend that is always on the pulse and beat of new trends. I confessed to her I was jealous of a certain influencer, who showed up online looking immaculate every day without fail. I moaned about how it wasn't fair that some people are blessed with such genetics. She replied to me with a puzzled look on her face and said, 'Phi, you do know she's documented all her surgeries on enhancing her body like a boob job, liposuction and Brazilian butt lift, right?'

In addition to physical enhancements, we also have all the filters and editing tools! Filters that alter the structure of your face. Filters that mimic cosmetic surgery enhancements, such as bigger lips. Filters that remove any sign of texture from your skin. It's leading to a universal look which appears part alien and part ambiguously exotic, though with a predominately Western base. This doesn't just apply for photos anymore; technology has advanced to the point that bodies in videos can also be altered. The lines between reality and fantasy are blurring. Editing and enhancing has become the norm. It's inspired new procedures such as the fox eye lift (which blows my mind being targeted with slanted eye racial gestures for being Asian). The women undertaking these surgeries are getting younger and younger. Cosmetic enhancements are the norm with the introduction of approachable entry procedures such as 'baby Botox'.

Beauty standards are thinly veiled in ageism. Society celebrates youthfulness so we do everything we can to avoid signs of getting older—grey hairs, wrinkles and sagging bits. Ageing is what comes naturally with being human and is a blessing, an indication of living longer!

With all this hyper-focus on body and beauty, women become either idols, competition and/or sources that trigger other women. I've been triggered and in turn activated too. I've judged women because they weren't wearing many clothes. I've seen women in tune with their sexuality, dancing in their lingerie online, and judged them for being weirdos. Guess what? All these actions act as a mirror for your own beliefs.

After I saw all of this, I deemed myself as not sexy or hot enough. I was the cute, funny girl next door not the sensual goddess. My conditioning of my body has always been sexual in nature. I've always been super self-conscious of my small breasts—member of the itty bitty committee here. Based on social conditioning, I felt like I wasn't 'feminine' or 'womanly' because I lacked curves. I felt like I wasn't sexy enough. I would always wear padded push up bras. In fact, I can't tell you the number of times I've gone down the rabbit hole researching breast augmentation surgery.

Our bodies are so sexualised that I personally lost touch with what the purpose of my body was supposed to be. It wasn't even about sex and pleasure; it became a means to being validated and loved.

THE UNLEARNING

Let's love our appearance as we are. Let's appreciate our bodies for what they do.

In order to reconnect with the purpose of bodies, we need to go back to basics. You are not your body. Your body is a vehicle which carries your soul, the real 'you'—your spirit and essence. You are a soul with a body, not the other way around. Think of it in terms of property, your soul is renting your body. Whilst you're in this long-term rental (or short, however you look at life), you want to take good care of it. Having a body is a huge part of the human experience. At times having an appearance and body can be exhausting, especially when there is a war waging inside your head.

Here's the thing, your existence is a divine experience! Your body allows you to have incredible experiences. You have eyes that capture turmeric skies and the dew condensing on glistening green grass. Ears that absorb the chatter around cobblestone streets and shrieking laughter around the dinner table. Lungs that are strong enough to enable you to climb mountains and gentle enough to allow you take in the sweetness of cinnamon cookies. Hands that trace along the spine of your lovers back and brush up against paperbark trees. A stomach that enjoys silky strings of spaghetti and plump mandarins. Legs that allow you to conquer hard terrain and traverse crimson dirt roads.

How lucky we are to have this body that does so much for us without asking for anything in return. Your body pumps blood to carry oxygen from your lungs to the tissues of your body. Your body has a heartbeat, that is the primary centre of your circulatory system, to send oxygen and nutrients all around your body. Your eyes blink without thought to ensure they are lubricated and free from debris. You have hands and legs that are capable of so many functions including gripping and walking.

It must be said, I am sharing this as someone who is able bodied. For those who have disabilities, you deserve to be seen as you are without constant staring and without judgement from others. Our bodies, all bodies, deserve to take up space and be embraced as they are, as being human. There is no such thing as universally 'normal.' Let go out of what others think and start telling yourself you are incredible as you are. You deserve to have a body that houses inner peace as it is without changes like surgery or weight loss. Having a body means that you are alive and that is what is most important. Enjoy it.

Our bodies are designed for function, not aesthetic. Women's stomachs aren't meant to be flat and empty. They have essential organs that men have, *and* also fit our reproductive system in alongside. Fat and tissue are needed and engineered to protect these vital organs. All in all, every body is different. Every body has different needs.

Eating has a natural purpose: to sustain life through energy. Let us unlearn judging ourselves for how much we eat or how little, the most important thing is to eat. All in all, our body keeps us here alive. It lovingly protects you from all sorts of germs and disease. It does its best no matter what, even when under attack—whether it's a negative comment from someone or a virus. Yes, your body may look different, it may be exhausted, it may be sick, but at the end of the day its sole purpose is to ensure you survive. Don't go through life hating the very same source that sustains life. All your body has ever done is love you, why hate it?

Your body is living evidence of your resilience. It has been by your side for every battle. It has felt every emotion you've experienced. It is your most loyal companion, always willing to try. Scars are evidence that you survived. Wrinkles are evidence of experience. Your body is incredible because it holds life despite how hard life can be.

I have a true appreciation for my body. I attended the world's first women's only Wim Hof Retreat. For those who don't know, Wim Hof is known as the ice man and is well known for his ability to withstand the freezing cold. He developed a method called the Wim Hof Method which combines breathing with cold water immersion. I decided to go on this retreat after the first wave of the pandemic. I wanted a challenge. Not only that but I have always been averse to the cold and needed extra layers of clothing. I've been afraid of even a drop of cold water in my showers. I thought it would also be interesting to test my mind and discover the power of my body. Especially being the asthmatic kid that was always picked last for physical education sports teams.

You will never forget the first time you willingly descend into the icy cold water. You'll question your sanity. I did when I saw Leah, my instructor, chipping and cracking away at the ice with a sledgehammer that tightly hugged the lake. As I hit the water, pain and shock immediately seeped into my flesh and bones. My lungs gasped and struggled to take in the crisp air and snow-capped mountains. I felt the cold crawl under my butterfly thin skin, turning it shades of blue, white and grey. I felt the cold cracking into my fingers and toes. You feel it all, truly with the irony of thinking you'll freeze.

As you drop out of your mind and into your body there comes a stillness. In that space of eternity within your body, a wave of euphoria drip feeds through. The cold becomes refreshing and invigorating, like the first sip of water after a hot sunny day. You feel the warmth of your blood like an inbuilt radiator in the core of your stomach. This experience gave me a newfound appreciation for what my body could do and loving my body for its strength as opposed to just its appearance. This experience also highlighted the importance of mindset, which would go on to be a foundational cornerstone of my methodology and approach to coaching clients.

Imagine if as a society we focused on the shape of our minds instead of the shape of our bodies. That self-critical voice that drags down your body is only your mind, no one else can hear it. No one else would likely believe it. Don't bash your body because somebody bashed your mind. The productivity obsession in society programs you to resent your body when you're ill or burnt out because it interferes with getting things done. I remember thinking how inconvenient getting sick was because it meant I would miss deadlines or have a tonne of work to catch up on when I was back. I would avoid taking a sick day (even though they are an entitlement for that very reason). The sad thing is that your body hardly ever has a rest, it's still working when you're sleeping! We believe that we have to deprive ourselves to earn or deserve something. It may be nice new clothes when you've lost weight or earning a meal after working out. You can eat whenever you want to and buy nice new clothes for your body as it is now because you already deserve it. A healthy self doesn't just refer to your physical body (wellness is wealth!). It's also your mental capacity. Healthy self = heal thy self.

Beauty isn't just how you appear on the outside; there are so many aspects of yourself that are beautiful. Smiling makes you beautiful. Your kind heart makes you beautiful. Your compassion for others makes you beautiful. Your helping hands make you beautiful. Your very existence is beautiful. What good is beauty if it isn't matched by what's on the inside. It's like being sold a beautiful home with an ugly interior. Be a beautiful soul. A beautiful soul radiates warmth and joy. A beautiful soul is sunshine and brings light to all those they interact with. A beautiful soul touches hearts not just tickles the eyes. Beauty can't be measured by how much you weigh on a scale or how you look. Want to know how you to make yourself look 'good'? Move on from the past. Overcome your negative self-talk. Prioritise yourself. Invest in yourself. Love yourself. Work on yourself. Become more conscious and intentional. Reaffirm your boundaries. Be grateful. Feel your feelings. Yeah, that'll make you look really good. Beauty isn't about what you see in the mirror, it's about how you feel and see yourself. Beauty cannot be obtained because it already exists within. By you just being you!

However you aren't *just* beautiful. You are so much more. You aren't here just to be beautiful while walking down the street. You aren't here just to be beautiful when you're having sex. You aren't here just to be beautiful in photos. We've become obsessed with beauty—looking beautiful, feeling beautiful, being beautiful but what you're truly looking for is to be lovingly embraced as you are. To look, be and feel. Pursue beauty all you like but unless you get to the heart of self-embrace you will end up in an unhappy and endless chase. You weren't born to only exist for appearance's sake.

The best weight I ever lost is the self-limiting beliefs I learned from life. The experience I had while staying at a farm in Byron Bay was a pivotal moment. I went to Byron Bay for a work trip to do human design readings. A human design reading offers an energetic blueprint of who you are which is completely unique to you. It offers profound insights into your soul's purpose, key themes you will experience in life, your strengths, how to best make decisions and so much more.

I endlessly scrolled Airbnb without luck until, just before midnight, this place caught my eye—panoramic views of lush green valleys and the iconic lighthouse in the distance. I was captivated by the photos alone, so I went ahead and booked it, only to then become aware of the actual title of the place: Clothing Optional. I was mortified, how did I miss that! I was nervous. The idea of being naked, even for a minute, was confronting. Growing up Catholic, I was programmed to believe nudity was sinful and degrading. Adam and Eve though born naked, covered their bodies due to the shame of falling from innocence and obedience. All my life I've felt very uncomfortable while naked for this very reason, alongside all the cultural conditioning we absorb. As I've dived deeper into my understanding of why I felt uncomfortable, I slowly removed all the limiting layers. Breaking free from the realisation that I've been brainwashed to believe, nudity is sinful.

When I first arrived, I headed to the outdoor shower. Dipping my toes into the water of being naked. Not to mention I was also severely sweaty after taking hours to find the location (I'm horrible with directions). The shower happened to be located outside of the house which happened to have two other guests staying—a mother and daughter. My host assured me that I didn't have to go clothes free, it was optional, and that they were out in town anyway. This alleviated my fears: *'Isn't it awkward to see naked people?'*, *'What if they judge me?'*, *'Is one of my boobs bigger than the other?'*, *'No one's seen me naked for the past three years apart from my ex-boyfriend, this is strange'*. Given they weren't present, I ran to the shower paranoid that perhaps my host would see me (we had just met!). But it was such a tranquil experience. The sun glistened on my skin and the birds chirped in the palm trees. Though this experience soon became temporarily disturbed by loud footsteps as the mother and daughter walked past. However, without flinching, they waved. I waved back. It wasn't as bad as I thought it would be. The metaphorical Band-Aid was ripped off.

After that moment, I embraced the nudist philosophy. A copy of Tan, the Australian Naturist Magazine, sat on the coffee table. I flicked through it, feeling confronted by the images of naked people of all sorts of shapes, sizes and ages. Though, I had to chuckle at the three-legged race. Once I got over the initial shock, nudity strangely became the norm. Especially during my stay at the property. I began dancing naked with all the house blinds closed, because, hey, why not? I felt like me! As I built my confidence, I opened the blinds and became a literal naked chef as I made a winter warmer: vegan noodle soup (again embracing the hosts philosophy).

I want to point out that the farm is twenty-two acres and situated in the Byron hinterland on the outskirts of town (a ten-minute drive). Apart from the mother and daughter staying downstairs, I was alone. However, the host lived next to me with his wife and child. The host was an older man who labelled himself a hippie. Up to this point, I had worked my way up to being comfortable being seen naked by other women, but a man? This thought was challenging because I had only ever been naked in front of a man for sexual purposes. I felt narcissistic thinking, 'What if he sees me naked and gets an erection!' Given my parents divorced while I was young, I didn't have a man in the household for the majority of my life, particularly in the years I went through puberty.

The host invited me on a tour of the farm to see their sustainable and organic practices. He explicitly told me he would be naked and wanted to work on his tan lines. Fair enough, me too. Previous versions of me would never have entertained the thought of being naked around a man I wasn't sleeping with. I danced with the invitation. I went back and forth between feeling uneasy to feeling bold. I decided to go ahead with the tour, but I would wear a button up shirt to cover up. I thought I would be more shocked to see him out there on his tractor naked, but I wasn't.

Tuning into my body, I actually felt comfortable. My host was very kind and understanding. He would answer all the questions I had about the guests he'd had and his thoughts on being nude. His parents were nudists and, initially, he had been uncomfortable, wishing they would cover up. I then had flashbacks of my own mum being naked all the time and I would avoid seeing her by staying in my room. As the tour continued, I decided to unbutton my shirt. I had also just cut my hair so I knew it wouldn't cover my boobs anymore (my boobs were the most self-conscious area of my body). He would probably see a nipple! The host didn't flinch, he didn't make any advances towards me. He didn't act any different. This was a breakthrough moment for me!

Truly being free was so liberating. Being in the moment without a care for my appearance—no need to look in the mirror or wonder if someone was judging my stomach for being too round. No readjusting my clothes so that they fit a certain way. No draining concern whether I looked hot or not. Through this experience, I realised that being desired is not enough to make you happy. Being 'sexy' doesn't satisfy your soul.

Have you ever evaluated how much money you've actually spent on your appearance and body for superficial purposes? Can you imagine if you'd used that money to build a business or invest in your future? Can you imagine all the mental, emotional, and physical energy you would get back without worrying about your appearance? Imagine being able to enjoy a night out with friends instead of worrying how your legs look. Given this, I didn't want to be surface level and superficial. I wanted to be at peace with myself as I was, that was the real deal.

For the rest of the week, I enjoyed being naked. It gave me a rush of excitement. It felt wrong in ways because of my deep-set conditioning but all in all, it also felt right. After all, we are born naked. The rush soon transformed into a soft inner contentment that radiated within me. I would wake up in the morning to make a banana smoothie naked. I meditated in the sun naked on the balcony, the sun soaking into my skin. I even recorded social media content naked (from the shoulders up). I wiped down the kitchen bench top and cleaned the dishes naked. I am even writing this chapter, right now, naked on the couch. It was truly a beautiful week. I felt so vulnerable, not only physically, but mentally. I was a week out of a three-year relationship, so the experience was healing for my mind, body and soul. A revolution for myself.

Let's embrace radical self-acceptance. This looks like body neutrality and takes into account non-physical characteristics and abilities. This is to embrace yourself as you are regardless of trends and weight. Embrace your moles, freckles, body hair, and birth marks. The body you have right now is the only one you will ever have. Your body isn't your enemy, it is your ally. Your body has given you everything that it possibly can. When you die you'll miss your body, for it was the vehicle that allowed you to experience your life. It has given you the most amazing gift, so much more than what you can consciously appreciate. When you die, you won't be remembered by your jean size. You won't be remembered by what you ate. You will be remembered by how you lived your life. The impact and influence you had on the world around you. How you made your dreams come true.

Embrace your body as it is now. Experience a synergy between mind, body and soul. You are your body, and your body is you. Fall deeply in love with being vividly and wildly alive. The journey is not easy, but it is so beautiful and rewarding. Should you choose to walk this path, you will find self-love, self-compassion and self-acceptance. You will be stripped of the fears and thoughts that hold you back. You will swim freely in the waters of liberation.

YOUR GREAT UNLEARNING

1. LOVE AND ACCEPTANCE OVER HATE

Become aware and conscious of the self-talk with regards to your perception of your body and beauty. Write these down and for each negative one, find a thought which supports your highest self. For example:

>Thought: *I am fat.*
>Alternative: *I perceive myself to be fat. I perceive myself to be many things but that doesn't necessarily mean it's true.*

Thought: *I don't like the way I look.*
Alternative: *I acknowledge that I would like to change parts of how I look. In saying that, I also acknowledge that I like many things I cannot see such as how helpful I am in my community.*

Thought: *I eat too much junk.*
Alternative: *I believe I haven't been eating the most nutritional foods for my body and I would like to eat more nourishing foods.*

2. MIND TO BODY TO SOUL

Commit to developing a stronger relationship with your mind, body and soul. The central component being your body. You can use the following prompts to facilitate a connection.

- How are your heart and soul today?
- What is your body craving right now?
- What helps you connect to your body?
- How can you have more fun with your body?
- How does your body communicate with you?
- If your body could talk to you right now, what would it say?
- How does it feel to be you right now?

3. BODY INTIMACY

Create a private and safe environment. For example, you may want to light some candles and play some soft, calming music.

The aim is to become more acquainted with your body. You may do this clothed or not. You can do this in front of a mirror or not.

As part of this exercise you may:

- Run your hands over your body with the intent to admire and caress yourself.
- State out loud compassionate affirmations and compliments.
- Reflect on what you appreciate about yourself.

- Show love towards your body by using essential oils or massaging yourself.
- Practice being naked, whether it's for a minute or an hour.
- Do something that feels good to you.

If negative thoughts creep up, acknowledge them, thank them for sharing and then release them. Know that the thoughts that arise are not necessarily true and that you get to choose the thoughts that feel loving and supportive.

SELF-PLEASURE

THE LEARNING
A woman's self-pleasure revolves around sex yet it's taboo to talk about masturbation and orgasms.

Beautiful souls, it's time to liberate ourselves from the chains and constraints of pleasure that have been placed on us. When it comes to pleasure, the first thing that might come to mind is sex. Let me start the unlearning early by saying pleasure isn't just found in the bedroom. It isn't about feeling orgasmic 24/7. Sex is an important aspect, but it's not everything. Pleasure isn't just 'getting off' and boisterous moaning. Pleasure has taken a backseat in our busy lives and is relegated behind closed doors. Pleasure is presence. It's in being and in your being.

Pleasure is being connected to your body and open to all the feelings and sensations that arise. It's the ecstasy of life. It's being turned on by the fullness and richness of the moment. The vibe? It's you, turning yourself on first and making love to life. It's you making life your lover. You don't even have to touch yourself if you don't want to! It's your exquisite expression. It's sunlight dancing on your skin. It's basking in the serene silence of being underwater. It's savouring the sweetness of strawberries in your mouth. It's the seduction of smooth silk sheets caressing your skin. It's bopping your head to the euphoric beats of the drum and bass in your ears. It's bursting into tears during sex not because anything is wrong but because you are able to fully surrender to the moment. It's wailing from experiencing such a huge release. It's laughing uncontrollably.

Our inherently conditioned belief of pleasure being sex is dominated by the male gaze and perspective. Female expression, on the other hand, is marked by criticism, judgement, shame and scandals. This is a stark contrast to our natural inclination as children.

Many of us may recall getting acquainted with our body from an early age. We start stimulating and touching our genitals, discovering that it feels nice to be touched a certain way. I vividly remember being six or seven and rocking and rubbing myself against pillows over the boys I fancied at school. At age eight or nine, I touched myself under the bed covers. For one reason only—it felt great. At the time I had no idea I was masturbating. What intrigues me is at the time it didn't feel like I was being bad or weird. Naturally, as a child I knew it felt good and I wasn't ashamed. Pleasure is encoded in our DNA. Especially for women as men have sexual organs that also provide a bodily function. Women? The sole purpose of the clitoris is pleasure. Pleasure is play, enjoyment and bliss.

My parents skirted around the topic of sex. One remarkable thing I remember from my childhood is that I genuinely thought babies were delivered by storks via heaven. My mum then told me, 'Phi, you came out of my vagina. Your dad and I made you. You didn't come from the sky.' The lack of education continued throughout my formative years at high school. We didn't have sex education at my high school, but we did have health classes. I only remember one time during my seven years of schooling that I had a class relating to sex; we watched the teacher put a condom on a banana.

After reminiscing with my friends, they had mentioned that I had apparently missed the class where they had watched a woman giving birth via a projector screen. That was it. Nothing more said about sex—what it constituted, consent, techniques, nothing. My best friend in year ten, Sonia, asked me if I knew the physical makeup of a penis. This was before I had ever had sex. I replied, 'Yeah, of course, it's like the thing that's filled with air…' If you're face palming and laughing, I am too.

It's no surprise that many women don't feel comfortable talking about sex or exploring the endless possibilities to their sensuality and sexuality. I had accumulated many beliefs around sex.

Let's talk about the perpetuating Madonna-Whore complex that society has. You're either pure, saintly and untouched, or you're a sex-crazy nymphomaniac fiend. You're a good homemaker or a bad whore. Nowadays, sex has evolved much like levels employment do. We start with an entry level role yet that comes with a long list of requirements, including education and experience. When it comes to dating, you need to be an innocent virgin that has the capacity to please him by being 'freaky' and 'nasty' in bed. Go figure. If you don't have sex, you're labelled prudish or frigid, yet you're called a slut if you enjoy having sex. God forbid you have sex with more than a certain amount deemed appropriate, while men are championed for bedding as many women as they can. Let's also highlight the irony of men slut-shaming women for sex work and having accounts on platforms like OnlyFans, yet they are the biggest consumers of free adult pornography. (Please note, women do this too.)

Let's talk about the vagina. Even saying vagina and writing about the vagina feels edgy. Perhaps it feels unnatural or repulsive. Maybe you feel uneasy hearing or reading the word. I want to discuss the word 'pussy'. It's one of the many terms for vagina, like vajayjay, box, downstairs, fanny, flower, lady garden, lady bits, poon, clunge, beaver, muff, nooni and the list goes on.

The term pussy is also used as an insult to insinuate being scared and wimpy: 'Oh, don't be such a pussy.' Fuck that (ha ha I have to point out the playful use of word here). It's time for us reclaim the words pussy and vagina. The vagina and having a vagina is amazing. Vaginas are strong—they give birth to new life. Your vagina can stretch out and accommodate a baby the size of a watermelon. Vaginas endure consistent bleeding. 'Vagina' is a beautiful metaphor for being soft yet strong and powerful. I love the way Trevor Noah sums it up, '*You realize vaginas can start revolutions and end wars... There's a reason men have sought to oppress it for so long. The vagina is frighteningly powerful.*'

Growing up in a Catholic household, I came to understand that sexual activity was seen as bad, sinful and shameful. The Bible made it clear: God ordained sex to be an act shared by husband and wife mainly for the purposes of continuing the human race and male stress relief in the Old Testament. I believed I had to abstain from sex until I was married to ensure I was pure and a 'good' person. I equated sex to a one-way ticket to hell—the inferno and being punished by the devil. I held these beliefs until after dating my high school sweetheart when I was seventeen. After being together for a year, I started to question why having sex with someone I loved and was in a committed relationship with was so bad. What was so bad and evil about that? Whilst I overcame these beliefs physically, they mentally plagued me throughout my twenties. I felt guilty touching myself. I found it hard to relax and orgasm during sex because it felt dirty.

After being cheated on, I enjoyed being single (admittedly, I did this to recoup my shattered self-esteem). A new belief then came in. Slut. Let's talk about this. Whilst I enjoyed the freedom of being single, I had a confrontation with my mum. She had noticed nights where I would not come home. While I didn't tell my mum what I was up to, she knew—mums just have that sixth sense, don't they?

One day I was at home, painting my nails white. My mum gasped and in Vietnamese called me, 'con đĩ', which essentially translates to slut/whore. I was taken aback and cried for hours. I felt dirty and ashamed.

A week later, my mum apologised. She confessed that she was envious of how sexually free I was. I was shocked. She shared with me that women were not able to freely date when she was growing up in Vietnam. She told me that I would've been beaten up, scolded and disowned, if I had my grandma (her mum) as my mother. Whilst Western societies like Australia are more open, not without their own challenges, sexuality was very conservative in the seventies and eighties in Vietnam. My mum was in her early twenties during these years. My mum gave me great insight into Vietnamese culture. She stated she was taught having sex before marriage would soil you and diminish your chances of a 'good' marriage. Marriage was considered critical in Vietnamese society and demonstrated by language. People would not ask, 'Are you married' but 'Are you married yet?' My mum and I have come a long way since this incident. In fact, she once sent me a picture of cucumbers on sale for Valentine's Day when I was single. Hilarious.

My sexual awakening in my early twenties and my overall pleasure journey hasn't always been 'high vibe'. Sex and pleasure have felt forced or as though it involves a lot of effort. There have been times where I haven't enjoyed sex because I didn't feel connected to the person. I have forced myself to have sex even though I didn't want to or felt uncomfortable to because I felt bad if I didn't. I've faked orgasms to appease men and it didn't seem weird or abnormal.

I have numbed myself by consuming copious amounts of alcohol as an escape so that I could have sex. Alcohol was a great excuse for dissociating. I could be a 'sexual person' and wouldn't worry if I did anything to embarrass myself. I could blame it on the booze. I would have sex to seek the validation, love and approval that I didn't have within myself. I would weaponise sex to try and secure commitment (it never worked). I've also lost my sexual spark, which left me feeling flat, stagnant and stuck. I've been stuck in my head and unable to connect with my body, then forced myself to find a way to orgasm quickly.

It's experiences like the above mixed with our thoughts, trauma and tension on a physical, emotional, mental and/or energetic level which can develop into what is called 'armouring'. It often happens unconsciously. Whilst it's not exclusively sexual, it often happens in the context of sex, particularly with our vaginas. Armouring, as the name suggests, is your body guarding itself through means of shielding and defending. Whilst armouring protects us, it also restricts us—it cuts us off from having a full, multidimensional experience when it comes to pleasure and sex.

Physical signs of armouring include, but are not limited to, clenching your vagina involuntarily, lacking sensitivity, numbness, and pain during intimacy or intercourse. Nonphysical signs include, but are not limited to, a discomfort in expressing your sexual desires and feeling energetically closed off. The practice and purpose of de-armouring is to release these blockages, leading to greater freedom, feeling and flow. I've included more on de-armouring in your great unlearning exercises at the end of the chapter.

THE UNLEARNING

Self-pleasure doesn't just come from sex. It's time to reclaim our pleasure and, in turn, power and presence.

Beautiful soul, it's time for your pleasure revolution. I'm aching for you to reclaim yourself and your pleasure. Drop out of your head and into your body, feel the presence. Meet yourself as the full, authentic and multidimensional woman that you are. Worship your beautiful self and incredible pussy. Give yourself permission to explore what sex and pleasure means to you. Know that it is a dynamic journey. You can explore who you are attracted to. The vagina exists for more than birthing a baby; explore the depths of the universe and tap into magnetism, sovereignty and presence. It's not just about touching yourself but touching your power, fullness, freedom, authenticity and Queendom.

Everything involved in exploring your pleasure and sexuality safely and without judgement is oh, so right. There's nothing wrong with enjoying sex—anchor into connection and bliss. There's nothing wrong with touching yourself—appreciate your damn fine body. There's nothing wrong with experimenting—have fun with it. At first this might feel odd, uncomfortable and wrong, but hear me out. I've been there too. One of the funniest and most insightful things my mum has ever said to me is that we touch our phones more than we touch ourselves. Too true. Be patient and enjoy the journey, it will serve you well.

Through one of my dry spells (metaphorical cobwebs and more), my dear friend Grace blew my mind when she said, 'You know, you don't just have to have sex with someone to enjoy sex.' That is how I came to purchase my first sex toy—a vibrator—at the age of twenty-four. I walked into Honey Birdette, sweaty and intimidated, and came out with a game-fucking-changer! Do yourself a favour and invest in the Venus. It's allowed me to gently dip my toes into the pleasure pool and work my way into greater depths.

One of my most profound pleasure moments came from allowing myself to delve into my sexual shadow—exploring what turned me on, even that which I judged 'bad' and 'wrong'. The experience was uncomfortable at first, but the end result was worth it: I met my full embodied self without shame and fear. I let myself discover my taboo and kinky side. This allowed me to let go and step into my power.

I had an empowering moment with a fuck buddy, Ryan. He was very confident and extremely attractive, and he knew it. He was tall with a beard and worked in the engineering and construction industry. When we matched on Tinder, he refused to get to know me initially and instead told me to just come over because that's what all girls he'd been with did. In this case, I was not like other girls and refused (though I've been that girl before).

We had drinks at a bar and, as the months passed, I found myself in his bed watching a movie. Getting intimate with Ryan awakened a primal instinct. We explored our impulses and urges in a safe way. With him I got to experience dominating a man. It felt freeing to unleash the wild woman within; a dimension of me that I had previously believed to be sinful. It sent shivers down my spine, and his too, when I had him lie down on his bed, blindfolded, with his hands tied up. I wrapped my hands around his neck. The subversion of norms and power was hot. Being in control and on top of Ryan, who embodied the stereotype of a man, was hot. Your desires are dynamic, not static—they're allowed to change, and they're allowed to evolve.

In contrast to this, I have experienced tidal waves of tingles with my ex-boyfriend, Malcolm. Having sex with him, a beautiful soul I loved, was so nourishing and fulfilling. We made love, which was gentle, slow and tender. Cascading waves of pleasure rippled from my head to toes. Seriously, I was in ecstatic bliss, the type where your eyes are rolling to the back of your head and you're in a whole other world... galaxy. We had sex under the stars on a cliff to the sound of roaring ocean waves. The thrill of getting caught was exhilarating. At home, we had a wall-to-wall mirror, so you can imagine how juicy it was making love, fucking and watching ourselves do so...

Before meeting Malcolm, I had been single for eight years. It's no surprise I'd had a delicious smorgasbord of sensual experiences and sexual encounters. With an open mind, I've explored many curiosities and I encourage you too as well in a safe manner. It's normal and healthy to do so. Humans are naturally sexual. Discover what turns you on. Figure out your edges and boundaries. It's okay and normal to have sexual fantasies. Some are to be explored in your reality and others are best left as a fantasy. Many people have fantasies they would never act upon in real life. In your sexual exploration, I trust and empower you to have the discernment to figure out what to act upon and what to leave as a fantasy or imagination.

I've kissed girls and I liked it. I've had one-night stands. I've explored countries and their men. I've watched adult only movies. I've role-played fantasies. I've had my toes sucked and armpits licked (personally, not for me, but it turned me on that he got so much joy and pleasure out of it). I've had friends with benefits, such as Johnson, an appropriately named, handsome German American surfing architect who looked like a Swedish God.

As I write this, I reminisce about one particular Friday night. I went over to Johnson's place, extremely stressed after work. He created a disco in his living room complete with tacky neon flashing lights and we danced the night away to the soundtrack of his old school vinyl records before going at it in bed. Eventually we both got into relationships, but he was one of the first people to tell me he was so happy I met someone and one of the first to check I was okay after we broke up. I digress and share because he and a few others dismantled my belief that all men wanted was sex, that they didn't actually care about women's feelings or wellbeing at all.

Exploring your pleasure and sexuality can look like journaling to reflect upon your desires and beliefs. It can look like listening to sex-themed podcasts or reading erotica. It can look like working with a sex coach or therapist. It can look like attending a workshop or seminar or exploring a sex shop. Try a yoni massage or find out your erotic blueprint. Tune into your sensuality through physical means like tantric yoga, belly dancing, bachata and pole dancing. Drop into your body and explore what it feels like to move with what is alive within you—to gyrate and circle your hips, to pulsate and shake. Refer to the *Great Unlearning* at the end of this chapter for a greater exploration in a fun pleasure party exercise.

The nature of sex and pleasure for women is ever evolving. Some seasons you'll be horny, going at it like a rabbit, and other times you won't. Different times in your life call for different desires. You're here to experience pleasure as a woman not a man. You don't have to follow the typical male programming of being instantly turned on and ready to go, rushing to orgasm. You don't have to follow the beliefs of what sex should look like from a male perspective and put on a performance. You don't have to moan loudly and look sexy all the time. You don't have to partake in fetishes or be subjected to acts of sex that you may not be comfortable with, such as choking, spitting, humiliation, pain and name calling. You don't have to act out and engage in sexual acts that have been normalised in adult videos. Straight up: you don't have to do anal unless you want to and it's pleasurable for you. You're allowed to voice what you *really* want and teach him to please you, because that's what he wants!

It's my hope in your unlearning, that you see pleasure as not just a process or practice. I hope that pleasure becomes a way of life for you. I hope that you feel pleasure so fucking good it makes your toes tingle. I hope that pleasure has you dripping in feeling good and you soak it all in. I hope that pleasure enables you to meet layers of yourself you hadn't before. I hope that pleasure allows you to wildly express yourself in every aspect unapologetically. I hope that pleasure connects you to how incredible you are and how much love is encoded within your DNA. You deserve pleasure in whatever form that looks like for you (may that be multiple orgasms or a strawberry smoothie). Here's to your pleasure revolution, beautiful soul, it's cumming… ;)

YOUR GREAT UNLEARNING

1. PLEASURE PARTY

It's time to experience a pleasure party. It's time to rediscover what pleasure means to you. The pleasure party isn't just limited to sex as well. Let's start with the pre-party by answering the following questions:

- What would I like my definition of pleasure to be?
- What does it mean to be in my body?
- How do I connect to my body?

Now the main event.

Based on the unlearning above, we are redefining pleasure as presence, feeling good and giving into the ecstasy of life. A fun way to do this is to tap into your senses… your sensuality. What sense-based activities can you do that give you pleasure? I've listed some examples beneath each category.

Touch

- Receive a massage.
- Make something with your hands! Try a pottery or cooking class. Tap into your inner child and play with Lego, slime or play dough.
- Hit the beach. There's a variety of textures to experience there. The sand between your toes, the water lapping against your skin, and the feel of running your hands over nearby trees or rocks.

Taste

- Eat your favourite meal and savour every bite.
- Eat with presence, at the table, with no distractions (don't

read a book or watch TV or listen to a podcast).
- Taste foods at different temperatures and varying levels of spice. Explore the unique taste senses: salty, sweet, sour, bitter and umami (my personal favourite).

Smell

- Bake choc chip and caramel cookies because the smell is seriously divine.
- Light up a candle and take in the scent.
- Literally stop and smell the roses! Go for a walk in a lush natural reserve or park.

Sight

- Visit an art gallery.
- Experiment with coloured light bulbs in your house.
- Go somewhere new.

Sound

- Listen to ASMR videos.
- Try a moment or day of silence.
- Listen to an erotic audiobook.

2. GETTING TO KNOW YOUR BODY

What you'll need:
- A safe, comfortable and private place.
- Ample time.
- A handheld or pocket mirror.
- A full length mirror.
- Body oil or lotion.
- Lubrication.
- Trimmed nails (self-exploration is not fun with long nails—they can induce sharp and painful sensations).
- A journal and pen.
- Optional support tools such as a vibrator, dildo or crystal wand.

For this exercise you may want to start fully clothed and work your way up to undressing. Use your hands to explore every area of your body. Make a note of what feels good, what sparks an *oooooh* and *mmmmm*.

Use sensory experimentation—hot massage oil, cold ice cubes, ticklish feathers, a dry brush or being blindfolded.

Along this journey you may find it helpful to journal and document what comes up. Often, as we touch our body, unconscious stories may arise. These tell us how we feel about our body.

One of the areas I felt discomfort by and actively had to acquaint myself with is my breasts. Lovingly touch your breasts and massage them. Try circular motions with varying pressure and strokes. Play with your nipples.

Explore your vagina. I never even knew what my vagina looked like because I only knew it from a straight on, external perspective in front of a mirror. Use a handheld or pocket mirror to examine your vagina. Get into a low squat position to see more. You may even like to print out a diagram of a vagina and familiarise yourself with the anatomy and nerve clusters.

Set aside the time, intention and space to familiarise yourself with your vagina. At first, you may just touch the outside. As you become more comfortable, you may like to explore what your vagina feels like with your fingers or even support tools like a vibrator, dildo or crystal wand. They key is feeling safe and creating a pleasurable environment. Use lubrication for a more sensual experience.

I suggest lying in bed with a few pillows behind your head so that your body is slightly upright. Don't push yourself if you're uncomfortable. Work your way up to a finger or two. Deep breathing helps you relax. When we are tense, we tend to clench our vaginas.

I like to use crystals as another method of self-exploration. I love the energy and intent behind them. I use a small rose quartz crystal wand because I like pink, and it symbolises love. I explore with the wand in a hot bath where I can relax. Light some candles to create a soft environment too!

Another variation of mirror work, which you may need to work up to, is to explore what it feels like to watch you pleasure yourself. This is ideally done in front of a mirror. You may want to surround yourself with soft blankets and pillows to create a comfortable and safe space.

3. DE-ARMOURING

De-armouring, in the context of pleasure and sex, can involve examining your beliefs around pleasure and sex and reframing them in a way that serves your highest self and your desires for your intimate experiences. You can explore this through the framework below:

My current beliefs around pleasure and sex and *what I want to believe instead.*

Here are some questions to help you become aware of your current beliefs:

- What is pleasure to you?
- What is sex to you?
- What do you think you've gotten wrong when it comes to sex and pleasure?
- What memories can you recall and associate with pleasure and sex?
- Would you consider yourself sexually free and what does being sexually free look like to you?
- What was your mum's approach to pleasure and sex? (Or your closest motherly/female figure.)
- Where did you get your beliefs about pleasure and sex from? Was it through a person? Perhaps an event or experience? Maybe it was from being affiliated with a certain group (e.g. culture/society).
- Imagine all stigma, judgement and shaming didn't exist. What incites curiosity within you when it comes to pleasure and sex?

Stimulate areas of tension, contraction and pain. This can be done through bodily movements and physical interaction such as shaking, jumping and dancing. When it comes to the vagina, this may involve using your fingers or a wand to support you. You may also want to investigate 'yoni mapping' for more detail.

Emotional release—feeling is healing. This could look like grunting, groaning, screaming into a pillow, moaning and crying.

Reconnect to yourself through means such as touching with soft strokes, hugs and self-massage.

Breathwork—slow inhalations and exhalations. Taking in deep breaths and imagine circulating the energy around where you feel your armour.

SELF-MADE

THE LEARNING
You have to be another class of special to be self-made.

Self-made. *Adjective.* Dictionary meaning: *used to describe people who have become successful through their own efforts and actions.* Yet, it's funny, when we think of self-made individuals, we believe they weren't born with money (*cue the controversy of the now retracted Forbes article on Kylie Jenner being the world's youngest self-made billionaire…*). We believe they didn't have help. We believe they are special (*maybe they're unicorns*). We believe something has enabled them to live the life of their dreams and be wildly wealthy. We all know the self-made stories, the rags to riches tale. '*It's so nice but it can't or won't happen for me.*' '*The grass always looks greener on the other side. Can life really be that good?*' If you're anything like me, you're not only doubtful and sceptical but resentful too. Guzzling down coffee, knee deep in anxiety and a never-ending-to-do-list, thinking about how easily these 'self-made' people have it. '*Why can't I be as lucky as them?*' '*They've got something that I don't have and it's unfair.*' '*What is their secret?*'

When it comes to being self-made, we may also jump to the conclusion that it means being an entrepreneur and starting your own business but that isn't the only means of being self-made. To me, the essence of being self-made is building something from the ground up. Going somewhere that hasn't been ventured before by those who came before you—whether it's your family, friends or society.

I am proud to be self-made. I never had a connection that handed me a job. If anything, it was harder for me because of my foreign name

(*Phil? Is it a typo? Oh, you're not a man? No, it's Phi, pronounced 'fee'*). Being first generation born in Australia, nothing was handed to me. My family came from Vietnam to start a new life with no existing ties or connections to Australia. I have worked hard for everything I have. I climbed the corporate ladder as a Woman of Colour through grit, determination and a work ethic that nearly killed me. As a child of refugee parents, this way of life has been instilled in me. I am grateful I even held a job in a country free from extreme violence compared to poverty in a war-torn country (which makes you feel so guilty when you are miserable, but your bills are paid, and you have food on the table).

This chapter is about taking the leap of faith and going at it on your own because this is the current chapter of my life. For many of us, we get caught up in the rat race of working for someone else. The fantasy and dream of starting something on your own is alluring yet it's the security and stability of the traditional career path that holds us back. Don't beat yourself up, it is not your fault. As a species, the notion of safety is hard-wired in our DNA. Safety is a fundamental, evolutionary need for our species. We make decisions based on either maintaining our baseline or improving it. Our ancestors faced constant threats: wild animals, the elements and more. Whilst we no longer face these fears, this drive is embedded in us. So, we follow what is familiar, the playbook passed down by generations before us and our parents. Go to university, get the job, save for a mortgage and buy a property. This doesn't necessarily mean we feel happy or fulfilled but a stable job certainly fulfils the need to be safe (however, this is no longer the case with the job cuts and reductions seen by the global pandemic).

More people are waking up to alternative lifestyles and means to make money. There has been a rise of *#bossbabe*, *#girlboss* and *#sidehustle*. What's stopping you? The blocks and fears you face are in your mind. The idea of having your own business terrifies you. It feels dangerous and risky. What if it all goes wrong…? When really you should be asking yourself, '*What if it all goes right?*' Are you willing to risk it all, to have it all?

So here comes the truth bomb: you can feel the fear and choose to do it anyway (I certainly did and that is truly why I believe I am living a life beyond my wildest dreams). If you can dance with the fear, sneaky self-talk might come interrupt with excuses: *I don't know what I could do; I don't have time; I don't have money; I don't have what it takes*... and the list goes on. There will always be an excuse. The key to being self-made is being solutions-orientated and getting creative. There has never been a moment in time like this where it has been easier to be self-made and follow your dreams. We have the internet! We have technology! We have so many free resources! All you have to do is be willing to learn and find the time and willpower to start.

When I started my business, I didn't intentionally set out to do so. It was an anonymous passion project on mental health that led to me becoming the life coach and writer that I am today. Typically, we believe if we work hard and make money, we will be happy. When really, being happy and doing what you love will make you money. You just have to start. Of course, the stories about when your sister's best friend Jessie tried to start their own business and lost lots of money or how your uncle John says it's better to play it safe in life. These are all valid opinions, but this is your life! The only way to know for yourself is to try firsthand. To be in control of your dreams and destiny, not your family or the opinions of people you hardly know. Stop listening to the world and start listening to yourself. Listening to the world has us believe that we would be happy with a high-paying job and an enviable job position. Nowadays you don't even need to quit your job to start a business. Some people like to though, putting everything they have into it but I started my business on the side. I would work on it before my full time job and after. I replaced binging Netflix with my passion. For every problem or challenge, there is a solution!

It is important to note that I won't sugarcoat the self-made journey for you. It is not for the faint-hearted and those who aren't truly aligned with their vision and purpose for what they want. There have been moments I questioned if I made the right choice by leaving my corporate job because it looked like I wouldn't have enough money for the month to pay off all my expenses. I created scenarios where

I would need to get a second job or potentially move house. Yet I've never had to and every time, I have been able to not just meet my expenses but thrive. Having your own business can wreak havoc on your nervous system until you learn to adjust to the waves.

Social media has portrayed the idea that getting what you want and living your dream life looks easy, breezy, fun and beautiful. We've been sold the dream that anyone can do it! While this remains true, I do believe anyone can do it, but it won't always be smooth sailing. It's far from it. At the beginning I put in hard work and hours to build a strong foundation. That meant working before and after my usual 9-5 *(really 8:30am-5:30pmish/6:30pmish)* for nine months. From my personal experience, it came at the price of time which could've been spent with loved ones but now that it's up and running, I have so much time to spend with loved ones.

Don't let that stop you from building something amazing though. It may seem like the hardest thing in the world to achieve until you do it and then you'll wonder why you didn't start sooner. When you are truly devoted to yourself and why you are doing what you do, you will have the strength to commit, to be there during the good times and the bad *(just like a marriage!)*. You don't give up when it gets hard, at least not without a fight and some serious effort.

Sometimes our ego and pride get in the way. Sometimes we experience the fear of failure. Personally, I don't see someone who started a business only for it not to work out as a failure… I see it as brave because if it were easy, wouldn't everyone do it? The biggest failure is to not even try at all and be burdened with regret. It's better to do things poorly than not at all. Reading a few pages of a book is better than nothing. Going for a walk when you wanted to go for a run is better than nothing. Baby steps are okay. Baby steps are progress. At the end of the day if you 'fail' now, you'll 'succeed' sooner by learning from your experiences.

THE UNLEARNING
Anybody can be self-made.

If you're reading this and feeling uncomfortable, it's probably because you know deep down that you're here for more than what you have now. I never thought or dreamed of being my own boss and running my own business yet here I am. It's absolutely surreal to be writing this chapter in divine timing a week before the anniversary of when I resigned from my job on the 13th of September 2021. Wow, what can I say? Since officially finishing up and leaving my job in November 2021, so much has changed. I am writing this chapter in my new home which is a stone's throw away from Australia's most iconic beach. A home which I got approved for and pay for through my own business! I also recently had the privilege of being able to pay for my beautiful virtual assistant Ellie to come visit Sydney so I could meet her in person. She has been a game changer for my business. She has allowed me to do what I love by freeing up my time and now she's going full time in her own business too! I am fulfilling my lifelong dream of writing a book and being a published author (an opportunity that was finalised months after leaving my steady corporate job!). In my first year of business, I had the privilege to travel to Singapore, London, Brighton, Wales, Seville, Portugal, France and Monaco whilst working from my phone! Everything you desire, you can give it to yourself when you are self-made.

Despite the name, being self-made isn't about doing it alone. Many people in your life will play a part, whether it's moving your business forward through an opportunity or being by your side when things get hard. I couldn't have done it all on my own without the support of my coaches: Tiff, Kristina, Paige, Charlotte, Tameera and Patti. They are incredibly powerful women. Some are younger than me, some older than me. It doesn't matter—it's all about the soul that can help me best (something I had to learn after being conditioned to always have an older male mentor—hello familial father conditioning).

I always get asked, *'When did you know it was time to take that leap of faith and go all in on your business?'* It's cliche but you just *know*. Even if it doesn't work out, you will live the rest of your life in peace knowing that you tried, rather than allowing the what ifs to eat you alive. I thought I would leave my job with $10,000 saved up but the truth was when I ended up doing it, I had no savings, but I had to trust the pull of my heart and soul. Pain is inevitable in life, even if you make all the logical decisions, so you might as well try. I truly believe when you are in alignment with your purpose and trust yourself, you are wholly supported by the universe.

Knowing my human design also helped. I am a 2/4 Manifesting Generator with an emotional authority. To sum up what this means as succinctly as I can, I am a multitasking energetic powerhouse. The best decisions I make involve my gut instinct and it's advised I wait to make decisions in order to gain clarity as my emotions are the biggest influence. The 2 is my conscious personality which means I am a 'natural' genius at what comes easily to me (such as human design, I am self-taught!). The 4 is embedded in my soul which means I am a people person and in terms of business, referrals are a vital source of clients.

Just before going full time, I crossed paths with Molly Jane, the co-founder of WELLWEB, a digital wellness platform. She had seen a few of my posts on social media and contacted me to get in touch with Amarra Bowkett to be a part of the platform as an expert. I would go on to record a series on human design and relationships. After doing a human design reading for Amarra, she referred me to many individuals including a particular beautiful soul, Rebecca (Bec) Duffield. Bec is the founder of Zero Point Yoga Studios. Bec is true to her powerful design, a 5/1 Generator who's destined for greatness, who holds guru energy. The number of referrals I received from Bec planted the seed in my heart. Yes, I could do this full-time.

A year after that very reading, in July 2022, I was invited to be a facilitator at Bec's retreat at SOMA in Byron Bay. A true pinch me moment as the stunning location is the backdrop for the series *Nine Perfect Strangers*. Such a surreal moment to be doing what I loved and getting paid for it all thanks to Bec. At the retreat I met one of my very first human design clients Tas Spurigan who would also play a key role in referring so many of her friends to me. This exemplifies an invisible interconnected network of angels supporting me in my business. You just never know who you will meet and how they may play a key role in your life!

In May 2022, I visited Cannes in France. I happened to be in Europe when my friend, Mili, whom I virtually met in a mastermind, would be at the same time. It's funny though that this pivotal moment in my life nearly didn't happen. I wanted to go to Cannes, but I was feeling worried about money and so flew a day later than planned. The day I was meant to arrive was the day Mili happened to get tickets for a daytime premiere of a film at the Cannes Film Festival. I was so annoyed with myself, but at the end of the day the reason I would be in Cannes was to meet her in person! In a turn of events, I would end up attending the premiere of the film *Nostalgia*. I also got to walk the red-carpet solo. You have no idea how surreal it was. Flashing lights. Seeing myself on the jumbo screen. Rubbing shoulders with the who's who of the film industry. All thanks to Mili and her partner Ale for getting me tickets. A year prior in my old job as a strategy manager at a cinema advertising company it was my job to be on top of the news for Cannes from behind the computer screen and here I was attending the premiere as the CEO of my own business. Life is crazy. Life is wild. Life is surreal.

You don't need to be perfect to be successful. All you need to do is start and be true to you! People don't want perfectionism; people want your potency. Your true authentic, unapologetic, radiantly magnetic and magnificent self. I was told to act as an authority, to avoid being 'messy' online and so I would tell myself, 'You can't show up like this, you have to be well-presented, you must have your make up on and hair done.' Yet I'm known online for being myself and showing the true raw, messy parts of my existence and book out regularly. I'll show up bare face, messy bun in an oversized t-shirt and all. In the aftermath of my break-up, I uploaded multiple stories online where I cried and wailed hysterically. In fact, I share myself crying a lot because I do experience a lot of painful moments even as I live my dream life. That's the reality folks. Living your best life and having everything you want doesn't mean that you're immune from feeling sad and being unhappy.

Forget the rules and what you think you need to do, whether that is showing up and posting online every day or doing what everyone else in your industry does. It's your damn business. Do what you want. Do what lights you up. Run it your way. This is why you're starting a business. You are the boss. Don't let yourself feel like you're working for someone else when it's your own business. Your business, your rules. The biggest turning point for me was when my business was still a passion project in June 2020 with a hundred followers. I became aware of Men's Health Week and at the time online no one was talking about it. I was in disbelief given in Australia alone, 1 in 8 men will experience depression and 1 in 5 will experience anxiety at some stage in their lives. I was apprehensive to do a post about it because *who was I?* My mental health page 'inhervitality' was aimed at women. I wasn't a man or a coach just some Asian Australian woman who wanted to make a difference. I knew in my soul that I needed to spread the message even if only one person saw it… overnight it went viral globally and I gained 10,000 followers. Sure I had some online trolls but I was so glad I did it. I stepped up and became a leader not because it was handed to me but through the choice I made.

There is no business without you. You must also remember that your business is not you. It may play an important role in your life but you are more than just a business. If someone doesn't work with you or buy your product, it doesn't mean there's something wrong with you. If something doesn't work out in your business, it doesn't mean you are a failure. Your business is an incredible channel for you to offer your products and services with the world. Your worth and value isn't determined by your business.

Business seemingly never ends and that's okay. There's always more you could be doing for your business no matter what level you reach. What's important is *you*. Taking care of your mind, body and soul so that you can be at your best. Your clients are paying you to ensure your optimal health so that you can operate and share to the best of your abilities. Don't be afraid of the masculine elements in structure.

After leaving my job I experienced extremes. At first, I tried to recreate the same routine into my own business by pushing myself to hustle all the time. In that pursuit I forgot why I started my own business in the first place. I wanted to experience more joy, freedom and pleasure without sacrifice. So, I reigned it back and became petrified of routines and working on a Monday because it gave me flashbacks. Being in the free flow of life was wonderful but it started to get overwhelming when I got side tracked or forgot to do something. Eventually I found balance by understanding my own human design. I am designed to experience flow with routines, not rigidity. A routine that doesn't have to be stifling or take away from your freedom, instead it should liberate you so you can do what you love! Having my own business has helped me heal my inner masculine. Don't get lost in building a business that you forget the very reason why you started in the first place.

The self-made journey isn't straightforward and it's certainly not a walk in the park, but it is very much worth it. Take the judgements, concerns and opinions of others off that pedestal and tune in to yourself. I'd rather be labelled 'weird and crazy' than be an unhappy follower of tradition and status quo.

In this sacred journey, you will meet yourself in a way you never have before. Just like how relationships can bring out different parts of you, so will your own business and career. Being self-made will activate you over and over again. In pursuing the path of being self-made, you will receive deeper invitations to grow, transform and evolve. To meet the edges and confines of who you are, yet to continually stretch and expand. It takes true determination to build something you love from nothing. It takes true confidence to be illogical by following your heart and soul. It takes true courage to walk away from the safe and traditional in pursuit of more. It takes audacity to take risks knowing they don't guarantee success. Dare to be bold and blaze your own trail. You don't need anyone's permission to do so. It doesn't have to make sense to anyone but you. Trust that you have the capacity and ability to make your dreams happen. You deserve the life you desire. Now, go make it happen.

YOUR GREAT UNLEARNING

1. SELF-MADE BUSINESS

Know that you want to start a side hustle or business but not sure what you could do?

Here are some prompts to help you get started:

- If money weren't a thing, what would you love to do?
- What are you good at?
- What is something people praise you for and compliment you on?
- What is something that you're naturally good at?
- What is something you wish could be invented to help your life?
- What is a service you wish someone would do for you but isn't available right now?
- What problems are you good at solving?
- What resources do you have at your disposal to start a business?
- What are you willing to skill up on or learn?
- What's an idea you've always thought about but never made happen?

2. FINDING TIME

One of the biggest barriers to starting a side hustle or business is time. Write your 'must do's' every single day for a week based in half hour blocks. Identify activities that are not essential and could be substituted. You will see that you have more time than you think. An example on the following page.

Mondays

7am	Wake up
7:30am	Breakfast
8am	Gym
8:30am	Work
9am	Work
9:30am	Work
10am	Work
10:30am	Work
11am	Work
11:30am	Work
12 noon	*Lunch Break—Spare time*
12:30pm	*Lunch Break—Spare time*
1pm	Work
1:30pm	Work
2pm	Work
2:30pm	Work
3pm	Work
3:30pm	Work
4pm	Work
4:30pm	Work
5pm	Work
5:30pm	Work
6pm	Home
6:30pm	Dinner
7pm	*Usually Netflix—Spare time*
7:30pm	*Usually Netflix—Spare time*
8pm	*Read book—Spare time*
8:30pm	*Read book—Spare time*
9pm	*Social media scroll—Spare time*
9:30pm	Spare time
10pm	Wind down for bed
10:30pm	Sleep

That's four hours! You could keep two hours for yourself as downtime and use the other two on your business.

3. SOLUTIONS ORIENTATED

Part of being self-made is being able to be resourceful and figure out your own answers. You can use the below table to help you.

Problem:					
What resources do I have?	Who can help me?	What does the internet suggest?	Potential Solution 1	Potential Solution 2	Potential Solution 3

Problem:					
What resources do I have?	Who can help me?	What does the internet suggest?	Potential Solution 1	Potential Solution 2	Potential Solution 3

Problem:					
What resources do I have?	Who can help me?	What does the internet suggest?	Potential Solution 1	Potential Solution 2	Potential Solution 3

Part 3
INNER BEING

Finding out most people believe they spend most of their energy, time and life at work or even at home isn't uncommon... the real truth is we spend all of our time inside our mind, body, heart and soul.

THOUGHT WORK

THE LEARNING
Everything you think is a fact and must be true.

Isn't it fascinating that when we start school, we are taught about animals, history, mathematics and science but not our own mind? Given how much our mindset dictates our reality, this baffles me. One could argue that the reality we experience is that of how it plays out in our brain. We unconsciously live on autopilot where we automatically believe the thoughts that pop into our mind. If we think something, we believe it's fact. The truth is, just because you think something that doesn't mean it's true.

Don't believe everything you think! This is such a simple statement, yet I feel many of us don't come to this realisation until later in life. It would have been helpful to know when I was thirteen; just because I thought I was ugly doesn't mean I was. Your thoughts are simply what's being offered to you by your brain. This is shaped by a whole variety of factors: your upbringing, your programming, your conditioning, your past and so forth.

Our minds are great storytellers! The voice inside your head has created 'you' and your reality by weaving together pieces of your past experiences, how you interpret the present moment and what you believe to be true. It creates an overarching narrative you believe to be reality. It all pieces together perfectly like a jigsaw puzzle. Only certain pieces make it into this jigsaw puzzle because they fit your current belief system. Think of this as the current operating system on your computer or phone. Have you ever observed or noticed this story telling? These narratives shape the story of our lives. How we view ourselves, our life, our relationships and what we do.

As a result, ironically, we live most of our life in our head. All the possibilities and scenarios. What if A happens? What about Plan B? Goodness, could C happen? If you're constantly in your head, you are missing out on living your life! You watch TV and scroll through videos on your phone, but do you ever watch your mind? Your thoughts are so powerful. Believing them gives them power. They are the internal navigation system. Your thoughts could make you go bungee jumping or make you cry. Your thoughts could make you run away or cook a gourmet meal. The personal-development world has established the fact that your thoughts create your reality. Circumstances are neutral and have no inherent meaning. It is your thoughts that create meaning and in turn influence how you feel and what actions you then choose to take.

Your thoughts aren't the issue. We all experience negative self-talk, it's a part of the essential experience of what it means to be human. 'You're not good enough.' 'You look ridiculous.' 'No one cares about you.' This is the way we are hardwired, the negativity bias, as a means to protect us from potential threats. An example of negatively biased brain behaviour is the feeling that the negativity will always trump the positivity. Five good things could happen, but you may focus on the one negative. Your brain is more likely to think of everything that could go wrong instead of everything that could go right. You can remember and recall negative experiences more clearly than positive memories. It's also the reason we are more likely to leave negative reviews as opposed to positive ones. It takes uncomfortable, intentional and conscious work to overcome the negativity. It's difficult to do on your own and much easier with a life coach (such as me!).

The issue at heart here is your resistance to your thoughts and trying to get rid of them. It doesn't matter what you do, you cannot control or get rid of your thoughts! It's up to you to choose who is there to meet the thoughts. You and your highest self or the autopilot version of you with its past pain, patterns, stories and conditioning? We will do the craziest things to avoid facing our thoughts. We will indulge on food, sex, drugs, busyness, obsessions and fantasies, you know how it is… the list goes on and on. By accepting and allowing our thoughts, we melt the resistance we feel when trying to control something that is uncontrollable. We allow in the reality that thoughts are a non-negotiable fabric of life.

Your mind is also extremely gullible. Whatever thought pops up, it believes it. You don't intend to believe the mean things but imagine if you intended to believe in the good things, the thoughts that serve you well! Your brain is also lazy. It loves to be comfortable at all costs. It likes to repeat thoughts you already have had, even if they are negative because they're familiar (apparently 95% of our thoughts are repeated!). I hate to break it to you, your brain is also a liar! It means well because it wants to protect you and keep you safe, but it lies to you.

The common way your brain lies is through catastrophising. Every little setback becomes a huge hurdle—the sky is falling in. You make a problem more significant than it is. Imagine going on a date with someone who doesn't want a second date. Then you think you'll never find love again…

Everything is either black or white and you overlook the possibility that there's a spectrum of shades. We're under the impression that we are either a success or a failure. In reality, our lives include a mix of successes *and* failures.

Another common way your brain lies to you is through personalisation. When you make everything about you even though it has nothing to do with you. *'That person doesn't want to date me because I'm not good enough,'* when, really, that person just got out of a long-term relationship and isn't ready to commit to anyone.

You're not at fault for believing these lies. Stop blaming yourself. Negativity is just easier. Your brain loves to be efficient and has so many things to do and because of that, taking the more familiar negative route is easier. Think about it. Your brain ensures you subconsciously breathe, blink and circulate blood. It uses so much energy to keep you alive therefore it likes repetition because that means comfort. If you're always complaining, your brain will latch onto this. The more you do it, the more it will happen automatically as the neurons work together. Your brain thinks, *'Why build a temporary bridge when I can build a permanent bridge since this human loves to do it all the time?'* So it does. As the saying goes: *'Neurons that fire together, wire together.'*

THE UNLEARNING
Your thoughts are not facts, but they do form your reality.

At the end of the day, your thoughts are *just* thoughts. We are conditioned to believe our thoughts should be or need to be a certain way but they don't. I know what it's like to fear your thoughts. We all have dark or inappropriate thoughts such as wanting to disappear or desiring revenge. There is no shame in thinking them. Just because I have them or maybe you've had them doesn't mean we desire the physical manifestation of these thoughts. Be kind and compassionate to yourself. It's one thing to think thoughts, it's another to act on thoughts. You don't need to attach yourself to the thought because it's just passing by. You're human. We have brief, random and convoluted thoughts. Remember you are not your thoughts!

We also must be conscious of the structures and logistical make up of our thoughts. As Alan Watts puts it, *'We seldom realise, for example, that our most private thoughts and emotions are not actually our own. For we think in terms of languages and images which we did not invent, but which were given to us by our society.'* Indeed, the power of words! Words have the power to make people cry and feel loved. Words can touch our hearts and speak to our soul. As seen on social media, *'Words cast spells. That's why it's called spelling. Words are energy. Use them wisely.'* We get to be our own magical alchemists by consciously creating our reality with the language we use.

So, who are you if you're not your thoughts? Consciousness. To truly 'awaken' is to realise that you are not the thoughts but, rather the silence, the emptiness, the space, the void, the awareness, the watcher and the observer behind the thoughts. A word of advice from your soul: The quieter you become, the more space you create in your mind and the more you can *truly* hear. If you believe every thought in your head is yours then who is the one listening? You have to be the one listening! The moment you witness your thoughts is the beginning of separating yourself from them.

We've established that it's impossible to stop thoughts. You can try to run away from them high in the mountains or in the middle of the jungle, but this is only a temporary fix. The solution is to be at peace with them, to not be distracted by them and to not be so egotistically impacted by them. Free your mind.

You deserve to be free. You deserve to have peace of mind. This is what we know as meditation. Meditation gets this wrap for silencing the mind when it actually does the opposite. You don't meditate to get rid of thoughts and feelings. You meditate to become more aware of your thoughts and be with them instead of struggling with them.

Meditation doesn't need to be performed sitting with your legs crossed. Life can become your meditation method. When you're brewing a cup of tea or going for a walk. Meditation allows the thoughts to go by like the clouds in the sky, rather than getting deeply involved and entrenched in them. Letting thoughts flow without attachment is a skill in itself. It is through surrender we gain the feeling of control. It's how you take your power back from your mind. You're no longer in the passenger seat but driving the car. Meditation brings the focus from the past and future into the present, what is going on right now in your brain. Be mindful, not *mind-full*, know the difference.

One of my favourite quotes by Osho is, *'The mind is a beautiful servant but a dangerous master.'* Thinking is not a bad thing. Thinking is an incredible tool. You will achieve what your mind believes. When we consciously use our mind, we are no longer at its mercy like an untrained leashed dog dragging you around. Instead, the dog is tamed and trained. Limiting beliefs are formed from negativity and insecurity. You become a prisoner of your mind by listening to the voice in your head that says stop or you can't do it, before you've even tried! The only limits are your mind and what you believe. Step back and see that you can claim your power by choosing not to believe these thoughts. Choose to believe that anything is possible. Choose to believe anything can suddenly change for you. Choose to believe in the infinite spectrum of possibilities and outcomes. It doesn't matter what you see. What you hear going on in your brain matters, what you *believe* matters. Afterall, beliefs are simply repeated thoughts you have.

Alongside belief, is perception. When it comes to consciousness, perspective is everything. You get to choose your perspective. Are you experiencing discomfort or room for growth? Pain or power? Rejection or redirection? Failure or a lesson? Wounds or wisdom? Reframing your perspective is power.

Something I read on Instagram to this day still makes me cackle, *'Don't be afraid to be open minded. Your brain isn't going to fall out.'* Nothing changes if nothing changes. If you choose to have the same thoughts, you will get the same results. If you want a new outcome, you must have new thoughts! You are the creator of your reality. Use different words. Reframe your language. Live a life by design. This is thought work. As Wayne Dwyer says, *'If you change the way you look at things, the things you look at change.'* Use the mind for what it is, a thinking machine for your benefit. If you hear a song you don't like on the radio, you don't just listen to it, you change the channel! Do the same with your thoughts.

Our greatest misery, dread and suffering stems from our mind. As Eckhart Tolle eloquently explains, *'Have you ever seen an unhappy flower or a stressed oak tree? Have you some across a depressed dolphin, a frog that has a problem with self-esteem, a cat that cannot relax, or a bird that carries hatred and resentment? The only animals that may occasionally experience something akin to negativity or show signs of neurotic behaviour are those that live in close contact with humans and so link into the human's mind and its insanity.'* Your mind is naturally going to point out everything that could go wrong. You choose, let your thoughts stifle and throw you off, or choose to rise above them.

Our whole reality and everything we experience is shaped in our mind. All states and emotions begin with us, whether happy and joyful or angry and scared. Thoughts are like visitors. From time to time unwanted and unexpected guests will arrive. We may not want them there, but we can choose to be respectful and polite. Some may overstay but eventually the less attention and focus we give to these guests, the more likely they will end up leaving themselves. This is what it means to let go. This is what it means to liberate yourself from your mind. When you are aware of your true nature (soul and consciousness) you will find peace. You will no longer be chained to the constant chatter of your mind. You will be able to let go, flow and see things for what they really are, so you can make better decisions.

YOUR GREAT UNLEARNING

1. (META)PHYSICAL THOUGHT WORK

Our thoughts are invisible. When I'm feeling stuck or overwhelmed, I find taking a somatic approach helps. Try some of the techniques below:

- Imagine Ctrl + Alt + Deleting your thoughts.
- Act out the action of pulling out thoughts from your brain.
- Imagine washing away the thoughts that do not serve you.
- Imagine unhelpful thoughts floating away in a bubble.
- Imagine a windscreen wiping away your thoughts.

2. BRAIN DUMP

When you are overwhelmed with thoughts, possibilities or a combination of the two, brain-dumping can be useful.

- Get a piece of paper and put a timer on for five minutes. Write out everything that comes to your mind.
- From there you can systematically go back and see what is on your mind. What thoughts are repetitive? Is there a main theme that pulls them together?
- If you're trying to solve a problem, brain-dump a specific list of the problems and then a list of potential solutions.

3. OVERWHELMED

When you are bamboozled with a tonne of thoughts, simplicity is best. What I like to do is focus on my breath. Holding a thought is difficult when you're consciously breathing! The simplest way to breathe and alleviate tension is to ensure your exhalation is longer than your inhalation, that's it! I also find breathing as if you are sucking through a straw really helpful.

HAPPINESS IS EVERYTHING

THE LEARNING
You should be happy all the time (everyone else is!).

What do you want in life? The most common answer you'll hear is not money, fame, love or a house. It's happiness. Even if someone answers differently, if you dig deeper and ask them why, they'll respond with, *'To be happy.'* Society is obsessed with happiness. The United States of America's declaration states, *'The right to life, liberty, and the pursuit of happiness'*. The irony is that as humans, we aren't designed to pursue happiness. We are primarily built like animals to survive and reproduce as a species.

Why do we obsess over happiness as a society and species? Or is the question, *Are we obsessed with it or its absence and the search for it*? I think we can admit that we're afraid of being sad and what it entails: pain, disappointment and heartbreak. It hurts. Broadly speaking, it's as if we believe some elusive magical formula for happiness exists. We believe that happiness comes from outside of ourselves. We believe there's a benchmark for happiness levels that everyone needs to live up to and if we don't meet it, there's something wrong with us. We try to crowdsource happiness and fulfilment, but it doesn't work.

In the pursuit of happiness, you can do all the right things and still not find it. You can have a good life on paper. You can have money. You can exercise. You can work harder. You can make time for friends and family. You can donate to charities. You can volunteer. You can eat more vegetables. You can have more vitamins. You can meditate. You can self-care Sunday. You can be in a romantic relationship. The truth of the matter is to ask yourself, *how is your heart and soul today?* This is one of my most favourite questions I get asked from my dear friend Mili and now in turn ask others.

If I could sum up my upbringing with a mantra, I would choose, *'Don't worry, be happy'*. A sweet sentiment that was actually downright toxic. I would attempt to override my thoughts with happy shiny thoughts and affirmations. Beneath the surface, I ignored the negativity until it accumulated and I couldn't take it anymore. I tried doing things I believed would make me happy, such as travelling the world or going out with friends. Pretending to be happy, doesn't make you happy. Happiness isn't one of those things you can fake until it happens. Maybe for a while you'll believe it but deep down in your soul, you know you aren't.

These days toxic positivity is perpetuated on social media. We're told to *'look on the bright side of life'*. Splashed across our feeds are *'good vibes only'* across a plastering of pretty pastel posts. Social media is a highlights reel. On social media we see the perfect poses, people flaunting their new purchase, holiday, partner or wealth. Whilst you see that, what you fail to see is the emotional state the person posting is actually in.

I am always so surprised by the amount of people and clients that think social media is real. Having worked with well-known influencers and celebrities, I know firsthand that it's not true. I had a session with one who would post happy snaps of her on holiday but in our sessions she would cry because she was so unhappy and stressed from the pressure of keeping up appearances on holiday. That I could definitely relate to. When I went to Europe in early 2022, I smiled but behind the scenes I was going through a heartbreak hardly anyone knew about.

Somehow happiness is about keeping up appearances, yet appearances can be deceiving. I've had messages flooding my inbox from people who thought I seemed so happy when in reality this was not the case.

After achieving my goal of quitting my corporate job and going full-time as a life coach, I thought I would finally be truly happy. Based on popular culture, I had come to believe that happiness is found in things and achievements. Indeed, I was happy! Don't get me wrong.

However there were moments of sadness and overwhelm. Adjusting from being surrounded by people to working alone from home. Lots of spare time with no one to spend it with given most my friends worked 9-5. Not to mention the moments where I processed the anxiety and burnout that had accumulated from my job.

I was successful in my own right, yet my relationship was not going so well. Even as we were galivanting across Europe. I felt so disappointed when he didn't join me in Spain. We would even upload stories of us happily out and about in Brighton when afterwards we would quickly escalate into arguments over something stupid, like attending a family friend's BBQ. It felt like I was living a double life. The worst thing about it was that I felt so guilty for not being happy. There I was travelling to incredible places yet beating myself up for being ungrateful and unhappy. When you're truly happy you're not thinking about happiness as a mental concept because you're too busy living it.

Funnily enough, some of us are afraid to be happy because we're scared we will lose it. Subconsciously we create a need to maintain a certain level of happiness otherwise something has gone wrong in life. The ironic notion of feeling *too* happy because you're waiting for something to take it away. You don't want to fully feel it in case it's fleeting, or it disappears. In fact, there's a term for this, *cherophobia*, from the Greek word *chairo*, which means to rejoice or be glad. I don't think we fear happiness itself but rather the bad things that might follow it. Perhaps it's feeling undeserving of happiness or having unrealistic expectations of what it will do for oneself and their life. It could even be self-sabotage (been there!). When I've reflected on life, I've realised that sometimes happiness evades us because we have things to learn from sadness that we cannot from joy.

THE UNLEARNING
You don't have to be happy all the time. You say you want to be happy but only when you're a certain way or something in particular has happened in your life. That's not happiness. That's self-imprisonment.

Sure, you can chase happiness but really it can't be bought, caught or obtained. You see, so many people seem to miss that happiness doesn't suddenly start in the relationship, the job, the degree or money… happiness isn't an object. Happiness is a state of being and therefore happiness truly comes only from within. It starts with your thoughts and what you tell yourself every day. I don't want to contribute to toxic positivity so I would like to acknowledge that sometimes life deals us a hand that truly does suck. It can be exhausting to force yourself to see the bright side. Sometimes all we can do is call it a day and accept that we aren't happy. In times like this, the best things to do is take care of yourself and find support.

Happiness is one of those airy-fairy concepts… we go with what we believe it to be yet we never take a moment to stop and actually ask ourselves, *'What truly makes me happy?'* That's the unlearning. Doing what you want, not what your mum, casual acquaintance or society wants. You're not responsible for anyone else's happiness. Do what makes you happy, not what you *think* will make you happy. Happiness is sweeter when you are present and in the fullness of the feeling. Happiness is being your true authentic self and acting accordingly in alignment.

While our minds are very aware of our pain, misery and suffering, they aren't as perceptive of moments of joy and bliss. We seem to hold onto the rain and forget the days of sunshine. You have to consciously and consistently savour moments of joy to rewire your mind. By doing so, you also extend your happiness. Compound the joy. In saying that we cannot have happiness without sadness. They need each other. Even sunshine all year around can get tiring. Flowers need rain to bloom.

Striving will not always lead to happiness, but it might lead to contentedness. I've heard stories of people turning down promotions because they didn't want to take on more. Once upon a time, I would have thought they were crazy. A promotion means more money and more status! What's funny is I would go on to turn down a promotion and more money to stay in my corporate job and turn down an opportunity to work for one of the biggest companies in the world who were trying to poach me. The less you need, the more you will have. It's true. You don't need much to be happy, but that doesn't mean you should only have the bare minimum.

Happiness truly can be found in gratitude. I am grateful to pay taxes because it means I have a job and earn a considerable amount. I am grateful for my round stomach because it means I have plenty to eat. I am grateful to vacuum and scrub the toilet because it means I have a home to live in. I am grateful to walk a long way to my car because it means I can walk and have a car. I am grateful that my alarm goes off because it means I'm alive and get to live another day. I am grateful for the moments of joy I find in the small things. Lazy Sunday mornings. Picking up a paintbrush. Falling leaves. Find pockets of happiness in your day through the small things.

If you truly want to be happy, you need to stop saying, *'I'll be happy when...'* I'll be happy when I look a certain way… I'll be happy when this happens in my life… I'll be happy when I weigh… I'll be happy when I have *insert dollars*… I'll be happy when I'm in a relationship with someone… I'll be happy when I'm on holiday… I'll be happy when I buy… You may never get that. You may not have the next moment or tomorrow. Happiness isn't found on a pedestal or in a destination. Happiness isn't pre-packaged or predetermined.

Conditioning has led you to believe when you have certain things or look a certain way you'll be happy… It's the dangling carrot that keeps on dangling—an illusion. You think you've got it and then another carrot appears, and you'll start chasing that one. Why do you need something to be happy? Do you need something to be happy? The conditions you create on happiness keep you trapped in your unhappiness. What if happiness could be your default state of consciousness and you've been led to believe otherwise? As Adyashanti says, *'There's only one thing that's better than getting what you want: it's to know that you can be happy whether you get it or not.'*

Yes, you can simply be happy right now, despite whatever is going on in life because happiness doesn't need life to be a certain way. Happiness is your being! Happiness is being with loved ones on holiday, not the holiday itself. Happiness is making a cup of coffee, not the coffee itself. Happiness is doing what you love, not the money you get from it. Happiness is already here. The question is, are you open to happiness? It's up to you because with true mindfulness and consciousness one can choose to find the happiness in every situation. Sure, it won't always look like elated joy, at times happiness is simply acknowledging that a lesson has been learned in life.

Happiness isn't everything but it is an important part of life. That's not to say you won't feel sad or down. How we feel makes up the whole picture, our existence and experience of being human. So, here's to happiness—enjoying it when it's here in the moment. To happiness in the little things. To happiness in gratitude. To happiness in contentment. To happiness in consciousness. To happiness in choice. Happiness is felt nowhere else more than in your heart and soul. You deserve to be happy, beautiful soul, and you are allowed to be happy. Deliriously, stupidly and simply happy.

YOUR GREAT UNLEARNING

1. THE GRATITUDE IN MY ATTITUDE

Here is a list of ways to tap into gratitude in your daily life:

- Straightforward: a gratitude list.
- A gratitude jar. Write down something you are grateful for everyday and put it into a jar. This will accumulate and when you are feeling down, you can read through each and every single one in the jar.
- Set an alarm every few hours to as a prompt for what you are grateful for.
- Rename your alarms on your phone. e.g., my morning one is I am grateful to be alive.
- Switch your thoughts from 'I have to' → 'I get to.'
- Switch from the term 'gratitude' → 'appreciation.'
- Take a gratitude walk, put on a feel-good song and intentionally think of everything you are grateful for.

- Whatever in your life you are bored with or dissatisfied, ask yourself 'when did I not have this in my life?' and 'if I didn't have this in my life anymore, how would I feel?'
- Add depth and substance to your 'thank-yous' by explaining why you are thankful when you say it.
- Imagine a past version of yourself in your shoes now, what would this version of you be for grateful for?
- Have a gratitude keepsake such as a stone or crystal on your bedside table or under your pillow. Every night before you go to bed hold it in your hands and think of one thing you are grateful of. You'll charge it up full of gratitude energy!

2. THE FLIP SIDE

The following exercise will help you reframe a situation that takes away from your happiness. Write down everything that is getting you down, annoying you or frustrating you right now. Flip it to reframe it and see it in a different light. For example:

- He's not texting me back and I feel rejected → by him not texting me back, I am being given a redirection by the universe to text someone who can't wait to text me back.
- I didn't get the promotion because I'm not good enough → The promotion was not meant to be but that doesn't mean I'm not good enough. Maybe it means a new door is opening for me somewhere else.
- I'm stuck and lost; I don't know what to do → Being lost is an opportunity to find myself and discover what I want.

3. CREATING HAPPINESS

Write a list of the things that make you happy followed by a list of what you usually do every day. Compare the lists. How can you incorporate more of what you love into your everyday? Often, we can find and create happiness in the mundane and ordinary moments of life.

THE FEELS

THE LEARNING
Feelings are scary and should be avoided at all costs.

We live in a society that is ruled by the mind. We must do the logical thing. We must analyse it. Feelings have become foreign. We are scared of feelings. Feelings are uncomfortable. The conditioning of feelings starts from an early age. We aren't taught to understand and process them. Displaying our emotions is seen as being irrational. We are taught not to care too much. To not be the one to say *I love you* first because it's downright embarrassing if it's not returned. We disregard an emotion as silly or the enemy, *'Don't be stupid, use your head, not your heart'*. We avoid them anyway we can and buffer—we'll eat too much, drink too much, work too much and have too much sex all with the aim of not feeling our feelings. We are taught to bottle our feelings and hide the truth. This is reinforced in the workplace where showing emotions are unacceptable and seen as a lack of emotional intelligence. Take the emotion out of that email. Stick to the facts. Be professional.

By the same token, we are programmed to take a logical and rational approach to feelings. We operate from the belief that we need permission to feel. We try to understand feelings. Why do we feel them? Why is this feeling coming up? It's a very human belief to think that if we understand something enough, we can heal from it and move on with our lives. However, it can lead to over-analysing and getting stuck in the past, which conjures up anxiety, melancholy and trauma. When you truly think about it, approaching our feelings logically doesn't make sense because they *aren't* logical. The truth is it's okay to feel something for no reason. We don't have to have a step-by-step detailed manual for our feelings. Maybe there is no reason at all, it doesn't make them less valid.

Validation is vital when it comes to feelings. Not only does society tell us how to feel, but people do also. Perhaps you've been told not to cry or to get over it because it's not *that* bad. If you have, try to have empathy for those that have said this. It's likely that their feelings were also invalidated and they are projecting onto you.

If I displayed any sign of emotion in my childhood household, especially crying, I was told *nín đi*, which literally translates to 'shut up'. I was expected to be stoic like my Vietnamese parents. I'll never forget hysterically crying when I told my dad that my first boyfriend had cheated on me. My dad remained silent. I don't think he knew what to say. He then said, '*I knew he wasn't a good person.*' That was heartbreaking. All I wanted was for him to acknowledge my pain. I believe he felt uncomfortable with all my emotions and thus replied in what seems like an egoic way.

My first boyfriend was very emotional in a time where we had been programmed to believe men weren't to display their emotions. In hindsight, he was before his time. In fact, I labelled him sensitive and went on to be labelled the same thing by others. Ironically, later in life, I would end up desiring a partner who was more in touch with their emotions. My second boyfriend, would label me as *difficult to be with at times* because I was so emotional. He would say things like, '*It's understandable to feel this way but you're being overdramatic/ oversensitive/over the top.*' It was always *over* something and I would be bucketed into emotionally intense. Yet, when we broke up, he couldn't stop crying. He felt a whole spectrum of painful emotions that led to him feeling suicidal. Despite everything, I'm proud that he ended up seeking help and going to therapy to process everything, because men have also been conditioned to supress when it comes to their feelings.

As for women, societal conditioning is complicated and can feel like imprisonment. As women, we're taught to push down and hide our anger. We're taught to cage our rage and resentment. We're taught to be small, sweet, soft and submissive. To apologise for having feelings.

We're taught to 'tone it down' or 'calm down' and to 'just relax.' In fact, society fears a woman who is able to fully express and feel her emotions. Not just the ones deemed negative, like anger and sadness, but also the positive emotions. If you're too happy, you're a smug bitch. If you're abundant and enjoying your wealth, you're selfish and evil. Society is all too happy to label women who feel as 'crazy', 'a drama queen', 'psycho' and my all-time loathed, 'sensitive'.

Sensitivity is a label that has often stung me. It has been deemed a personality flaw. Being told, *'You're too sensitive'* doesn't feel good. It conjures up all sorts of feelings: stupidity, immaturity, childishness and embarrassment. It feels like a bad thing, an insult. It dismisses how you feel and puts the blame on you. It feels as though something is wrong with you. It can be used as a form of gaslighting and other forms of psychological manipulation. The world tries to tell you to toughen up but you're soft at heart. You're an empath. As a result, this leads to a fear of being vulnerable. A state where you feel scared to be exposed or fully seen. Accordingly, you become emotionally constipated instead. Cold. Blocked. Repressed.

This suppression of emotion is stereotypical of Asian culture. In fact, the very act of doing so is called 'saving face' and calls for you to maintain your dignity and respect. Expressing emotions is taught as a sign of weakness, which makes you feel guilty because it wouldn't just impact how people view you but also the way they see your family. The love language in Asian culture is predominantly acts of service, such as cooking a meal or providing a home to live in. It wouldn't even matter if you were displaying positive emotions, if you were too expressive you would be scolded for being unladylike. I remember my mum conditioning me to believe that the only acceptable feelings were 'positive' in nature. To be happy and smiling all the time. I can understand why she did this, she always kept a brave face despite heartbreaking things happening to her. Haven't we all believed if we smile enough, we will eventually become happy?

This very attitude has led to 'toxic positivity'. A well-meaning intention of happiness but at its core, is poison. It's an oxymoron really, if it's toxic, it isn't positive. I'm all for genuine positivity, after all I am known as the Positivity Queen. However, I am against toxic positivity. Toxic positivity refers to the illusion of being happy all the time, a relentless focus on joy no matter what. It hides behind sayings like '*stay positive!*' and '*just think happy thoughts*'.

When my dad passed away, I put on a brave face for the world. The last words my dad ever said to me were '*be brave.*' I thought I understood what he meant at the time but I didn't. I kept smiling even though my dad died. I went back to work after the weekend off (red flag!). I was upbeat and cheery telling all it's not that bad! (*it obviously was!*) I did this to avoid processing everything. I did this so my friends and family wouldn't worry about me. I did this so as not to be a 'downer' on conversations. I did this because I didn't want people to feel sorry for me. I'm happy to say that as life has gone on, I have come to understand the significance and depth of my dad's last words to me.

THE UNLEARNING
Feelings aren't scary. They are what make us human.

To me, being brave means going headfirst and facing your fears. In this instance, feeling your feelings.

Deal with your feelings or they'll deal with you. The irony is that when you avoid your feelings because you don't want to feel pain, that's how you create pain and suffering. Suppression is not the answer. When you suppress negative emotions, you're also suppressing everything else in life, including the good. Suppressing is invalidating your feelings and your experience. 'Negative' emotions are not bad, they are beacons. Lend curiosity to what is going on beneath the surface. See feelings as if they are information, your body's way of communicating with you. To hear and receive the message, you first have to be conscious and present. Don't confuse feelings as facts. Just because you feel like you're a bad person doesn't mean that you are a bad person. Feelings can be intense so take a step back and gain some perspective.

The key to processing emotions and untangling ourselves is in the power of presence. Consciously choosing who is meeting the feelings and responding, not reacting. Don't run from yourself and your feelings. Running won't bring you freedom, flowing will. Sit with your feelings. Hold space for your feelings. They want to be acknowledged and heard. When you are ready, run towards them. Get acquainted. You don't have to necessarily understand them (if you don't there's nothing wrong with you). Feelings are complex. Just because you don't understand them, doesn't mean they aren't valid. Just because you don't agree with your feelings, doesn't mean that you can't validate them. Your feelings are feelings and nothing makes them less valid. They are your internal experience. No one can jump into your skin and speak for you. They are very real whether you want them there or not. Embrace them. Pay attention to them. Listen to what they have to say. Then lovingly escort them out to make way for new energy and new experiences.

Through unlearning everything I had about feelings, I have so much wisdom to share with you. More so because I am an emotional authority in human design. Your authority is how you make the best decisions. There are several types of authorities including sacral (gut), emotional, splenic (intuitive), environmental, self-projected, lunar and ego. This gave me so much validation to being someone who is designed to truly feel it all. Imagine your emotions are the waves of the ocean. Waves of emotion will ebb and flow just as the waves of sea do. Sometimes these waves take the form of riptides or tsunamis. Sometimes these waves are still, peaceful and tranquil. We don't know what is truly going on beneath the surface of the waves. We don't know what's lurking beneath. We don't know what might emerge. But even a tsunami wave doesn't last forever. When a tsunami hits, it does so with mighty rage and force. It cannot be reckoned with. It uproots you and displaces you somewhere else, lost, shaken, ravaged and suspended in reality. You cannot fight it; you must flow with it. Allow it to swallow you. Go with it into the darkness. Into the depths. Into the unknown. Dive headfirst into the shadows... and then it will pass. Then light will appear. And it's clear. Just like that. All in a moment.

At times you may feel lost in the inescapable and intense waves. Even when tsunamis and storms come to rock you, there is a safety within.

It's not about what's happening around you on the outside, it's about what is happening on the inside of you, your internal world. You can deep dive underwater and still come up for air. It's easy to be strong when life goes to plan. It's easy to be strong when life is going the way you want. Real strength comes from braving the storms, riding the waves and withstanding the hurricanes. Life doesn't get easier, you get stronger. So, let it all out. Let it go, let it come and let it flow. Free your emotions and self, it's safe to do so. Don't apologise for feeling, save the apologies for mistakes. How you handle your emotions will be very different to how you feel them. There is nothing wrong with genuinely experiencing your emotions.

Let's dismantle the learned conditioning and amp up the UN. UNlearning. UNveiled. UNapologetic. UNbridled. UNrestrained. UNfuckwithable. UNplugged. UNruly. UNstuck. Feelings don't discriminate. It doesn't matter if you're rich or poor. It doesn't matter if you're a 'good' or 'bad' person. It doesn't matter if you're famous or unknown. You'll feel heartbreak, disappointment and loss in your life. It's okay to feel. You're a human being not a robot. Being authentically human and simply expressing your feelings is much easier.

You're here to be a multidimensional woman. We want all of you unconditionally, your full spectrum. Feelings are a portal to our pleasure and the gateway to being fully A L I V E. Your feelings are a superpower. They allow you to pick up on the details and subtle nuances that others may not be able to. Sometimes what you feel expresses more than words can. Your feelings are an intrinsic wisdom that speak to and permeate through your being. Your feelings are an invitation to embodying your highest self. There is a reason you feel so deeply. This might feel like a hinderance and an inconvenience but embrace your sensitivity and empathy. Your emotions are guiding you to your soul and alignment. Own your power and presence, beautiful soul.

The key to this all, is to express yourself in a way that is healthy and doesn't drag people into a storm or hurt them. You can be mad and go for a jog, don't hurl dishes at someone. Feelings aren't inherently dangerous or harmful. They carry no morality. They just are. We are their channels. After all, emotions are energy in motion (*e-motion*). When we don't process them, we trap them inside our body and, by doing so, allow them to manifest physically, begging for attention, to be heard. They want to move through you. You may come to realise not all the feelings you carry are yours. They could belong to others or other versions of you: past feelings being unloved and unseen.

Feelings are not always simple. There will be times you find it hard to find the right words to articulate how you're feeling. Language isn't just about words either. You can express language through song, dance, movement and art too. Find the right language for your feelings and emotions. There is also a duality to your feelings. You can be sad and happy at the same time. I definitely was after the end of my three-year relationship. I mourned the loss while enjoying living my dream by spending long sunny days at the beach and writing this book. My writings went viral on social media to an audience of five million. I never quite expected that my heartbreak would resonate with and help so many. It was certainly healing for me too.

You can express your feelings by sharing them with others. They can be so heavy to carry on our own. We try to hide them in the cupboard no one will open but when you let people in, the heaviness lifts. You feel lighter and see clearer. Start a conversation. Talk about what you're going through with someone you trust. Another reason why having a life coach is great because it's our job to hold space for you and listen. Get it off your chest. Cry. Crying is cathartic. Cry when everything is too much. Cry when your pain has been going on for too long. Cry because your heart longs for a release. Cry because you are frustrated. Cry now because you can. Cry even if there is no reason. Cry until there are no more tears to shed. Crying is so powerful and soothing. By crying we crush the stigma and taboo around it. Let your tears mend your heart. Let your tears heal your wounds. Let your tears be a soft embrace.

To those who feel deeply, there is nothing wrong with you. You aren't being an attention seeker. You aren't being dramatic. You aren't overreacting. What's so wrong with being soft at heart? Cry during movies. Check to make sure someone is okay. You are the compassion and kindness this world needs more now than ever. Don't let anyone make you feel bad for being soft. I know how hard feeling it all can be. It makes your bones ache and tugs at your heart. You feel it in the warmth of your skin and in the electricity of your veins. You feel it in the pit of your stomach and shivers down your spine. It truly is a superpower. You get to feel every single sensation of what it means to be alive. Wild, untamed… raw. Every touch, every breath, every feeling. Here's to you, sensitive soul. Feeling is freedom. Feeling is healing. Feeling is medicine.

One of the most beautiful moments of growth you'll experience is the day your feelings go from foreigner to friend. In this process you learn the art of emotional alchemy and transforming our feelings into healing. You'll find the silver-lining. You'll find the nuggets of gold. You'll turn wounds into wisdom. You'll transmute energy into expression. At the end of the day, feelings are just sensations. You're strong enough to handle sensations. It is the dynamic nature of feelings that makes life so interesting and enjoyable. Turbulence is scary but it makes for a fun ride. Feelings are sources of passion and power. Feelings are the very thing that make us human. Feelings are incredible motivators which can inspire us to make our dreams a reality. Most of all, feelings help us to be skilled swimmers and surfers of the waves of life.

YOUR GREAT UNLEARNING

1. EMOTIONAL VOCABULARY

This exercise will help you connect deeper to your emotions and help you to express yourself. Language and words are so powerful (spells are literally words!). Developing a greater vocabulary to describe how you feel is highly beneficial. We often fall short when describing something as 'good' or 'bad'. Differentiate whether you're feeling something or whether it's a need or desire. For example, feeling safe is a need for security's sake. In turn, you feel safe, calm, relieved and relaxed.

Create your own feeling word bank. For example:

- Happy
- Joyful
- Ecstatic
- Content
- Cheerful
- Merry
- Jolly

Keep a feelings journal and tracker. Note down the various spectrum of feelings and moods you may experience in a day. Add context to the feelings: circumstances and timings. This is also serves as a way to distinguish patterns.

2. SELF-SOOTHING

A game changer for me was learning how to regulate my emotional state through self-soothing instead of looking to someone else to do so.

Examples of self-soothing practices are:

- Hugging or stroking yourself.
- Placing your hands on your heart (which psychologically releases the same chemicals as a hug).
- Placing your hands on your stomach (great for anxiety).
- Bringing attention to the soles of your feet on the floor (to ground oneself).
- Taking a shower or warm bath.
- Going for a walk.
- Deep breathing into the belly.
- Focusing on a colour.
- Lying down and placing your legs up on the wall.
- Performing a comfortable and easy task, such as folding laundry or washing dishes.
- Honing in on your senses, such as chewing gum or listening to music.

3. ENERGY IN MOTION

As discussed, emotions are energy in motion. Therefore, it is through transforming emotion into energy that we get out of a funk. Examples of this include:

- Shaking.
- Jumping.
- Exercising.
- Dancing.
- Screaming into a pillow.
- Unclenching your jaw and moving it from side to side.
- Bouncing your shoulders up and down.
- Rotating your head from side to side.

MENTAL HEALTH

THE LEARNING
There is so much stigma and discrimination around mental health.

Let's talk about mental health, whether it describes experiencing an overwhelming moment, a bad day, or having an illness. Many of us have come to believe that the term 'mental health' means to have depression, anxiety, schizophrenia or another condition. These are specific examples of mental health diagnoses, but the term mental health is broader than that. World Health Organisation (WHO) defines mental health as *'The state of mental well-being that enables people to cope with the stresses of life, realize their abilities, learn well and work well, and contribute to their community.'* There are so many myths and misconceptions around mental health. You may have even believed or heard of them at some point. *Everyone affected by mental health issues are on medication. You only need to take care of your mental health if you have a mental health condition. Mental health is only caused by family trauma.* None of these are true.

It's time we normalise talking about mental health because there is such stigma and taboo around it. Let's normalise feeling off and feeling unhappy (because hey, we are human after all—no one is happy *all* the time). Why should we feel guilty that our mental health isn't at its best at times? Your mental health does not have to be pretty or palatable for you to be loved and cared for. Mental health issues aren't dirty or a problem, they are health issues we ought to openly discuss as a society and as individuals. Our mental health isn't a weakness, it's the complete opposite. Surviving negative instances of mental health is an incredible strength. Even then, you don't have to be strong all the time. Having bad days doesn't take away from the good in all that you've done. Your achievements are still there. Your friends and family still love you. You can be having a negative mental health moment or illness and you'll still do amazing and wonderful things. At the end of the day, it isn't about impressing, it's about progressing.

Even with pure intentions, it can be deflating to hear critical comments, such as being told to think positive (it doesn't help or solve the problem). When it comes to societal conditioning and our desire to be happy all the time, we put up the visage of 'everything is fine' and 'I've got it all together,' when really we are crumbling and falling apart beneath fake smiles and a dismissive 'it's all good!' Mental health isn't easy so don't feel ashamed or afraid of struggling. You may begin to believe that you are a burden or problem. As a result, you will become convinced that you don't deserve to be happy or have a future.

This isn't true, it's your mind is tricking you. You absolutely do and you are more than capable of recovery. You are worth worries. People want to help you and love you, if you'll let them. It may take some time and that's okay. It won't be perfect and that's okay. Healing and recovery aren't a race so you don't need a timer. There are some things you simply can't rush. Setbacks happen. That doesn't mean you won't heal. With that in mind, we've come to believe that we need something in order to heal, whether it's an apology, an explanation or closure. Time is important but alone won't heal; you need to consciously choose to start where you are right now without anyone's approval or input.

I remember one of my first experiences with negative mental health and, to be honest with you, I didn't really understand it. When I was seventeen, my first boyfriend would randomly cry and have moments where he didn't want to leave the house. He would soon confess he had depression and anxiety. Back then, no one really talked about mental health, and I didn't know how to support him. Mental health wasn't discussed in my family and if it was it would be insinuating those with it are crazy, unwell and cannot function properly in society. He understandably had moments of frustration with me because I didn't understand. One time he blurted out, 'Honestly, Phi, it's a blessing you don't know anything about having a mental illness. I hope you never have to go through it yourself.'

Being human, of course I would go on to experience the impacts of mental health. My unwilling dance with mental health began with my dad passing away. I was overwhelmed by the mixture of emotions leading up to it. For a while I was traumatised by the memory of seeing him look as if he was pregnant because his cancer tumour had grown so much. I was speechless he was actually gone. I didn't know what to do with my feelings, so I numbed them.

I delayed my grief until it felt like everything was coming down on me. At university I had obsessive, spiralling thoughts about getting perfect marks for my grade. Soon after, I began experiencing heart palpitations. Then I catastrophised everything—'If I fail this assignment, I will die.' This was followed by a lack of appetite, having no motivation to shower or brush my teeth and isolating myself from my friends. My brain was on overdrive with endless looping thoughts and soon I was unable to sleep. First for a few days that would then turn into sleepless weeks. I felt like a zombie.

I had wished I was dead. I searched online for the best ways to end my life and was terrified to learn that so many methods would be incredibly painful. I plotted my death as I drove my car around town but didn't go through with it because I was scared I wouldn't die. I was scared I would end up a paraplegic. I questioned the purpose of life. I went to so many dark places.

Eventually you will come to the realisation that you don't want to die. You just want to escape your pain. The only way out, is through. I fell through the cracks in the system. It felt like waves were bashing my bruised body against menacing rock shards. At the hospital they told me that not being able to sleep wasn't a real condition. It was.

The stigma of antidepressants fried my brain. I felt weak and ashamed. Here's the thing, if we have a broken leg, we'll get a cast. If you're having bouts of depression and anxiety, the equivalent to a cast in some circumstances is medicine. After several attempts with different medications, a psychiatrist finally listened and diagnosed me with anxiety and depression due to delayed grief onset. He prescribed me with an anti-depressant that helped me sleep. Being able to finally sleep again was a relief, I had taken it for granted. It was such a relief to have someone finally listen to me and truly help me. Alongside having medication and working with a psychologist I was able to make a full recovery. With that being said, a huge shout out to my support network: friends and family, especially my mum who worked really hard to look after me. Even though I tried to push them away, they always made it clear they were here for me and were persistent with their efforts to connect with me.

I thought I wouldn't have to deal with something like that again. I thought I had experienced the worst of it in the aftermath of my dad's passing. I thought I had hit rock bottom and recovered… until I fell and hit it again. My mental health issues would sneak up on me while I worked in the corporate world. I experienced psychological abuse through battles in the office politics arena, long hours, psychopathic narcissistic bosses and repeated burnouts. I would swallow cutthroat criticism that burnt my throat and came out as tears. The worst part? I stayed silent; I wired my jaw shut. I wanted to be the stoic warrior and 'golden girl'. I wanted to not just climb but pillage through the rungs of the career ladder.

I continued to stay silent until my body's whispers turned into screaming. My body went on strike. In my early twenties, to my doctor's dismay, I was diagnosed with high blood pressure, despite the fact that I exercised regularly and had a healthy diet. She attributed this to stress alongside my other physical symptoms: coughing up blood, month long menstruation, a sore jaw from constantly grinding my teeth when I slept and blurred vision. I finally came to my senses when my doctor told me that there was a very serious chance if I continued life this way I would die young. I am proud to say that after years of silence, I found my voice.

Despite all this pain, I am so grateful because it led to my passion for mental health and becoming the life coach I am today. Even as a life coach I still have experiences with mental health. You don't become immune even when you live your dream life. Take it from me.

What I do know about mental health that I would love to share with you is to give yourself grace, kindness and compassion. It may take time and that is more than okay. Progress can look like eating more than one meal a day, showering more often, changing clothes. Progress is progress. Know that there isn't a minimum when it comes to pain and suffering. You don't have to hit a certain amount for it to feel a certain way to qualify for something such as compassion and support. How you feel is completely valid no matter what anyone else says. You don't have to keep it to yourself and go through your experience alone. You don't have to outwardly show signs of distress to seek help. You don't have to feel bad comparing your experience to another. You aren't weak for feeling this way and people don't think less of you. You are a human being. You're understandably allowed to seek a way to move through it all.

THE UNLEARNING

Your mental health doesn't define you. Mental health goes beyond illnesses and exists on a complex continuum of states and symptoms.

Why is that the person we are hardest on is ourselves? We seem to be so understanding and compassionate towards others, yet we forget ourselves. Don't be so hard on yourself, beautiful soul, you are doing the best you can with whatever is going on right now. You've been through so much already. You are strong. You are a survivor. Life is already tough; you don't need to make it harder. Perhaps you could be kinder to yourself. Perhaps you could bring more love to all parts of yourself. Perhaps you could make peace with all the doubts and worries that snake around in your mind. Perhaps you could meet yourself with more tenderness. Perhaps it's time to be less hard on yourself…

If only you could see yourself from the eyes of others. If only you could see yourself from the heart of others. If only you could see yourself from the soul of others. If only because in the moments you find yourself unworthy and unlovable—you would see, feel and know the truth. That truth is, that you are so deeply loved and cared for. The way you see the world is so uniquely beautiful. The way you walk into a room lights it up. The way you laugh adds more joy and soulful positivity into this world. The way you care adds so much depth and hope into this world. The way you love is so fierce, passionate and strong. All these things that you don't see in yourself, others do. When you face tough battles within yourself, it is my hope that you remember this all.

The beautiful soul you are right now has fought invisible battles and conquered wars with tender scars and a full heart. The beautiful soul you are right now has struggled in the seas of misery yet resurfaced to conquer the waves. The beautiful soul you are right now has had to die and hold funerals for past versions of self in order to be reborn. The beautiful soul you are right now has walked through fires of pain and suffering, to rise from the ashes. The beautiful soul you are right now has turned wounds into wisdom, anguish into achievement and trauma into triumph. The beautiful soul you are right now thought they could not make it, yet here you are. Yes you, reading this. I'm so glad because your presence is needed in this world. We want and need your light, magic and presence. You, as an individual, make a difference even when it seems small and insignificant to you, the little things matter. The red light on a traffic light. The screw in a piece of furniture. Small does not mean it has little impact, if anything it's vital. The little things add up. Your existence matters so much.

You offer so much to the world. You don't need to change the world on a massive scale to do so. You make a difference in the way you help others. You make a difference in the way you voice your opinion. You make a difference when you smile at a stranger. Sometimes we get so caught up in the big picture, we lose perspective. So, tap into the vibe of main character energy, you are the centre of your life. Without you, life is lost.

With regards to your mental health, it's so beautiful that you care so deeply for others but what about yourself? Are you okay? It's okay not to be okay. You're busy giving it your best when it comes to work, relationships and life. You're busy giving and checking in with other people.

We've all been there, in that dark place, where we feel like nothing is going right. When we feel like the world is ending. When we feel like it couldn't get worse, then it does. Never forget how strong and resilient you are. You're still here. You've made it through all the times you didn't think you would or could. Remember, asking for help isn't a sign of weakness, it's a beacon of strength. This lifetime wouldn't be the same without you. There's no harm in asking for help. You don't have to carry the weight of the world alone. You don't have to shoulder the burden of responsibility alone. You will experience challenges, but you don't always have to struggle alone.

Beautiful soul, you are allowed to slow down and take your time. You don't have to push, push, push, force, force, force and hustle, hustle, hustle. Your pain, whether physical, emotional or mental, is real. No matter what anyone else says. Feeling is not attention seeking or dramatic. You aren't being selfish or lazy. You are brave and doing your best. That takes true courage. Take it day by day. Moment by moment. Minute by minute. Even second by second. Your highest self and soul are waiting for you to prioritise yourself. Your highest self and soul crave to be honoured for the miracle that you are. Your highest self and soul yearn to be acknowledged for your resilience, strength and capacity. Hold on. You've got this. You are creating a beautiful life for yourself.

When you feel weak and sad, remember that you are made from the same stuff that makes the stars shine so bright. The same stuff that makes the ocean ebb and flow. The same stuff as the sun that bursts joy into the sky. Healing is a journey. You have fought many internal battles and wars that no one knows about.

Healing is a funny thing. It can feel slow. It can feel arduous. It can feel as if nothing has changed. It can feel like the past has a grip on you. It can feel like your mistakes will catch up to you. It can feel like you are doing so much yet so little at the same time. It can feel like you are on the edge of an abyss and only slowly moving back. It can feel like the dark void, and it can feel like fullness. And then, one day, you'll realise how far you've come. You'll realise that healing isn't sudden. You'll realise that you've been healing the whole time. Every step counts whether big or small.

Good things are coming. Good things are waiting for you. Good things are about to happen. Life has its highs and lows. Life has its setbacks. The weight of sadness, grief and pain. The ache of a broken heart and stress of an overwhelmed mind. The frustration you feel being stuck with nowhere to go. The paralysis of anxiety and perfectionism. The yearning for hope and relief... there is more to come. Old energy is clearing and the new is ready to rush in. In the meantime, be kind to your mind, be kind to your body, be kind to your heart and be kind to your soul. Move at your own pace. The good is inevitable. Better days are on their way.

YOUR GREAT UNLEARNING

1. CIRCLES OF CONTROL

When facing negative mental health moments or illness, it can be easy to feel weak and as if you have no control. This is where this exercise comes into it. This exercise will prove that you have power and influence. This exercise will help guide your energy into what you can change instead of what you can't.

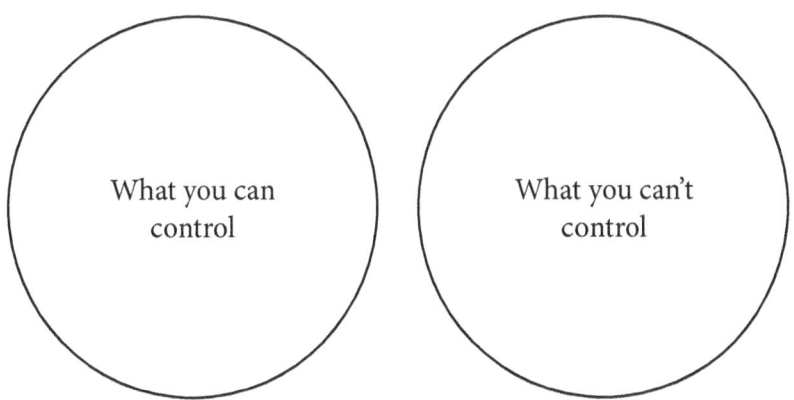

2. SITUATIONAL CONTINUUM

This exercise helps you see the different outcomes of a situation, so you avoid following the all or nothing theory.

Best Case	In Between	Possibility	Worst Case

3. MENTAL HEALTH MANTRAS

The following mantras can help when you're having a tough day whether you say them to yourself or write them out.

- I can do hard things.
- Better days are coming.
- It's okay not to be okay.
- I was designed and built to survive.
- I matter and I am significant.
- I am strong and resilient.
- This too shall pass.
- I choose love and kindness.
- I deserve to be and can be happy.
- I have made it so far and I will continue to make it.
- I prioritise myself.

GRIEF AND HEARTBREAK

THE LEARNING
It's hard to love and care. Loving and caring will lead to grief and heartache.

Good *mourning* to you. As I write this chapter, I wear the watch my dad got me before he passed away. Loss, grief and heartache are inevitable for us as human beings. They are natural parts of life and happen to everyone. They aren't something you can avoid or escape.

Typically, we think grief and heartbreak have something to do with the relationships we have: our family, our friends, our partners and our pets. A majority of the time, my experiences certainly have been. You can also experience grief and heartbreak outside the realms of a relationship. Grief is universal. Grief can be the loss of an opportunity, the loss of possessions, the loss of time, the loss of a goal. However, loss can be collective too. Grief is also a wonderful quality to life because nothing lasts forever and losing something can help us truly value and appreciate what we have. We get to embrace change, cycles and the present moment. Really, loss is a privilege because you had something to lose in the first place. It means you loved something deeply. Not everyone gets to experience love of this magnitude.

There is no right way to mourn. There is no normal way to process grief. There is no standard timeline or expiry date for grief. You may not cry. Initially, when my dad passed I cried but afterwards, I didn't. I hadn't processed the gravity of his passing because I was traumatised and overwhelmed. This is not to say that after a certain amount of time you'll suddenly feel okay and ready to move on (do you remember the urban myth that it will take you at least half the amount of time you were in a relationship to get over it?).

Looking back, I felt a spectrum of emotions processing grief. Prior to being diagnosed with cancer, my dad discovered he had diabetes. He did the 'right' thing by exercising more frequently and completely changing his diet for the better. As a result, he lost a lot of weight. What no one realised was the dramatic weight loss was actually due to undiagnosed cancer. So unfair. The worst part was when he did finally find out, it was too late. Whilst bowel cancer is often curable, it had been left undetected too long and spread to his liver which is very difficult to cure. I was mad at life because he hadn't been retired long and was only in his early sixties. I was seething rage when I unexpectedly caught him smoking cigarettes towards the end but then proud because it was his final hurrah, he was going out anyway and did it his way. (Cue his funeral song: *My Way* by Frank Sinatra.)

Loss leaves a mark on your life. The timeframe between my dad's diagnosis and his death was short, perhaps only six months. I'll never forget being told he had several cancers. I couldn't stomach or comprehend it. I was so shielded from negativity growing up that I wasn't familiar with cancer at all. I knew it was a condition with different types but that was about it. I didn't even interact with any media to do with cancer in any forms such as books or movies. In fact, my stepmum would call me out on it. That was heartbreakingly tough but needed. I never asked about how he was going or updates on it at first because truth be told I didn't want to know. Ignorance was bliss. I didn't want to admit to myself that my dad was very sick and dying. It would take a while for me to even admit he had it. I was in denial from shock and sadness. Honestly it breaks my heart writing this because I was so naïve and young. I was only twenty-years-old.

My dad went from bike riding with me to barely being able to move. His face went from full to hollow and gaunt. The arms that once carried me became stick thin and frail. He became more agitated, understandably battling intense cancers with only paracetamol to ease his pain. That itself caused so much anguish and drama with everyone. My dad wanted quality of life over quantity. He didn't have any chemotherapy (it would only extend his life slightly anyway, however, at a punishing cost to his body and mental health from his perspective). Whilst I was upset at first, when I understood his reasoning behind it I was fully on board and to be honest, it wasn't my decision anyway—respectfully it was always his. To my family's comfort we found out from his doctor that a similar man who did do chemotherapy passed away around the same time frame as my dad anyway.

I remember feeling so worried and guilty when he insisted I still lived my life and went backpacking around Europe for my first overseas trip and solo too at eighteen. I burst into tears when he was still able to pick me up from the airport. Little did I know he lived longer than expected to do that (he'd secretly been given only three months from diagnosis).

It was a very surreal experience. In the aftermath of all this, I felt cripplingly lonely at times even though I was loved and supported by those around me. The grief felt ginormous, like it would swallow me whole.

His death was a blackhole of emptiness for me. I was overwhelmed and stunned. His passing was the first experience I'd had of death. His funeral was the first funeral I had attended. In fact, my whole family was so greatly impacted by the event that I planned the funeral myself. It was so confronting to see his body in the open casket, once so full of life. Seeing him at peace gave me peace though, my dad was no longer suffering or in pain. Looking back, the whole thing feels like a blur. I feel like my mind disassociated because it was so painful. We all wore white headbands as a sign of respect in Vietnamese culture and tradition.

My emotions beset me. I was sad, angry and disappointed. Holding this grief inside me was so heavy. What hurt more was how even when his death occurred, the world continued. This made me feel like the loss I'd experienced was insignificant. I suffered… yet life around me went on as normal. People still went to work. People still celebrated special occasions. Bills still needed to be paid. With so much going on in the aftermath I isolated myself. I didn't want to see anyone. I didn't want their pity or empathy. I didn't want to explain what had happened. I didn't want to relive the experience. I completely shut down. I cut myself off from the world. I disappeared for a few months.

I would lie on the floor of my living room and wish I was dead. The heaviness eventually turned into numbness... I repressed my feelings to the point that I couldn't feel anything. I hadn't felt joy in a while but feeling nothing was worse. It felt so strange. I was not only detached from life but also detached from myself. I remember purposely trying to watch sad movies like *The Boy in Striped Pyjamas*. *Nothing*. I watched the news during Melbourne Cup and heard about the horses being put down. *Nothing*. I felt like I was a monster. Especially because the horses being put down moved my mum to tears and she had to have time alone.

My healing came from reconnecting with my feelings and body. Loss deserves to be mourned. Your world shrinks when you suppress grief. Appreciate the smallest details in life like breathing and being alive. This is how I learned to feel again. I wasn't taught to... however, it was the silver-lining from this dark period in my life.

How much I had grown became evident after I processed and dealt with my grief at the end of my relationship with my ex-boyfriend Malcolm. I posted the following on Instagram the day we broke up: *'Beautiful soul, I know it feels like you'll break from the weight of the world on your shoulders and the heavy ache of your heart. I know it feels like you wish you could rip your heart out and not feel every ounce of pain. I know if feels like you're sick of crying, it is as if the tears will never end. I know it feels like you will not be able to carry on, that the world has forced you on your hands and feet. I know it feels like everything is crumbling and collapsing, leaving you trembling in the wake of the void. I know it feels uncertain and scary in the clearing of it all, even though you know, it will all be for your highest good. I know it feels like you're alone and no one gets it. I promise you, it will be okay. Hold on and keep going. I believe in you. All is on your side. Have faith and have love. You've made it through and so much already and will continue to. You got this.'*

I truly felt every fibre of my feelings in the journey of breaking up. Initially, I felt disheartened when cracks appeared after a period of tension over Christmas that we spent time with my family. To give you context, my dad passed away a few days before Christmas so often the end of the year is difficult for me already. Being with my family did trigger Malcolm understandably as he hadn't seen his family in three years, though that didn't take away from my pain hearing 'Christmas in Australia wasn't real because it was sunny and spent at the beach' or 'no offence, Asian food doesn't count as Christmas food.' It highlighted the cultural differences between us and I felt unappreciated as I had gone to the effort of cooking a roast dinner for him on Christmas Eve. Not only that my family welcomed him with open arms and we often had hybrid meals at Christmas such as XO lobster noodles and a roast ham. It felt like the final straw given I felt I had done so much for him… buying him a MacBook for his birthday, my mum got him an iPhone and my stepmum a car.

In January and February, I broke up with him several times but it never stuck as we had already booked in November a trip to Europe in April. Leading up to the trip, I was anxious about meeting his closest loved ones, knowing we would break up after the trip. We temporarily filled in the cracks of our relationship by ignoring them and for me at least knowing the future outcome helped: it would be over soon. Spending time with his loved ones brought me so much joy. I enjoyed the classic Sunday at the pub and taking Reuben, their sweet border collie, for a walk. I felt so much sadness as I said goodbye to them knowing it would be the last time we'd ever meet. Despite everything, we did truly deeply love each other so much. I was heartbroken when I said goodbye to him at the airport knowing it may be the last time I ever held his hand and looked him in the eyes.

Romantic grief and heartbreak are very difficult to deal with. They encourage so many questions. What happens to love when we break up? What happens to love when it's unrequited? What happens to love when they don't even know you exist? What happens to love when there are no labels? What happens to love when they aren't there anymore? What happens to love when they forget about you and move on? What happens to love when things get complicated? What happens to love when you keep trying but it never works out?

What happens to love when they slowly fade and disappear? What happens to love when they find it with someone else?

Love will always come back to you in one form or another. Love is abundant. Perhaps your experiences of love have hardened you. You don't have to carry mountains of pain. You don't have to fight wars that don't belong to you. Being hard won't let love in and it certainly won't heal your heart. You build walls and think you're protecting yourself but what you're really doing is preventing love from coming in. Be soft in love, beautiful soul. So soft that you melt the sharpened edges. Being soft is not being weak. Being soft is strong and soft looks beautiful on you.

Grief goes beyond the person or event. Grief is an intricate tapestry. When you lose a parent, future hopes of being together become impossible. My father won't walk me down the aisle, he won't join in on a father/daughter dance and he won't meet my future children. My dad loved technology and I find myself wishing he was here to see how far computers have advanced or new innovations that he would've loved.

When you lose a relationship, you lose the vision of travelling the world together, owning the home with the big backyard and taking your children on road trips in the Range Rover. Grief can be messy. It inevitably spills out over every area of your life. It changes the way you interact with people. It changes the way you see certain things. The most important thing is to be kind and compassionate with yourself as you move through a life-altering event.

THE UNLEARNING
The act of loving and caring is worth the inevitable heartbreak and grief.

Grief isn't just sadness, it's a myriad of emotions. Anger, guilt, denial, regret, remorse, shock, sadness, acceptance and hope. Grief is fluid. Grief blazes its own path. Grief strips you naked. Grief isn't a problem to be solved. Grief is raw, real and evolving. Time will heal but you do need to put energy and effort into your healing.

I have come to understand that grieving is not problematic. Grief has no concept of time. It doesn't just suddenly disappear after a year or ten. It's a *lifelong* journey that you learn to deal with. Grief is a natural human response to loss. You can't *just* think your way through it. You have to get out of your head also *feel* your way through it. Yes, it's uncomfortable. In times of grief your job isn't to be strong, it's to be brave. You must be brave enough to feel all the feelings, to continue on with life, to open your heart and love again, to trust that the loss was for a reason. Bravery will lead you on a journey where you will find your inner strength. You will realise how strong you really are. You will realise what you are capable of. You will realise how resilient you are.

Grief and death initiates us. Thus, grief became the spiritual practice that tore my heart open for greater growth and to be reborn. The gigantic blackhole of grief spat me back out after chewing me for an eternity. I had to face the world again. I slowed down and surrendered. I let go and turned inward. I reconnected with my soul and what made me human. I rediscovered my appreciation for life. I opened my mind and dropped into my body. I realigned with my body and felt the sensations.

Grief becomes a part of your life, but it isn't your whole life. You can continue to take steps to move past it and forward into the future. You'll feel fragile but really, you're incredibly tough while you continue to live life. There will be hard moments, but you can do hard things. Even though you feel alone while you process your loss, you aren't. Silence will amplify your pain and suffering. Let people in. Let them support you. Don't feel guilty, they wouldn't offer if they didn't want to. I am so grateful I had an overwhelming amount of support from my family, friends and colleagues.

I know that when our loved ones cross over to the other side, they are at peace, and this warms my soul from a spiritual perspective. They may be physically gone but they live on in our hearts. There's nothing more haunting and surreal than seeing the chair they once sat on and their clothes still neatly hung up in the cupboard. Traces of their existence surround us. They live on, above and beyond in paradise and joy. You feel them in the melting of harsh winters and spring morning time. You feel them in the salt of your tears and the bleeding colours of the sky. You feel them in the soft sunlight shining on your skin and the wind that glides. You feel them in the mighty roar of the ocean, of rolling, turning tides.

Our lives are beyond what we see in the physical reality. The soul is eternal. There is no pain or suffering anymore where they are. They are always with us—their love, their protection and their guidance. You can call upon them and they will be there straight away.

I like to call upon my dad at my altar, a memorial dedicated to him that I made at home. It includes a photo of him, crystals in his favourite colour (green), a special candle and a carrot cake bar (because it was his favourite!).

When I reach a milestone moment, such as his passing or birthday, I like to communicate with him. I ground and energetically protect myself before I declare my intention out loud to speak with him. I light the candle, speak and meditate. Being clairsentient (feelings-based), I often feel him touch my shoulders and then I receive answers in my mind—in the space of the third eye or in my heart. Strangely at times I feel closer to him now that he's on the other side. He's more emotive in his communications than he was Earth side.

It's okay to feel a mixture of emotions. Joy and grief can coexist. Memories may fade, their voice a distance memory, their touch a cruel distant linger but their love runs deep. It's etched in your blood, bones and soul—it cannot be forgotten. To this day I still feel sad about my dad's passing.

Sadness is like an old friend; someone you've known for a while and who feels familiar. You don't keep in touch often, but you always remember the memories you've shared together. When sadness comes to visit, it may be expected or unexpected, nevertheless sadness' impact is known. You may ask: *Why are you here? Why are you visiting me now? Where are you going? What are you here to teach me this time? When will I see you again?* We should welcome sadness like an old friend, they are only here for a visit… for sadness doesn't stay forever.

At times, sadness shows up at your doorstep unexpectedly or as something that has been closely following you. Sometimes sadness is a friend that ambushed you out of nowhere with full force. Sometimes sadness is a friend we dance with everyday not knowing what the next move will be. Sadness comes in all forms. Whatever form sadness takes for you, know that you will be okay. Sadness' visits are bittersweet and allow us to feel the depths of our emotions, which makes us human. When sadness visits, we learn and grow beyond comprehension in happiness and joy. The breakdowns lead to breakthroughs.

When times get hard, think about what the person you lost would want for you. Given the fact that they deeply loved you, they want you to be happy. For you to continue living your life. To live life to the fullest in honour of them. I've had my fair share of guilt trips after I forgot the anniversary of my father's passing because I was stressed from work. Both times this happened, I became distraught and broke down in tears in the office. It's okay. You're allowed to move forward with your life without constantly remembering their passing. It's what they would want. You're honouring them by living life. You're honouring them by taking care of yourself. Meeting your basic needs after you experience loss is important. The little things like making your bed and flossing your teeth are important. If it feels right for you, find something you can contribute to in their honour. My closest friends and I did in The Colour Run in honour of my dad and raised money for the Cancer Council. This book is also dedicated to him. Perhaps one of the greatest things I have found in grief is the ability to help others deal with and process their grief. You don't have to be a life coach to do this, simply listen to a friend and be there for them because you've experienced tremendous loss too.

As I progress deeper into my spiritual practice, I had an incredible insight about grief. I am so happy to share it as I certainly didn't see this in any grief resources I have come across. We can place the deceased on a pedestal, idealising or even idolising them. I certainly did unconsciously, I only saw the good in my dad yet saw the worst in my mum who was still alive. Since having this lightbulb moment, that's certainly levelled out now. When someone dies, I believe collectively we feel bad, and we feel obliged to portray *only* the good in someone. A focused optimistic spotlight on the deceased if you will. If we want to truly honour them and their life, I think it's through a balanced perspective. Seeing them for who they really are holistically. We are all humans. We aren't perfect. That doesn't make us less lovable in any way, shape or form.

Pedestaling reminds me of rose-tinted glasses. Especially when it comes to relationships. Hindsight isn't always 20/20. Don't just take the rose-tinted glasses off, shatter them because they create an illusion. At the end of a breakup, we remember all the good times and neglect to recall the hard moments. Remember: the breakup happened for a reason. To overcome this, you need distance and perspective, not just yours but that of those outside of you.

Grief is a beautiful and tragic thing. Many good things come to an end but that doesn't mean it's your end. Sometimes loss is necessary for gain. Finding gifts in grief isn't ideal but it's what we receive. A new perspective in life. A deeper understanding of ourselves. Happy *mourning* to you, because happiness is possible whilst experiencing sorrow. Shattered in pieces, broken like a mosaic—there is beauty in your grief and beauty in your heartache. It won't always be pretty but with the passing sands of time and softening of sorrow, there is a pearl of truth. There is life after death and sunshine after rain.

YOUR GREAT UNLEARNING

1. GRIEF MURAL

As an exercise to process your grief, find a wall that you can stick Post-It Notes to (alternatively use a big piece of paper or a journal). This is a dynamic exercise. On the Post-It Notes you can:

- Describe any feelings you're experiencing.
- Reflect on any memories that you shared together.

- Write messages to your loved one.
- Creatively express yourself through a poem, a song lyric or a drawing.
- An intention.

As time goes by you may change them and move them around. It can be useful to keep a journal to place old Post-It Notes in and reflect on the changes you've made on the wall of grief.

2. JOURNALING PROMPTS

The following prompts will help you connect with your grief and heartbreak providing points of reflection.

———————————

What makes me the saddest is…
What has been the most difficult thing for me…
My favourite memory together was…
I feel most connected to my loved one when…
Painful times we shared together include…
If I could change anything, it would be…
If they could speak to me right now, I think they would tell me…
Since the loss…
When I am alone…
The best way to honour the loss is…
What I miss the most right now is…
The best way to describe my grief is…
Right now, in my journey of loss, I…
The emotions I feel associated with the loss are….
What I fear in the aftermath of the loss is…
The loss has changed my belief system in terms of…
What gives me comfort right now is…

———————————

3. IN MEMORY OF

Create a ritual of how you can best honour and connect with your loss. You can turn to this practice when you're feeling sad and when there is a special occasion (any time really!).

- Create an altar for them.
- Make their favourite food or meal.
- Listen to a playlist of songs that remind you of them.
- Keep an item on you that reminds you of them (jewellery, crystal, etc.).
- Write a letter to them.
- Light a special candle.
- Write in a journal you've dedicated to them.
- Honour them in a public way (via social media or planting a tree in their name, etc.).
- Look at photos of them and reminiscing with loved ones.
- Celebrate special dates (perhaps going out for a meal or a glass of champagne).
- Embark on a commemorative pilgrimage or holiday somewhere.

LIGHT AND DARK

THE LEARNING
Life consists of battles between the light and the dark.
The light represents everything good.

Sometimes life feels like one giant mystical movie where light and dark battle for the win. We see the light as 'good' and 'positive' and the dark as 'bad' and 'negative'. We are attracted to the light like moths to a flame. We want innocence, happiness and kindness. However, darkness is an innate part of life too. Unfortunately, it's not always love and light, despite the desire to turn a blind eye to the shadows that lurk. The thing is, we can't have one without the other. It's the light itself that creates the shadow. The brighter the light, the darker the shadow. The concepts of polarity and duality exist not only in the world around us but within ourselves. We are here to weave the light and dark together. We are the union of light and dark.

This polarity has conditioned us to feel as if we are fragmented or broken and looking for wholeness. I hope you learn to love the light within but appreciate the darkness too. There is such thing as too much light—the pollution in the city that stops us from seeing the stars is the very thing that drives us into the darkness. Let's talk about the concept of your 'shadow' self. Funnily enough, shadow work is the highest form of light work that you'll perform. These two are inevitably intertwined. Your shadow self is the person you wish you weren't. Your shadow self is made of the demons and secrets you hide. Your shadow self is the repressed, disapproved and disowned.

So how do you make friends with your shadow? Through work. It isn't pretty or comfortable but has so many benefits. It's acknowledging what you do not like about yourself. It's acknowledging your pain. It's the journey of learning to love your wounds. It's using your deepest pain as a springboard for your self-love and power. As Carl Jung stated, *'Knowing your own darkness is the best method for dealing with the darkness of other people.'*

Welcome to the darkening of the light. Just like the dead of winter or the dark night of the soul, we need darkness to find the light. We need darkness to use as a veil to shield and protect what is growing beneath the surface. What will surface is your endurance to channel your crisis into change. It's time to surrender your heart and soul to the universe. Shed what no longer serves you like a snake sheds its skin. Let go and flow with the stream of life. Listen to the rhythm of your heartbeat. Follow the pulls of your soul. Release your fears and doubts, child of the universe. The stars and angels support you. When the world is dark, your inner light shines bright.

Life is a rollercoaster of experiences and emotions driven by the highest of highs and the lowest of lows. It can be excruciating to feel so deeply. Heartache and pain contrast liberation and ecstasy.

From a spiritual point of view, your soul chose to get on this ride. I suggest this perspective to you as I do with my clients, *'How does it feel to go through life knowing your soul chose this curriculum for your personal growth?'* To grow. To expand. Your soul is hungry for experiences and emotions that nudge you into alignment. The depth of the darkness and shadows you feel also open the limitless love and joy you can feel.

However, we dim our own light. We fear our own light. We shrink ourselves smaller to appease those around us. We're afraid to stand out from the crowd. We think we're too much for everyone. We don't want to seem overly cocky, arrogant or confident, so we downplay our achievements and successes—watering down who we are. We're suffering from tall poppy syndrome (something we like to say in Australia). Tall poppy syndrome is the fear of being better and more successful than others because those who are become criticised. If you were in a field of poppies you'd cut the taller ones down so they were in line with an average sized poppy.

The sad thing is, in the age we live in now, we need more of your light. Right now, at the time of writing this book, there is a heaviness in our hearts from all that has happened globally. COVID-19. War. Suffering. Climate change. Silencing of women. Controlling women's rights and bodies. Mental health crisis', especially for men who make up the majority of suicides globally. Perhaps the light is absent because we still have a few things we need to understand about the darkness.

Mainstream media has pushed the narrative of a time where the world is divided. Source, spirit and the universe are pleading for the message of love. To respect one another for our differences because in doing so we love, and love is unity and harmony. We are one. Connected to the same source. When we hurt another, we hurt ourselves. When we criticize another, we criticize ourselves. When we condemn another, we condemn ourselves. When we love another, we love ourselves. When we support another, we support ourselves. We are all on a different path, but our purposes are intertwined so we can help one another.

How can we first achieve balance and harmony in our lives before we help the world? Without integrity we cannot preach the message of love. *What legacy as an individual and as a collective are we leaving for generations to come?*

It's in these times that the light shines through. I hope for a world united by love, peace and light. I hope for a world led by love, not fear. I hope for a world where we ascend together. I hope for a world that is healed from the ground up. I hope for a world where the truth prevails. I hope for a world that overcomes trauma and suffering. I hope for a world where troubled hearts are comforted. I hope for a world full of compassion and empathy. I hope for a world where mind, body and soul align. I hope for a world filled with open hearts and open minds. I hope for a world where creation overrides destruction. I hope for a world where trouble is met with serenity. I hope for a world where strength comes from support. I hope you shine brighter rather than wishing for the darkness to go away. I hope, I hope, I hope.

THE UNLEARNING
We need shadow and darkness in our lives too.

We are all one. Masculine and Feminine. Light and Shadow. Chaos and Order. Body and Spirit. Creation and Destruction. What happens in our lifetime does so to bring us together in harmony and unity. To rise above divergence and separation. To not battle one another but come together. We do not have to act, feel and believe the same things to be unified… it is love and light that brings us together. Peace and community. A powerful energy and force beyond the comprehension, stories and fears of the human mind. We are shifting into a paradigm of love. A spiritual evolution and revolution. It's something you can't read or learn; it has to be practiced and experienced. There is no separation between us, all for one and one for all.

As our hearts ache with heaviness and sadness, beautiful soul, do not forget the positivity that happens every single day despite what you see on the media. There is so much that goes on that we never see. Children are born. Communities come together. Courage in the face of fear. Consciousness rises. Countless celebrations and spiritual awakenings. Laughter and smiles. Bountiful harvests. Random acts of kindness. Generous hearts. Unsung heroes. Love and light will always underscore everything.

The truth is, we need your light now more than ever. People may be jealous of your light, but they won't be jealous of your journey through the darkness. Never let another's darkness impact your light. Some people will not see you not because you don't shine but because they do not want to acknowledge your light. For others you will be too bright and that's okay. They will find your light blinding and would rather you dull to a small flicker instead of being the sun that you are. Shine bright, beautiful soul. It doesn't matter if you don't receive applause or validation, what you are doing by being yourself and contributing to this world is important. We have acknowledged the light within you. Your heart. Your desire to be happy and see others be joyful in this world. The way you smile even though life has been hard on you. It's imperative for you to feel lit up, energized, excited, and bursting at the seams. To not just live, but to truly be alive. Your light will glow and others will want to harness and cultivate their own because of you.

There will be times when you are lit up in darkness. When your life crashes and burns, and yet you remain a beacon. Embrace it—fan and feed the flames. There cannot be creation without destruction. Set fire to the old patterns that no longer serve you. Break free from what you think you should be doing. Burn broken beliefs to the ground. Surrender to your shadow. Release your heart from its cage. Destroy the masks you wear and reveal your truth authentic self. Rise from the depths of darkness and despair awakened—raw, wild and free. When times are hard, try shifting your perspective: *what if everything you're going through right now and have been through thus far is preparing you for everything that you want and have asked for?*

I know some days turn into nights and everything seems so unbearable you want to escape into darkness. When everything is dark, don't forget about the light. Turn within and whisper to your soul. Place your hand over your heart and feel the devotion that beats for you. Some of the best days of your life are yet to happen. Some of the best moments of your life are yet to be had. Some of the unforgettable memories are yet to be made. The people you'll meet are yet to be met. The souls you'll fall in love with are yet to be loved. The excitement you'll have that's yet to unfold. The mystery and magic of life that's waiting to reveal itself. Hold on because you're only on a single page while novels are being written within you.

When everything seems too hard, I hope you remember the strength and resilience that has kept you here despite all the hardships and heartache you've endured. I hope you remember how deeply you're loved. I hope you remember how much you've grown. I hope you remember the purity and innocence of your heart, with its vast capacity to love. I hope you remember how incredible it is that you're here and get to experience the greatest gift of all: life.

Do not be afraid of the darkness for you have the capacity to plunge into the depths of the ocean that is your soul. Even the darkest of nights end when the sun rises. It's always darkest before dawn. Even the biggest waves will surrender and subside. The moon will kiss the sun and see the light of day. Raindrops will refresh the barren earth. Gardens will sprout from your aching bones. Galaxies will emerge from the emptiness that haunts you. Love will pour into the cracks of your soul and mend your wounds. Stars will sparkle in the shadows of your soul. Flowers will bloom in the darkest crevices of your mind.

The darkest seasons of your life will precede the emergence of a light so beautiful it will ripple through you and dot your eyes with sparkles. The darkest season is full of painful kisses from the thorns of roses. The darkest season is a deep void that exists in the abyss and dwells at rock bottom. The darkest season inevitably comes with the pain of shedding who you were to become just that little bit more of your authentic self. This will all worth be worth it for the light that will emerge once again. The light of the bloom. The light of your wings ready to soar. The light of your heart, full of deep gratitude and experience from the darkest season.

You can only go as high as you've been low. Dark depths of the soul and shadows beneath the surface emerge because they are ready to be illuminated by the light. In this Great Unlearning, I hope you realise that you are whole in light and dark. We are taught that being whole means being perfectly happy, fully healed, optimistic, bright and shiny. Your Great Unlearning is to understand you've been whole the entire time. The whole human that you are—the light and the dark.

YOUR GREAT UNLEARNING

1. YIN YANG

The following exercise is inspired by the Chinese philosophical concept of yin yang, dualities that come together as a whole. It showcases how differences can be complementary. You can apply it to any situation or person where you're struggling to have a balanced view or alternative perspective.

The 'Good'	The 'Bad'
The 'Bad' in the 'Good'	The 'Good' in the 'Bad'

2. SHADOW WORK KICKSTARTER

Think of two people you're closest to and two people you dislike. Under each person's name write three things you dislike about them.

This is your shadow talking. We dislike what we see within ourselves and because we're familiar with these flaws, we easily recognise them in others. Think deeper and try to relate. In what ways have you exhibited or do you exhibit the behaviours or traits you dislike in others? Our ego likes to ignore these behaviours and traits but the world is our mirror. Our internal reality reflects our external reality.

3. LIGHT AND DARK SPEAKER

A reflective exercise for you.

If the light within you could speak, what would it tell you?
If the shadows within you could speak, what would they tell you?

Part 4
RELATIONSHIPS

A book on personal growth and empowerment must touch on relationships. Love is everything, the beating heart of everything we do. Love is all about the Romeo and Juliet meeting, the Rom-Com twist and the fairytale ending… right?

ALONELY

THE LEARNING
Being alone is a bad thing.

I started this chapter when I was still in a relationship, and I struggled to recount times I had felt lonely. I came to the realisation that from the moment we moved in together, we had spent every day together. Upon reflection we both came to the realisation at the beginning of 2022, prior to my solo trip to Singapore, that the most time we'd spent apart over two and a half years was three days! Admittedly, this wasn't by choice given the global pandemic and being in lockdown for extended periods of time.

In the immediate aftermath of the breakup, the haunting emptiness of living by myself in the apartment we once shared came up. It had gone from warm and fuzzy polaroids of us plastered on the walls, to bare and filled with sterile taped cardboard boxes. The house was so quiet. I could hear every drip from the kitchen tap, the hum of the refrigerator and slamming car doors.

Let's talk about the loneliness one feels after a breakup. This wasn't my first rodeo. In fact, after breaking up with my first boyfriend I couldn't even handle sleeping alone. I was co-dependent and had completely lost my identity. I would look at my empty eyes in the mirror and not know who was there. One of my best friends, Georgia, slept over for a few days to fill the gaping hole he left.

Being alone and feeling lonely after a break is difficult. Especially if you were the one to break up with them. I was the one to initiate separation in both the relationships I've had. I walked away even though I loved them with every cell of my body.

As I write this, I'm on my couch in my new apartment, after having a good cry (*the ugly, wailing kind*) because I decided to scroll through old photos and videos of my recent ex (*yeah, don't do it, it doesn't help*). I just had the best day too. I facilitated huge client breakthroughs and had my biggest month of sales—this is the duality of life. I thought I missed him but upon reflection, the lines between missing a person or missing the companionship of a relationship tend to blur.

What can we do with all this love and longing? Where can it go? We agreed it was best to cut contact whilst healing. It helps that he now lives on the other side of the world, but you know how it is with technology. The number of times I had written a text only to delete it. The number of times I came close to ringing him but didn't go through with it.

What do I do with all these pent-up feelings? Dating apps. Swipe, swipe, swipe. Ah! Old habits. Looking for validation. I got off the apps and channelled my energy into writing this instead of calling him. I'm happy to say my self-discipline muscles were strong in this instance, they haven't always been. Embarrassingly, when I was younger, I would get drunk and message guys I had a thing with or used to date... we've all been there, right? I blame the tequila! Ahhhh... cringe! I did that recently too; you'll see in a few chapters time. Back to it.

So, what's with the name of this chapter? Well, being alone and feeling lonely are two different things. Being alone is a physical state whereas loneliness is emotional. I'll be exploring these concepts through romantic relationships in this chapter, however, it's important to acknowledge these states exist outside this frame as well. I think most of us can relate to feeling lonely despite being in a room full of people. Most of us can relate to feeling swallowed by a big city or a vast open space. It's the urge and longing for more that accumulates in our bones. I have been very blessed to always have friends by my side, however, I know for some that isn't the case. Know that it's never too late to make friends no matter how old or 'weird' you are. Feel no shame for desiring connection, we are communal creatures.

Making friends as an adult can feel more difficult than when we were younger. Time is the most important factor in doing so. I love that meme on the internet that explains adult friendships as two people saying, *'I haven't seen you in forever, let's catch up soon'* repeatedly (too true!). It takes time to develop any sustained relationship.

When it comes to my clients, I suggest working on themselves to get to a place where they are able to put themselves out there. There are so many channels for making new friends, such as an online meetups, Bumble BFF (which I have used while travelling solo), through to a shared hobby (for me that's doing group meditations weekly). Don't be afraid to be the one that reaches out first, you never know, you could make a friend for life! One of my newest friends is Alexa. We met one crisp morning in winter as we were both swimming at the beach—there was hardly anyone else around. Alexa says she remembers we were being pelted by the sand in our faces due to the strong wind. That was a great conversation starter.

Society has painted being alone as a painfully sad thing, specifically when being single. We are projected onto and judged based on our relationship status. We are conditioned to believe that we're worthy of love when someone 'chooses' us. That we're only truly successful when we have a partner by our side. Perhaps you have been judged for not being far along your career as expected in terms of job titles. Maybe your relationship status has you feeling like you've fallen behind. The loved-up couples flaunting their love and happiness on social media doesn't help.

I'll never forget how lonely I felt during my first solo trip to Bali. During my twenties, I was single for eight years. I was always the single one, the third wheel, surrounded by happy couples. Heck, I've even been a seventeenth wheel once on a night out with my friends.

Let me set the scene. I was at La Brisa, a beautiful beach club with coconut palms, rattan beanbags with the most magical view of the sunset over Echo Beach. I was there with my now friend Lia, who I met on Bumble BFF. She invited a friend of a friend, a Scottish guy who she fancied so of course I ended up being the third wheel even on holiday!

Of all the places in the world, from the corner of my eye I spotted Adam, a guy I had a thing with after a big night out schmoozing clients years ago. I thought I had learned not to hook up with someone from work after my naïve, graduate heart was broken by a manager on my team who was levels above me...

Adam had moved back home to the UK (*yes, I used to have quite the thing for English guys*) so to see him again in Indonesia of all places was crazy. I desperately kept my head low to avoid eye contact. Once I finally got myself together, I was embarrassed to find that he didn't remember me anyway! Then, out of the pool emerged his girlfriend, a curvaceous red head, cocktail in hand. Meanwhile, here I was still single years later and alone again in Bali.

As I was sipping my long island iced tea, which I needed after all this, an astoundingly attractive man came up to me. His name was Seb, a tall, tanned DJ and surfer that turned heads. You probably thought I would lap up the fact that he wanted to get to know me but after ruminating over Adam I didn't think I was pretty enough or memorable enough for Seb to want me. My self-esteem was not at its prime. Here's the part in fairytales where you think, *'Well, this is perfect! It all works out. Sure, you ran into that guy you hooked up with and his new girlfriend but now you have the best-looking guy at the bar chatting you up!'* As it turns out, being with Seb would make me feel lonelier than I ever have felt in my life.

Even though I rejected his advances at La Brisa, we ended up reuniting at Single Fin in Uluwatu, a beach bar perched high on epic limestone cliffs that overlooks the best surf breaks. The fact that this attractive man singled me out from a crowd of girls throwing themselves at him was flattering to say the least. That gave my ego a great boost. It felt like a scene straight out of a movie. A magical golden honey apricot sunset, me on his shoulders, dancing the night away. Being in Bali was beautiful but I was alone and lonely, *alonely*. So, on a whim I decided to ask Seb to join me at my five-star hotel in Uluwatu. That's when it all went downhill.

After an epic night he became cold. He was always on his phone doing his own thing. I'd try to make conversation but his responses were short. Kissing him felt empty. It didn't live up to the fantastical story that I had built up in my head. Despite this, I didn't want to be physically alone, so I continued to spend time with him. Being with him made me wish I was alone.

On my final night in Bali, we went to see his friends on another side of the island. He was French-Canadian and spent the whole night talking to his friends. I felt so ashamed and disgusted with myself. Here I was in Bali with a guy I barely knew and his friends while they spoke French. I have, to do this day, never felt as alone and lonely as I did in that moment. When I got back home to Australia, I promised myself I wouldn't be with someone who made me feel that lonely ever again.

THE UNLEARNING
In being alone or lonely or both, self-love will be your guiding grace.

More often than not, we long for our own heart and love. When I was in my early twenties, the torture of loneliness would propel me into the arms of people who didn't deserve to hold me. It was an intoxicatingly temporary high that came crashing down the next day when I would feel emptier than ever before. Maybe you too have wanted to be wanted so badly by another that you put up with poor behaviour. When you're stuck in this loop, you'll be pushed and pulled into feeling like you deserve the inevitable pain of chasing people who will never respect and appreciate you. You'll blame yourself for not being lovable or worthy enough. You'll break your own heart. The way through this *alonely* journey is with self-love. Self-love feels shitty at times but it's better to hold your own hand rather than the cold hands of another.

We're always searching for home, a place to belong. Your place is this world. We look for a home outside of ourselves. In other humans. In a physical location. Where we just fit and click into place. Sometimes this leads to building a foundation for others, even decorating their home and bettering them, only for that person to leave and for you to end up with nothing. In this process, you forget yourself and as result end up neglecting yourself as if you're a temporary hotel or holiday rental. You'll end up wandering endlessly from place to place with no real roots or foundation. Create that home within yourself and you'll never be homeless. Be in a state of fullness within your heart and soul. Allow yourself to be your true unfiltered and authentic self. Allow yourself to be truly comfortable in your own skin. Find fulfilment within. As George Bernard Shaw stated, *'Life isn't about finding yourself. Life is about creating yourself.'* May home be somewhere where you are your best self.

Learning to love your own company is so powerful. Learning to embrace who you are is so powerful. There is no such thing as normal. I had no choice in the matter as an only child with a single mum who worked to provide for me. I honestly hated being alone. I didn't know how to be. I was that person who would desperately avoid having no plans on Friday and Saturday night. Heck, I would hang out with anyone who was free, even if I didn't like them because I didn't want to be alone. Being on my own scared me because in the silence I could hear all my thoughts and feel all my feelings, while I lay in bed until 3am. It was in the silence that my inner demons and shadows would surface. The first thing I grappled with was the fact that we are born into this world alone and we leave this world by ourselves.

There are so many benefits to spending time in your own company. In fact, I've come to crave it. As much as I love being social, I also need lots of alone time. My human design personality is a 2/4 which means an introverted extrovert. I am also single definition which means I am designed to feel a sense of wholeness alone and am naturally independent and self-reliant. Embracing alone time means to anchor deeper into your heart and soul. Tap into your true self—the spirit and essence of who you are. You are infinite love. You are divine source. Your true nature is love, compassion, joy, happiness and bliss. There is nothing missing from you as you are now, these are stories that past programming and conditioning will convince you of. You are not broken, pieces are not missing, you are already whole. This stems from disconnection and not feeling understood or not understanding. To reconnect within, meditate and go beyond the mind and into your true state of observer: consciousness.

I am now the most physically alone I've ever been. I live by myself, and I work by myself (except for my beautiful virtual assistant Ellie who lives in another state). However I am far from feeling lonely. I feel so fulfilled by my job (which doesn't feel like one because I love it so much). My heart is so full knowing that every day I make a difference in the world. I have helped clients live their best lives, whether they've become business owners with sold out services, reconnected with family members from a rift or are healing from heartbreak. If you are feeling lonely, know that you are never truly alone. In a dimension you cannot see, you always have hundreds in the form of your higher spiritual council with you—the unseen forces. Physically, someone will be willing to talk to you whether it's someone you know or someone at the end of the phone on a hotline. You are not a burden.

I have felt lonely on my own path at times. The path isn't really about spirituality at the end of the day but awakening. Awakening to your true self. It can be isolating to feel like you've woken up from the *Matrix* and snapped out of the illusions and delusions of the world. You might feel alone because you have a whole new perspective on life whilst others are stuck in the old. I would yearn to have deep conversations with everyone only to come to the realisation that everyone is on their own path, in their own time.

As they say, *'Your vibe attracts your tribe.'* I can confirm this. I have come out of the spiritual closet and embraced this aspect of myself, I have made more beautiful conscious connections. Shout out to Japna and Juju. I still maintain deep friendships with my friends who are not as into 'spirituality' as I am. I love having a variety of connections with differing things that bring us together.

In this journey of life there will be moments where you feel alone and lonely. That's okay. What is important is to know that you are never actually though. You are always loved and supported. The sun will always shine strength upon you. The whispers of the wind will remind you that you are supported. The grounds of the earth will hold you. The trees will remind you of your inner wisdom within.

YOUR GREAT UNLEARNING

1. BECOMING GROUNDED AND CONNECTED

Imagine you're a tree. Your roots connect you to the earth, ground you and keep you centred. What branches do you put out there to connect? What activities or thoughts keep you grounded? How can you nourish yourself—what do you desire from someone else? Whatever you answer, how can you give that to yourself?

2. SOLO DATE

You don't need someone else to go on a date and fall in love with. Take yourself out!

Some suggestions include:

- Going to a cute cafe for a coffee and reading a book.
- Being a tourist in your own city, go exploring!
- Going to your local art gallery or museum.
- Spending time outdoors, visit a new park.
- Pampering yourself, have a spa day either out or at home.
- Taking a cooking class.
- Leaning into self-photography.
- Going to the cinema and to a movie.
- Hitting the local markets.
- Enjoying live music at your local pub or at a gig.

3. SELF-CONNECTION

Below are some ways you can strengthen your connection with yourself:

- Before doing anything or speaking to anyone in the morning, check in with yourself. How are you feeling? Scan your body—notice and feel your current energy levels. What are your intentions and priorities for the day?

- Do something for yourself before the rest of the world.
- Journaling. Take notes of your thoughts and feelings. Freely express yourself.
- Spend time in silence.
- Touch yourself by giving yourself a hug, stroking your arms or exploring your body.
- Reconnect to your inner child. What did you dream of? Who did you want to be? Do activities that you enjoyed as a child.
- Listen to music that resonates with how you are currently feeling. Perhaps curate a playlist.
- Have 'me' time—consciously choose to be alone to do what you love. This could be an opportunity for self-care and to do nothing but rest.
- Do something nice for yourself.
- Thank yourself by writing a gratitude letter.

UGH, DATING

THE LEARNING
Dating sucks. It's a long, arduous process.

I know the concept of dating seems heartbreakingly hard. I know you wish you could skip to the good part. I know the bleeding calluses from holding on to letting go is hard. I know dating can be just another strong connection that fades and fizzles out. The barrage of texts turns into eerie silence. I know the envy you feel from seeing two lovers holding hands. I know the feeling of slugging multiple mixed drinks down your throat to get the taste of them out of your mouth. I know being unable to sleep at 2am because you've questioned every conversation and wondered if you interpreted them correctly. I know you've questioned whether the precious memories you made were even any good because they're not here now. I know you've replayed mistakes over and over and wondered how you could have acted differently. I know you've thought about the chance to kiss them again and they would change their mind. I know you've relegated memories of them to a tightly sealed box in the back of your mind. I know you've felt silly because you would give anything to spend a night with them again, just one more time.

There's nothing wrong with mourning for someone you weren't officially in a relationship with either. There's nothing wrong with you if they've moved on and you're still fighting back tears, trying to survive each day. There's nothing wrong with you if you miss someone you hardly spent any time with. You haven't missed your one and only chance at love. It's okay to mourn the relationship and life you thought you would've had with them. It's okay if it's been only a day, a month, a year or beyond. It's okay to miss someone because you don't have them in your life, especially if they didn't treat you well. You are someone worth fighting for, even if it's just you fighting for yourself. If the people you're dating don't appreciate you, it doesn't mean that you aren't lovable or that you are worthless. Don't settle for breadcrumbs, you deserve the whole damn loaf. When you realise this, the universe will say, *'Aah, finally, she's ready!'*

Why do we date? Well, many of us would agree we date for the courtship… We date to get to know someone and evaluate their potential as a romantic partner. We are conditioned to find 'the one'. This is ironic given that we are programmed to find our sense of self and worth through a partner yet when it ends, you'll be told by the very same society that instigated it, *'You don't need anyone to complete you'*. Don't beat yourself up for having so much love to give, it's a beautiful thing. Don't beat yourself for wanting love, it's one of the most precious things.

Your love never goes to waste. It's simply directed and recirculated throughout the universe in another shape or form. The intention is there, the love you give will always come back to you. It may or may not be through another person. Only time will tell…

In my early and mid-twenties, I thought I had bad luck when it came to dating. Was it because I broke the email chain by not forwarding it to seven people or because I didn't stare into people's eyes when toasting wine glasses?

The best way to sum up my dating life was not by a dozen roses but a dozen red flags. Maybe your pillow would tell thousands of stories of pain and heartbreak, mine certainly would. After a string of situations where men didn't want to commit to me, I stopped asking. Have you been in my shoes before? Have you thought you were 'hard work' to be with or that you wanted 'too much'? So, I diluted my desires and pretended. I put on the facade of the 'cool girl,' to make myself appealing to men. I acted carefree, as if nothing phased me.

Do not settle for less than what you deserve and desire on your dating journey. Don't cry oceans for someone who won't even go for a swim. They aren't ready to do your depths and beauty justice.

Maybe it will take a headache for you to realise they're constantly running circles in your mind, yet you don't have a foothold in theirs. Maybe it will take a hungry mouth to realise you're feeding them with love yet starving yourself. Maybe it will take sore shoulders for you to realise that you're carrying the weight of their unresolved baggage. Maybe it will take depleted lungs for you realise that you're breathing all your energy into their life without consideration for your own oxygen. Maybe it will take sore feet for you to realise that you're walking down this dating path without them by your side.

Consciously you believe you want *'that'* type of love. You know what I'm referring to. The fairytale stories of being swept off your feet. The all-consuming love. The one where they fight for you. The one that makes you feel safe, adored, appreciated and cherished. However, subconsciously you believe love is pain, loss and suffering. Maybe you lost someone. Maybe your heart has been crushed to pieces. Maybe everyone leaves. Maybe you didn't have the best role models for a healthy relationship. Maybe you feel abandoned. Maybe you've lost and sacrificed everything including yourself for love. When your beliefs don't match your actions, they result in an incongruent reality. It's time for you to examine the beliefs you have about love.

Honestly, examining my beliefs about love was painful. I had to face the truth that there isn't something wrong with men. Everyone is at a different point in their journey. No doubt some of the people who have hurt you really did care about you. That doesn't mean that they were ready or willing to do the work. Maybe their wounds are bigger than they show. Just maybe.

I looked at my string of dating experiences only to find out that there wasn't something wrong with dating culture. I couldn't blame everybody else… it was me. I wasn't dating healthy and available potential partners. I was dating painful patterns and festered emotional wounds. The commitment that I wanted was something I needed to give myself. I was looking for love in the dating Merry-Go-Round, when it wouldn't be found in another person but myself. When you hold onto connections that you feel disconnected from, it's no wonder why you feel disconnected from yourself. Know that you cannot force a connection. Know that some relationships have expiry dates.

Instead of wanting to be chosen, be the one who gets to choose. Be the Bachelorette not a contestant on The Bachelor. Want to know the best karma or revenge? Don't wish that they would come back, instead wish for your self-growth and evolution. Moving on, healing, happiness, success, gratitude, attitude, your upgrade, growth and glow up are all in your hands and within your power. You don't need *them* to make these happen. You don't need their apology. You don't even need them in your life. You need you in your life. Don't waste your time, like I have, wondering why someone won't commit to you. Instead figure out why you are an energetic match with someone who is emotionally unavailable.

THE UNLEARNING
*Dating can be fun. Dating helps you grow
and evolve as a person.*

All in all, think of dating like the plot of a novel. It starts out with anticipation, freshly delivered, full of promise and potential. The book shouldn't be judged by its cover for who knows what it will contain? You are a novel worth reading—full of chapters, poetry and prose. You deserve someone who's going to read every page and appreciate the details. The words, the plot, the structure… down to the use of words and punctuation. You deserve someone who will fix the spine with love and care if it all falls apart.

Many stories are being weaved together within you, but don't waste your ink and paper. Some pages will end up being torn and worn. Some chapters will be happy, some comfortable and others will read like a short story of the horror variety. Sometimes a chapter will only be a few pages and other times the chapter will go on and on, perhaps extending into volumes. Sometimes you may reread a chapter and hope for a different ending. Some have a straightforward plot whilst others are messy and tangled. You must close a chapter before you can fully immerse yourself in the next. The only way to see how the story unfolds is to turn the pages. Plot twists await as do new characters.

Dating after being in a long-term relationship has been a rollercoaster of a ride. Let's be real, it's scary to put yourself out there in the first place let alone after being in the safety and comfort zone that was your relationship. Dating is also awkward and full of cringe.

Let me share the story of "roses man" (surely my friends and I aren't the only ones who have code names for people we're dating). Let me set the scene. He's an older, good-looking and generous gentleman. I shared with him that I just found out I hit six figures in my business and he said we had to celebrate. How do we celebrate? Drinks. Lots. Of. Drinks. We have a great time and I ended up back at his apartment. The attraction we shared was undeniable on all levels: mentally, physically and energetically. Palpable chemistry hung heavy in the air between us. *That* tension just before your lips meets another. To be intimate with someone new for the first time in three years. It felt like sunshine after rain. Life after death.

After our passionate night together, this is where a whole heap of awkwardness kicks in.

I realise he has a meeting at 8am. He's in the bathroom getting ready and just as I'm about to leave he catches me trying to sneak off. I'm making his bed. He tells me I don't have to go but I don't want to inconvenience him, so he gives me a hug and kiss goodbye. More awkwardness kicks in. I am wearing my outfit from last night. A figure hugging little black dress showing ample cleavage, lots of leg and my stilettos. He lives in a fancy apartment in the central business district with views of Sydney Harbour. Awkward moment #2. I get to the lobby and the building manager is giving a tour to a group of men in suits. I sheepishly shuffled outside and waited for my Uber whilst people heading to work rushed past me obviously still in last night's outfit.

To be fair, it's a smoking hot outfit just not great at 8am on a Friday in the middle of the city. I'm also self-conscious. *Can they smell the sex on me?* It can't get any worse, right? But oh, beautiful soul, it can. So, on our first date, this gentleman tells me he had a thing with someone who turned into a stalker. After making his life hell by ringing him nonstop and showing up unexpectedly at his place, she sent him a single long-stemmed rose on Valentine's Day.

Most people order Uber Eats after a big night. What did I do? I ordered a guy I am newly dating a dozen long-stemmed roses as a joke. The irony is, at the time, I wondered *hmmmm, is this really a good idea?* My drunk ass said, *'You bet! I'm hilarious!'*

It wasn't until the late afternoon that I realised what I had done. I rang the florist to cancel and they told me it was too late and they couldn't call the courier. Damn it, drunk Phi. The roses were to be delivered on a Friday. Awkward. *What if he brings someone else home? Will she think the flowers are for her? Will she think he has a girlfriend?* It was the first time we had been intimate, oh goodness… Dead. Welcome to my dating life post-breakup.

Thankfully, he actually appreciated the joke and found it hilarious. I'm so glad because even if he didn't, I got a great story out of it. It's book worthy and I can laugh about it (thank you to my best friend Abi, for inspiring me to turn this awkwardness into my power). Whilst it didn't work out with him in the end (more on that in the next chapter), I'm proud of myself for getting back into the dating arena. After all this, funnily enough my humour would lead to me chatting stone cold sober with a famous Hollywood actor where he was impressed by a haiku I wrote about 'zombies.' It's stories like these that form the fabric of what it means to date. Be kind to yourself! It's not easy to put yourself out there. You're brave. You're doing the best you can. I truly believe if you are meant to be with someone no matter how ridiculous you are or how big a mistake you made, you cannot mess it up. Your person will understand and you'll work together through it. Trust that if they are your person, the connection is strong for not only you but them too.

As for meeting your person? Don't worry. You aren't meant to chase everyone you meet. You don't have to search and hope that every person you go on a date with will turn into the one. When you do that, you're looking for validation and not seeing the person in front of you. This will lead to inevitable heartbreak when the illusion is shattered, and they don't turn out to be the person you wanted them to be. Dating doesn't have to be taken seriously, like job applications. Dating is an opportunity to meet people you wouldn't usually. Dating is like sampling what's available at the buffet, you'll love some and hate some.

Don't obsess over finding 'the one' to the point that you lose sight of what already matters to you: your life, your friends and your family. Obsession restricts love. Romantic love is hyped up in society but why not allow yourself to enjoy love, whether it's plutonic or romantic? Enjoy loving. Enjoy being loved. Enjoy love itself. When that person does come into your life, it will taste so sweet because, trust me, there is someone out there waiting to meet you. You don't know it and neither do they, but you will find the friend, lover and partner you've patiently waited for.

Before you do find them, consider this: you want a soulmate but are you deeply intimate and connected to your soul? The number of people worried they won't meet their person outweighs the reality that many people will meet their person. Trust and know that everything will work out.

Don't be hardened by the experiences of dating that didn't work out. Difficult situations come into our lives for a reason. No one would willingly allow and choose them. However, they can be our greatest teachers if we let them. If you want a healthy, soul satisfying relationship, you have to actually believe that it's possible. You have to dismantle the beliefs that tell you otherwise.

Finally, don't take dating so seriously. It's meant to be a fun journey of discovery like a theme park ride. Enjoy it and make the most of it because you'll be with your person soon. You can learn something from every person you meet. Every date is an opportunity for you to grow. That's an empowering way to see dating. If not... at the very least you'll have some interesting stories to share just like I have in this chapter!

YOUR GREAT UNLEARNING

1. LOVE EXAMINATION

I want you to imagine that you are watching a movie of your love life. Go ahead and answer the following questions from this point of view to uncover your beliefs on love.

When it comes to love, dating and romantic relationships:

- Do your actions match your words?
- What do your actions show?
- What does your dating history look like? Do you see any patterns?
- What is love to you? (Base this on your actions vs your words.)
- Who are your role models for love? Do they embody a healthy love?

2. USEFUL DATING THOUGHTS

Below are some thoughts for you to try that will serve you well in the dating world, they have for me!

- This person could be the one, either way I can learn and grow from this date.
- I only want to be with someone who wants me back.
- I am worthy of the love I crave and desire.
- I have faith in the process.
- My person is out there and so excited to be with me.
- I am responsible for my own heart.
- Life will always surprise me, yay!
- Everything will work out the way it is supposed to.
- If it's meant to be, it will be, no matter what.
- It only takes one. One glance. One conversation. One date. One meeting.

- I am a catch. I am the prize.
- I am one step closer to my person.
- I don't force love, I allow love.
- I am responsible for my own happiness.
- Dating allows me to discover myself.
- Just because it takes time, doesn't mean it's not happening.
- I am a lover with or without someone.
- Love is my being.

3. SINGLES BUCKET LIST

Forget about waiting for a relationship, embrace and do all the things you want to do before you get into a relationship. This will ensure you feel fulfilled and accomplished prior to getting in one. It makes for great conversation on dates too! Bucket list examples:

- Travel to Norway.
- Volunteer at a women's shelter.
- Write a book.

LOVE STORY

THE LEARNING
Love conquers all.

Have you heard the theory about the three loves we are supposed to have in this lifetime? They say the first love is the all-consuming, fairytale puppy love. It gets you when you are whole—open, bright eyed and naive.

My first love, my primary school sweetheart, cheated on me (they don't talk about that in the fairytales!). Your first love makes you feel like you're soaring through the sky and floating with the stars. Your first love helps you appreciate your weird quirks even if no one else does. You wake up the next day feeling like you can take on the world. Your first love promises that you'll be together forever and there is so much to look forward to. Your first love teaches you about heartbreak: emptiness, endings and saying goodbye. Your first love shows you that not all pain can be seen and you'd much rather break a leg. Your first love promises that they'll never forget you until you see them holding hands with someone else. Your first love makes you look back and question whether it was really love. Your first love leaves you feeling broken and jaded. Your second love takes that all away.

They say the second is the one of the best because you learn to love again. Your second love is precious because you learn to trust and open your heart again. Your second love teaches you to be brave, to not be afraid of falling in love again. Your second love teaches you to be fully present in the moment. Your second love shows you that communication will make or break a relationship. Your second love emphasises the importance of not only loving them but also loving yourself. Your second love teaches you to be yourself. Your second love is brutal because it teaches you what you really want. Your second love teaches you not to be afraid of walking away. Your second love catapults your growth and makes you stronger.

They say the third one is 'the one'. The one that lasts. Your third love is unexpected and redefines everything you know and believe about love. Your third love doesn't follow any rules. Your third love just feels so right. You are more yourself than ever before with them. When you are together, you realise why it never worked out with anyone else.

Well, this chapter is dedicated to my second love, Malcolm, because he really did teach me a lot about love but not in the way that fairytales and romances do.

Before I met Malcolm I was in a situationshit (haha I love that I genuinely had a Freudian slip and wrote that instead of 'ship'). After letting this particular person back into my life, I realised that he was not ready for the exclusive relationship he had dangled in front of me. So, in tears, I angrily declared to the universe that I was done with finding love and getting messed around. I focused on myself. That was when love found me.

So, this is where my second once upon a time starts… with a boy from Brighton, England. This love story is a modern one. We swiped on Bumble and it was true love from first gif (not quite, love would come later but I just loved the pun—sorry, not sorry).

We first met on the rooftop of the Glenmore hotel with the fairy floss sunset trickling over the sweeping views of the Sydney Opera House and Sydney Harbour Bridge. Malcolm felt like a manifestation. He was very handsome and had a thick accent (so much so, I genuinely couldn't understand him at first).

A few weeks earlier, I had journaled about my desired checklist in my ideal partner: blonde with glasses, tall and kind (tick, tick and tick). Beyond that, our understanding of loss and death instantly connected us. Unfortunately, a few of Malcolm's friends had passed away due to accidents. It felt like he just instantly got me, so much so I felt comfortable enough with him to share about my dad which was unusual for a first date. I was not only attracted to Malcolm physically, but his sweet nature too. He was a disability support worker and hearing how much he loved helping people melted my heart.

Our second date happened just before my birthday. I was shocked at how much effort he went to celebrate it with me given we had only just met. This is in contrast to the guy I dated before Malcolm, who had previously cancelled my birthday dinner on the day of.

It was a spontaneous Friday night. Malcolm rang around and walked to all the local restaurants to find one that would take us in last minute. He succeeded and we enjoyed a lovely dinner at a pizzeria.

Just before I met Malcolm, I had moved into my new apartment. It was meant to be my summer bachelorette pad for a year. At the time I had inspected many places, but this particular apartment just drew me in. It had two bedrooms and was located close to the beach. To top it off, the street adjacent is *Brighton* Road.

I didn't need two bedrooms at the time because I was single and working a corporate job in the city that did not allow us to work from home (pre-pandemic days, remember them?). Six months later, due to visa requirements and the pandemic, Malcolm moved into my apartment.

Falling in love again was scary. I cried because he treated me in a way I thought only happened in fairytales and the movies. For Valentine's Day he strung up fairy lights on his balcony and played my favourite songs. He planted kisses on my forehead and swooped me into his arms to slow dance for no reason at all on a Wednesday night. He graciously dealt with me when I was hangry. He rubbed my belly when it was bloated. He made me laugh so much that my stomach would cramp. Most days we swam together at Coogee Beach—rain, hail or shine. We spent weekends away camping in the bush with no reception. One of our most memorable moments was when we nearly got submerged under a monster two metre wave off the coast of Byron Bay whilst kayaking to see dolphins and turtles. The metaphorical walls around my heart came down for him and with good reason. I felt safe and secure with him.

I can't pinpoint exactly when I fell in love with him, though it took me longer as he said it first (it sweetly slipped out early on). One random day it just happened. It was bound to. After all, is love not just an accumulation of the micro and macro moments? Love is like that, there is no formula to follow, a notification won't ping on your phone to alert you that you're in love. I just knew. You know someone is special to you when you're doing the most mundane thing, like vacuuming, and wished they were there with you. When five hours feels like five minutes. Falling in love is all-consuming and life is ecstasy. The air gets fresher, flowers smell sweeter. Your face hurts from smiling so much and you long to be around them all the time. The small things like going grocery shopping and feeling the tiny tingles of your fingers intertwined are exciting.

Here's the thing about fairytales… they are stripped and simplified into a fantasy that isn't real. I know the ones we grew up with were comforting and gave us hope but did you know that many of our beloved favourites have dark origin stories? I'll let you investigate that in your own time but share this: when Cinderella's stepsisters didn't fit into the shoe, they tried to hack off bits of their foot so the shoe would fit. Don't worry there's no blood and gore in this love story but there is a reality check. Malcolm and I went through many major life transitions together. The honeymoon phase quickly burst after he moved in with me. We learned that we had very different ways of living—I liked to clean dishes straight after eating whereas he would leave them overnight. I had that chair piled high with clothes whereas he liked to be meticulously tidy. Our once steamy sex life fizzled out.

Things became worse once I started my side hustle. Most of my time was spent building my business. I would wake up at 5am to work on my side hustle, then go to work from 8:30am to 5:30pm and then spend the rest of the night… working. It paid off because in nine months my side hustle expanded to the point that I was able to go full-time. When you go through something like that, you inevitably change. I had changed. My mindset on life and money particularly.

I had a higher disposable income to enjoy and more travel in my future plans.

Malcolm and I were one of those love stories that logically shouldn't have happened…yet it did. He was from England; I was from Australia. You'd think our cultures would be similar but really, they were a world apart.

When I first came across his profile, on a mental level I wanted to swipe left but I just had this feeling not to. He mentioned being a backpacker, which was the very type I avoided. Later, I found out that he didn't want to date an Australian because of the predicament we would later find ourselves in.

THE UNLEARNING
Love isn't enough. It should be but it's only the foundation, more is required.

I write these words with a heavy heart and tears streaming down my face. I knew before this chapter even unfolded that it would need to be part of this book. I feel vulnerable and scared letting you in because as this was unfolding not many people knew. I feared judgement. In my mind I knew it was foolish for my heart because of what would happen next.

I'm grateful for all that my heart feels. I'm grateful for the way it beats with pride and joy. I'm grateful for the way it floats with excitement and swells with tenderness. I'm grateful when it's heavy and anchored. I'm grateful when it feels like it's being crushed. I'm grateful when it swoons with delight and wonder. I'm grateful when it beats slowly and gently. I'm grateful when it races. I'm grateful when it aches. I feel every time it bleeds. I'm grateful when it rushes off the cliff and suspends itself for a moment. I'm grateful because my heart reminds me I'm alive.

I speak of my heart because of the enduring love *and* pain I put it through in this love story. By the end, I'll be honest, it felt like I had dragged my heart over hot coals and it begged me to stop.

I guess you could say our breakup was not conventional. After being together for three years, the cracks in our relationship formed. It all came to a head in January 2022 when I couldn't take it anymore. Coming to terms with the fact a relationship isn't working out and won't, is one of the most painful things you can go through. Losing someone hurts. You have to comprehend that the only way out is to walk away. Sometimes love means walking away. Sometimes we have to let go of what is killing us, even if it kills us to let go. Sometimes doing what's best for you, won't feel like the best. When there is no peace within the relationship, choose peace in yourself. Losing someone hurts but losing yourself hits so much harder. So, I walked away from Malcolm, not because I didn't love him but because we were growing in different directions. Sure, perhaps we could have overcome the cracks but for what? We wanted to settle down and start a family in two different places, 17,020 km apart.

I had to unlearn the belief that love was always enough. Love wasn't enough to compel me to move halfway around the world. Love wasn't enough to shake off the feeling that he wasn't the person I was supposed to be with. Love wasn't enough to overcome our cultural differences. Love wasn't enough to overcome our different values. Love wasn't enough. These words cut deep for a hopeless romantic. I was hopeless but I wasn't ignorant. I wasn't blind. I loved him. A part of me thinks I always will. No longer romantically but fondly as an important person in my life story. Love doesn't equate to compatibility. You can love someone and still not love them in the way they desire and require.

Typically, as breakups go, you move out and you part ways. The thing is, we had booked flights to visit his family in November 2021 for April 2022. After arduous conversations, we decided to proceed with the trip knowing we would break up afterwards. I would split the trip, half spent with him and half on my own or with friends. I also wanted to go for my own peace, in my mind and soul. I wanted to give it my all and have no regrets. I knew it would be hard, but it truly was more difficult than what my mind could comprehend.

I was nervous setting foot on the plane knowing what I was getting myself into. Even days prior to the trip I was having second thoughts and left packing until last minute. On the plane over, the man in the seat next to me started a casual conversation, asking my name and where I was headed. He gasped because his wife had the same name as me and he was headed to Brighton too—to visit family. The crazy thing? He said that his wife was from Coogee, Australia. He fell in love with her, they now have three children and he permanently stayed in Australia to be with her. You can't make this shit up, can you? It was a hopeful sign for me that the right person I am meant to be with would happily stay with me in Australia. I even told Malcolm who isn't spiritual at all, and he agreed it was too close to home to just be a coincidence.

Meeting Malcolm's dad was so sweet. When we first met in person, he gave me a tight bear hug. Bless him, he even tried to say hi to me in Vietnamese with his thick Irish accent. It was bittersweet. I got to experience the father figure that I had longed for in my twenties. His mum was a straight shooter and I loved that. She was refreshing with a huge heart. His brothers were lovely too. In fact, we did many things together, including a beachside sauna at Brighton Beach, a tranquil farm stay with his family friends in Wales and we even scoffed down scones after a swim at the world's oldest wild river swimming club in Farleigh, England. Malcolm and I also spent lots of time at the Brighton Spiegeltent and pubs with his friends too. Everyone in his world, I really liked them all so much, it made everything harder.

Despite agreeing we'd break up after our trip, high on the fantasy and bubble of holiday living, we really wanted it to work. It's not easy to end a relationship when you've invested so much of your heart, energy, time, and money into it. You feel as though you owe it to someone not to leave because of this. You don't just throw away or let go of something like that easily but if it doesn't work anymore, it doesn't work. You can't force two different pieces into a puzzle to fit, no matter how hard you try. They just don't fit. We didn't fit. We wished we did though.

For so long we held onto the belief that we could somehow make things work and things would change but we were stuck on a Merry-Go-Round going in circles. Each time we hoped it would be different but really it was the same. As we kept trying, we kept hurting each other. I loved him enough to know that it was time to get off this ride. You can love someone and know that not being together is for the best. Even as nice as the majority of our time in the UK was, I loved myself enough to know that I was sorry, but I was also done. I loved him enough to know that I felt stuck, and I had outgrown our relationship. As they say, *'Sometimes you have to make a decision that will hurt your heart but will heal your soul'*.

No relationship is worth sacrificing your growth for. If you're slowing down so they can keep up or shrinking yourself so you can be on the same level, then the sacrifice has already been too much.

I came back from Europe in the best state I had been in for a while. My soul purpose was taking off. I booked out 1:1 coaching and was set to go to Byron Bay to do human design readings at SOMA (*pinch me: doing what I love in the most luxurious and breathtaking location and getting paid to do so!?*). I was in a financial position to retire my mum early and afford my own two-bedroom apartment close to the beach. Malcolm was in a different place, looking for a job and barely surviving off what he had saved prior to us going away. It was a place of great self-love and devotion that led me to Malcolm and it would be the same that led me to leave.

Here's the thing about hard conversations: you want to avoid them, but they are the ones that need to be had. After Malcolm and I came back from our trip, it was clear I had my feet firmly planted back in reality and he did not. I reminded Malcolm of our conversation prior to the trip, and he was devastated. A holiday isn't reality, for the most part everyone is happy and tries their best to keep the peace. The reality of our relationship was that it was broken. We were comfortable with each other after almost three years together. We had grown apart. I was focused on my business. I wanted to travel more by myself and together. I wanted to continue making money to live an abundant life and enjoy my hard work. Malcolm was slightly older than me and ready to have a humble and comfortable life. He wasn't looking for a life purpose, he was looking for a job where he was content. He had never experienced wealth and wasn't interested in doing so.

Sadly, I think Malcolm realised he had taken me for granted a little too late. When he cried over our breakup, I wanted his tears to pour into me. When he did, I never knew that I would end up struggling to stay afloat in a sea of suffering. That's the thing about the sea, it can be gentle, but don't be deceived. The sea has the power to swallow you whole. Malcolm wasn't having the best time after being in his bubble of holiday dream land for two and a half months. He came back to Australia understandably devastated to leave his family behind and at the peak of a battle with his mental health. Unfortunately, from my perspective, it's true what they say, you always end up hurting the ones you love the most. I became his emotional punching bag and collateral damage.

Everything that had gone pear-shaped in his life was put on me. He had a huge task ahead of him, rebuilding his life from the ground up —he was newly single, needed a job, a new place to live, a new phone and a new car (both written off in accidents). What really broke my heart was at the peak of his anxiety, Malcolm was having issues with going to the bathroom. When I suggested he go the doctor and potentially check for any signs of bowel cancer, he was livid. With tears rolling down my eyes, I reminded him that not knowing the symptoms of it contributed to my dad's death. Malcolm was profusely apologetic, but the damage was done. He was in so much pain that he had no capacity to think about anyone but himself.

There's no sugar coating it, breakups feel like death. Due to Malcolm's situation, we continued to live together after breaking up. What felt like the world's most drawn out breakup finally came to a swift end in July 2022. Living together after one week became too difficult and downright toxic despite all the amicable love we had for each other. The pain of separating led to him becoming suicidal and I was in a difficult position where I had to look after my ex whilst trying to move on and live my life too. It got to the point where I couldn't leave the house for twenty minutes without him being extremely anxious and depressed.

Malcolm was devastated when he ultimately made the decision to move back to Brighton. Even though I intuitively knew it had been coming for a long time and had encouraged him to do so, it still hurt. He told me he would leave in two months, which became one month, two weeks and finally a handful of days.

I felt so much anger and resentment. I felt so much relief. I felt devastatingly sad. As life goes, when this happened so much was going on that I became overwhelmed. I had one week to prepare for my work trip to Byron Bay that involved eleven human design readings. Each reading is personalised and takes up a lot of my energy to connect to higher realms for intuitive information. I decided I needed to move out of our apartment we shared together despite it being amazing. I wanted a fresh start because it held too many memories. The morning he told me he was leaving, I kicked into action. I viewed an apartment on the beachfront at Australia's most iconic beach and secured the lease on the same afternoon. The most bittersweet circumstances led to my dream apartment! I ran on adrenaline while I packed up our apartment alone as I would have to move immediately after my business trip to Byron. The words I poured out from my heart and soul on Instagram to process this all unexpectedly went viral with over five million reached in a week and a half.

Monday 18th July 2022. The day had come to say goodbye to Malcolm. We had a lovely day together. We ate at our favourite local Italian restaurant, La Spiaggia, and went for one final swim together. We had shared many tears and hugs in the lead up to this moment yet still managed to cry as I drove him to the airport. Farewelling him at the departure gate was one of the hardest things I have ever had to do in my life. Despite everything, I still loved him. The memory of walking back to my car alone at the airport lingers in my mind. I thought I would feel empty but instead I felt full. My heart was full of love.

Moving on and forward was hard. My heart flinched and winced in pain. My heart longed to take a break from all the heaviness it held. My heart wished for a way to erase all the memories. It's hard hearing a song that reminds you of them. It's hard watching a show that you used to enjoy together. It's hard imagining them with someone else someday. It's hard when longing creeps in and nostalgia tortures you with precious memories you shared together. All in all, you think it's the ending that hurts but in truth, it's the thought of how much you invested in each other. It's the thought of what could have been if things had somehow worked. It's the thought of the deep intimacy you shared. The love was real, the love remains but the love transforms. So, then you slowly have to unlearn them. Unlearning the way they used to smile at you and hold you. Unlearning how it felt to hold their hand. Unlearning the sound of their laugh and voice. The unlearning kills, but it also heals.

So, what can you take from all this? Love isn't just butterflies and feeling as if you're floating in the air. Love isn't just sweet kisses and electricity surging through your veins. Love is also a crushed heart and disappointment. Love is also tears streaming down your face in utter despair. Without heartbreak, disappointment, betrayal, sadness, grief and loss we can never fully appreciate what it means to love. How would we know the sweetness and tenderness of a kiss without the sharp bite of pain? Love is the good and the bad. Love is the beautiful and ugly. Love is the truth and lies. Love is empowering and paralysing. Love is pleasure and pain. Love is sensual and a struggle. Love is freedom and commitment. Love is love, and we wouldn't have it any other way.

Don't go hating love and being bitter because love isn't lying to you. Love isn't manipulating you. Love isn't using you. It's the other person—plain and simple. Love is pure. Love will even heal you despite your hatred and heartbreak. With deep love comes a deep grief. The two are intertwined. A beautiful lifelong dance of tension, light and joy with shadow and heartbreak. To love is to expand your heart beyond your deep-seated fears, doubts and vulnerabilities. With that opening comes not only expansion and bliss but smashed pieces. No matter what happens in this life, beautiful soul, never close your heart. Never regret a fleeting moment. Never regret moments that feel like eternity, even if they don't last forever. It is through this opening that we receive. We feel it all. We ache in our humanness. This is the beauty of life. We feel, we feel it all so deeply it shakes us to our core and wakes up the divinity within us.

In the end, my second love really did live up to the theory of three loves. I learned that whilst our love is no longer romantic, it's still in our lives as friends. Isn't it sad when someone you knew so intimately and deeply becomes a stranger? You know everything about them—their secrets, their biggest fears, their pet peeves, their hopes and dreams… Time goes on, memories fade and they become someone you may not even recognise (this certainly happened with my first love). The love Malcolm and I had and continue to have (albeit in a different form) is immortalised on these pages and in these very words, this very book you are reading.

This isn't the fairytale ending one would have hoped for in a chapter called 'Love Story,' but it is a happily-ever-after story. It was never about the ending, but the love story and journey itself. Here's to love in all its glory, beauty and purity. Here's to love in all its wholeness: the butterflies, the tears, the elation, the sadness, the depth, the pain, the aches, the light, the shadow, the complicated, the messy and the rollercoaster. Here's to love at its fullest—for your lover, your friend, your family, humanity and kindred souls. Most of all, here's to love for yourself. The hardest, heavy hitting and the sweetest of them all. Self-love never leaves. There are times love is hidden under layers of learning from your programming and conditioning. Love is steady and loyal even when you don't feel it. In a world where it can feel wrong to love yourself, be the revolution, the spark and the choice… you are love. Your life is *the* love story. Whatever your love story is I hope you know how brave you are for loving so deeply.

YOUR GREAT UNLEARNING

1. YOUR BELIEFS ON LOVE

The following questions will prompt you to discover what your beliefs on love are and how they are formed.

- What was the relationship like between your parents? How did they show love? How did you know they loved each other?

- What were your favourite tv shows, movies and fairytales growing up? What did they teach you about love?
- How do you know you are loved? What does love feel like for you? How do you know if you love someone or are in love with them?
- What do you know about love? Is it easy or hard? Is it abundant or scarce?
- What have you learned about love from others? What stories have you been told?
- Who are the loves of your life? What did you gain from the experience? Has the theory of three loves applied to you?

2. LOVE LETTERS

Write a letter to the following people (write freely and unapologetically, you may choose to burn the letter afterwards).

To my last lover…

To the 'one who got away'…

To the one I just can't seem to shake…

To my current partner (if you have one)…

To my future lover…

To the one that disappeared…

To the one who hurt me…

To the one I hurt…

To the one I miss…

To the one who misses me…

To my first love…

To the one that was short-lived but impactful…

To the one I find it hard to let go of…

---

3. YOUR LOVE STORY

- What is your love story thus far? Imagine you are writing a book about your journey.
- Be clear on what you want from love. What do you want right now? What do you want in the future? When do you want it?
- What are your values when it comes to a partner? What is nonnegotiable? What deal breakers do you have?
- What do you expect in terms of communication?
- What teachings from the past do you want to take into your current and future love story?
- What were the best things about your previous relationships?
- Do you hold any pain or trauma from previous relationships?
- What does a healthy, conscious and committed relationship look like for you?
- What do you offer and bring to the table in a relationship?
- What makes your heart swoon and flutter?
- What does intimacy look like?
- How do you express your love and how would you like them to express theirs for you?

AFTER THE LOVE STORY: PLEASURE, POWER & LIBERATION

THE LEARNING
The ending of a relationship is just sad.

What happened after my love story? I entered a void that felt like a purge of mourning and grief. The void was a space straddled between two worlds. It was as if I was floating in a silent abyss. I lost my old self. It was the end of an era and an unforgettable chapter. I was no longer in a relationship; I was finally single again. I was no longer an employee; I ran my own business. I no longer lived in my home where I fell in love and started my side hustle, I was living in my dream place on the beachfront. Saturn Return really did live up to its reputation (an astrological transit that occurs around twenty-seven to twenty-nine, known for its momentous shake ups).

It was in the void that I allowed myself to unlearn and become undone. I descended into dark places and confronted truths within my soul that I was afraid to fully look into. I descended into despair as my heart felt flambéed alive by the pain and sorrow that comes with great change. The void can be mistaken as death, but it is far from it. The void is full of potential for new life.

When I originally wrote this chapter, I noticed that everything was defined by men (an old pattern of mine). I rewrote this chapter because I am not defined by men. This isn't a story about men, it's a story about me. Phi Dang. It's a story about my voice and power.

After the breakup, so much resentment bubbled to the surface. I resented the fact that my ex didn't show up in our relationship the way I wanted him to yet did after we ended things. After we broke up, we actually did a yoga class together and he started meditating. All I had ever wanted was for him to be open to the spiritual world I lived and breathed… to embrace and accept these parts of me that yearned to be loved. That made me loathe him. In reality, the person I resented the most was myself. I was angry. I had diluted who I was so I could be palatable for his ego. I was angry that I had shrunk myself so that he didn't feel threatened or jealous by my happiness and success. I was angry I had dimmed my light so that he felt comfortable. I was angry I tried to break up with him six months earlier and didn't end up going through with it because I didn't want to hurt him. I was angry I bent my boundaries and allowed him to live with me after the breakup where he took out his pain on me and it became toxic.

The anger was powerful because I had to face the blind spots in my personal growth. I had to own up to my shortcomings and take responsibility for the role I had played. I had felt trapped in that relationship. I'll never forget when he told me, *'I'm sorry. You always let me be myself, but I never let you be you.'* This was a familiar story. I had caused a lot of my own suffering for not speaking up. Something I thought I was past but here I was again. Why did I not speak up? I wanted to be the 'good girl', to be liked by others.

As a woman, I now yearn to love myself by being in my power and truth. To fully become my whole authentic self, I had to hold myself through all the pain. I had to tenderly meet and kiss my own wounds. As I integrated my insights and learned my lessons the raging storm within became a gentle breeze upon a still lake.

A month after the breakup, I had a dream that I was on a moving train with my ex. It was an endless loop of him stepping off the train and being killed. This upset me deeply and so in one of the loops, I reached out to stop him from stepping and in that moment… I *know* his highest soul spoke to be me. He grabbed me and reassuringly said, 'It's okay, Phi. I know what will happen. You can let go now.'

For those going through heartbreak, I know how much your heart aches right now. I know how it hurts to breathe. I know it feels like your heart has shattered into a million pieces. I know it feels like the tears will never end. I know your heart is hurting. I know you are in pain. I know you are sceptical of love. I promise, beautiful soul, one day when you are ready, your heart will open again. You will find love again. You will find love in being able to get out of bed. You will find love in an oversized t-shirt. You will find love in flossing your teeth. You will find love in the way the ocean kisses the shore. You will find love in the glimmer of the stars. You will find love again because it never left, it's always been inside of you. There will be a time when you're ready to put your whole heart back into finding love again. When you're ready.

Diving back into the dating scene in your late twenties is a whole other ball game. I had to start from square one whilst everyone around me had an engagement ring, mortgage repayments, a dog, a rough timeline for children and a pasta maker in the cupboard. I, on the other hand, downloaded dating applications (though that didn't last long), Googled what 'ENM' meant in profiles (FYI: *ethical non monogamy*) and had to figure out how to make my dating profile attractive yet approachable, hilarious but not too try hard.

It was daunting because I'm the person people go to for advice as a life coach or friend. The one who has the optimistic outlook and is passionate about people putting themselves out there. My motto was you'll either meet the love of your life or gain a new perspective or experience. Yet here I was getting back out there as my true authentic self absolutely terrified. I had to accept the fact that I wasn't the same carefree woman I was at twenty-five. I was now in the final years of my twenties with a deeper capacity to feel. Further to that being a writer too, I yearned for authentic experiences to inspire my words. Moreover, I was more intuitive with different capabilities such as being connected to the other side and spiritual world unseen through visions (clairvoyant), sounds (clairaudient) and feelings (clairsentient).

I started dating again, a month after the breakup. As much as I thought I had fully processed it all given the process really started half a year earlier than the actual breakup, it had crept up on me and took me by surprise. A month to the day of living in my new place, I was woken up by what appeared to be a shadowy gorilla leaping out from behind the door onto me and viciously choking me. I was experiencing sleep paralysis and a psychic attack.

The last time I had experienced this was a year ago when my relationship was having issues. I was lying in bed next to my best friend Abi and had a demon crushing down upon my chest, I felt defeated. I had attempted to move my hand to wake Abi up for help but I couldn't. All I could do was lie there with tears rolling down my cheeks.

However this time I was able to break free from the hold of sleep paralysis. I roared out at the dark entity to leave and called upon my spiritual guides to help me and in a matter of seconds, it was gone. I spoke my truth and found the power in it.

Speaking of which, the power in voice is linked to the power of pleasure. Did you know that your voice and your vagina are intimately connected? In fact, the word 'cervix' is the Latin word for 'neck'. Structurally, our larynx and uterus are similar. Our throat and vagina are potent channels for us to express ourselves in this world. Physically, your vagina and throat are connected by the vagus nerve, which regulates your nervous system. Tuning into your power is to use your voice *and* explore your sexuality.

I never truly realised how important my voice was until I was without it for a few weeks, not by choice. Countless social events and my grandpa's funeral were the precursors for losing my voice. I had laryngitis. Laryngitis is the inflammation and infection of your vocal cords. Not only was I suffering from this, I also had a cold. I was unable to coach or talk to anyone for days. It was a sombre experience, but it helped me realise that I had taken my voice for granted. It's one thing to choose to keep quiet, it's another to be forced. In my voice's absence I realised how grateful I was to live in a world where I could speak up if I chose to. In my voice's absence I realised that what I say does make a difference in this world. It was fitting that my personal theme for 2022 was 'truth'.

Accordingly, in my post-breakup world, I became reacquainted with sensual and sexual pleasure. This was an aspect I had lost through my past relationship. After being with someone for so long I thought I would find myself in the well-known 'hoe-phase,' (a promiscuous era known for sexual exploration). After only one experience, I realised I needed a deep emotional connection with someone to continue being intimate. I needed safety. In my journey moving forward, I needed not to be intimate with others, but myself.

THE UNLEARNING
After a breakup comes new life.

I took my sensuality and sexuality into my own hands (metaphorically and literally). For the first time I experienced energetically connecting to my womb, thanks to my friend Miranda who does Holistic Pelvic Care™. It felt so empowering and as a result I decided I wasn't going to outsource my pleasure or wait for a man to turn me on. I put on a saucy soundtrack and sexy lingerie. In front of the mirror, I seduced myself, stripping down to my bare skin, my fingers delicately exploring everywhere. I lovingly oiled and slowly massaged my breasts. I got on all fours and submitted to myself. I had the most visceral and brain blowing orgasm I've ever had. I moaned so loud I was sure my neighbours would hear me.

Continuing the confidence from this experience, I purchased a yoni egg set. Yoni means 'sacred space' in Sanskrit. They are smooth crystal stones designed to be inserted up your vagina to improve sexual health and strengthen your pelvic floor. After using it for the first time, all that came out was the string… I tried to push and force the egg out but that did not work. Honestly it felt like a sitcom gone wrong. This may be TMI but I'm definitely a woman who doesn't need penetration to orgasm. I used my fingers to go deeper than I ever have before to scoop it out, but it remained stuck. I conceded perhaps I needed to go to the hospital to remove it. Eventually, what felt like forever (which was only ten minutes), breathing in deeply, I surrendered in a squat position and out it popped. It felt metaphorical… I clearly had things I was holding on to within.

I went on to have an internal pelvic floor massage. I was nervous, I always associated opening up down there to a woman for pap smears (which are a necessity!). Whilst some women experience pleasure, the focus for mine was healing and releasing. Yes, I did feel discomfort at times and pushed through it mentally. Upon reflection I did this because a shadow part of me believed that it would help me heal quicker to call in the love of my life.

The session physically confirmed what my mind already knew. I had healing to do when it came to the masculine (spiritually the right-hand side of your body). As my pelvis was being cleared and swept, a flood of tears trickled down my face. Immediately what came to mind was the pain and disappointment of being let down by men in my life. My dad for dying young (even though he did not have a say in the matter). My ex. My first foray into dating after the breakup which didn't work out. I had to heal the belief that no man could hold me physically, emotionally and mentally. The healing came through rewriting my limiting beliefs by realising and seeing the amazing men already in my life (albeit platonically). In particular, the men that I coach, evidence of incredible men working on themselves to be a better partner and human being.

All in all, relatively smooth sailing so far post break-up, right? I'd like to say it continued this way but when does it ever? Doing all this work with my yoni, I was feeling so strong aided by the fact I was abstaining from physical intimacy with another. A deepened connection and opening with my yoni, went hand in hand with being able to allow more of my truth to flow onto these pages. That truth involves sharing painful details about the trauma of losing my dad ('Grief and Heartbreak' chapter) and the sting of reminiscing on dating experiences that didn't work out ('Ugh, Dating' chapter). The cherry on top? I had Chiron's astrological influence which happened to be retrograde whilst this all went down. Many of us are familiar with Mercury retrograde (known for causing communication mishaps including resurfacing ex's). Well, let's just say Chiron is a whole other level! Chiron represents your core wound in this lifetime. Already hefty, right? When you add in a retrograde which equates to intensity, you can expect deep wounds that surface to be healed.

As a result, the perfect storm came in to shake up my life that I never saw coming. They often do when you think everything is going so well… I feel that the universe orchestrates it so, ensuring you don't get complacent—that you continue to grow and evolve, no matter how much work you've done. I'm calling it 'BCE'—*big clearing energy.*

After freshly fleshing out the details in the emotionally charged chapters, I had a big night out celebrating a friend's birthday: caviar, champagne, the works! In my alcohol fuelled state, I decide to booty call, text, friend request, pigeon mail (not really but seriously I tried *any* way) "roses man" ('Ugh, Dating' chapter). To add to my cringe, even though I deleted his number, I somehow found it again (ya girl here really *really* wanted the D). I hadn't dated or been with anyone else since things ended between us three months ago, thus succumbed to the greed of lust whilst intoxicated.

To provide context on how things ended between us—After not seeing him for weeks and hearing from him occasionally once a week, he randomly sent me a six-minute clip of him on TV… so I voiced my truth and let him know that I desired a relationship not inconsistent mixed messages. He never did acknowledge or reply to it.

When his lips met mine again, I didn't even consciously realise how hungry I was… I was starving. He tasted of danger and temptation. Our tongues danced around each other like fire. It was fun but it wasn't the same—I didn't feel the spark and electricity like the first time before. When we fell asleep and I held his hand, it felt empty in my heart. It was a stark reminder of how I missed being in a relationship.

I thought I was past this all, yet I ended up hooking up with him. I'm a life coach. I consistently do 'the work'—regular sessions with my coaches, energy healing, identifying patterns, transforming triggers, practicing mindfulness and so forth… yet I slipped up… and that's okay! No matter how much work you do on yourself, you will inevitably fall, get back up then do it over again and again (hello, being human!). It felt so good in the moment to give into my urges but the next day I had hangxiety (anxiety served up with a hangover) alongside confused vulnerability and a slap of self-loathing. This experience was an intense activation of accumulating shadow work that was culminating behind the scenes.

I worked with one of my coaches, Patti, to get out of my blown-up spiral—to be kind and compassionate with myself. I had gone through huge changes in my life, in every facet whether personal relationships, my career and where I lived. A useful reframe that helped was: would this matter in ten years let alone next year? No. What would usually take at least a week for me to recover from, only took two days to my own surprise. I was ready for this huge release.

The medicine was to return to love, in my heart. I was triggered by his emotional unavailability. My inner child was subconsciously seeking the father wound of validation in the form of the masculine. I had to take ownership for building up roses man so much in my head and creating a fantasy happily-ever-after. Whilst I don't think it was unfounded (given what he would say to me alluding to a future, taking his last name in marriage and the smart, cute children we'd have)—I had to take responsibility for ignoring red flags and incongruent behaviour where his actions did not match his words.

The reality was healing because I found inner peace and closure. I was no longer secretly wondering what could have been and dreaming he'd come back someday because he was 'the one' all along. He didn't have the capacity or depth to hold me emotionally—and that's okay. His circumstances didn't have to be my reality. I have empathy for him because it's likely women he's been with before have hurt him and as a result he became closed off to emotions—I've been there. I appreciate his role in my journey because I didn't think I wanted anything serious so soon after my previous breakup, but our time together made me realise that I did. He give me a flicker of hope as the first man I could see as a potential life partner after my ex. Most of all this experience illuminated a blind spot in receiving the love I deserved.

As painful as it all was, it was perfect because I gained liberation and power in surviving the storm. I emerged stronger, wiser and back on track to hold space for the right person. After all, the perfect storms come in not to destroy you, but to clear the way… In the wise words of Haruki Murakami, 'When you come out of the storm you won't be the same person who walked in. That's what this storm's all about.'

Funnily enough, the next day after embracing everything that happened, my cousin Viv (who has no idea this all happened) sent me a text out of the blue saying, 'I just saw a butterfly and I had a sudden urge to tell you that your Dad is sending someone special to you.' I smiled—*you can't make this shit up*. A reassuring and reaffirming sign, validated by the tingles cascading up my spine as I read her message. A week later roses man appeared in my dream to tell me he was potentially moving overseas forever, I smiled and said I'd drive him to the airport.

In deep reflection of my journey after the breakup, I can see that I pursued a sensual path to reclaim my pussy, but I realise it wasn't just about that but my heart all along too. The pain of heartbreak and pleasure of my pussy cracked me open to a deeper love than I've ever known… myself. A raging release to ravishing, radiant rapture. To feel safe and supported in my own arms and heart. To surrender into deep union with all parts of myself, by softening when I wanted to harden. Ultimately, choosing myself and truth, over and over again.

Writing this book has been medicine for my soul. It has truly cemented coming (and cumming ;)) home to reawaken my power and pleasure. To finding my voice and not being afraid to speak my truth. I've finally broken free from the self-imprisonment of wanting people to get me. It doesn't matter if they do or don't because I know why I share what I do. To help people. So, I've had to get comfortable with people not understanding me. I've had to make peace with people not liking me. I've had to embrace people finding what I do and share as 'weird' or make fun of me. I'm breaking free from carefully editing and curating myself to be seen as perfect and to be likeable. I want you to feel the rawness of my fiery words. I want you to feel my heart and soul in everything that I do and say.

So very true are these words by Harriet Selina as I reflect on this chapter in my life, 'What once felt like heartbreak now feels like divine intervention.' I am truly wholeheartedly living my dream now as my highest, authentic and aligned self. I feel free to be my true self.

I am spiritually aligned and liberated. I live in my dream home on the beachfront in one of Australia's most loved and iconic beaches. I made six figures in less than a year full time in my own business. I am abundant and financially secure. I travel often and enjoy incredible experiences. I am surrounded by incredible people. I celebrate and revel in the joy of my life. I wake up excited because of my purpose and passion every day.

As for my new love story? Well, that journey is still underway at the time of writing this book. What I do know is that whoever I end up with will be a man who is ready, emotionally available and desiring a deep partnership like me. He will consistently show up for me and make an effort. He will stand by me despite the storms that may come. He will allow me to shine in the spotlight and celebrate my achievements. He will embrace my spiritual values and support the nature of what I do.

Ultimately, what is the focus of this new chapter in my life and overarching story? To have a greater impact and influence on the world, by helping as many people as I can. To make the most of life by cherishing every single moment. To be my most aligned and authentic self, and awaken you to yours too.

YOUR GREAT UNLEARNING

1. PLEASURE

Here are some ways you can experience more pleasure in your life:

- Learn more about the female anatomy and pleasure centres. They are full of nerves and sensations (it's not just about the clitoris!).
- Explore your whole body. Touch your face. Massage your breasts with luscious oils. Hold your own hand.
- Become aware of the physical sensations in your body when you do something. Take note of what makes you tingle and giddy.
- Soften and open your body.
- Go slow and savour the experience unfolding.
- Find the magic in the mundane.
- Alleviate stressors in your life. Empty them out. Write down your thoughts. Minimise to do lists. Have a good cry or scream.
- Express your pleasure vocally.

2. POWER

Below are some methods I use to tap into my power which you may find helpful:

- Connect to your inner voice. Find a quiet space, get comfortable and relaxed then close your eyes. Ask yourself: *'Inner voice, what do you want to say to me right now?' 'Inner voice, what are the truths I am holding back on?' 'Inner voice, what do you want to be known?'*
- Where are you leaking your power? How can you remedy that?
- What's something you want or know that you're afraid to admit to yourself?

3. ACTIVATE YOUR CHAKRAS

I like to do this in meditation. Go through the below list and visualise the colours. Check in with how each centre feels. Going from top to bottom for a clean sweep or you may do it the other way around if you're in need of grounding.

> 7 Chakra: Crown
> Colour: Violet
> Location: Above your head
> Themes: Consciousness, Spirituality, Self-realisation
> Affirmation: *I understand*
>
> 6 Chakra: Third Eye
> Colour: Indigo
> Location: Centre of forehead in between your eyes
> Themes: Intuition, Foresight, Imagination, Visualisation, Premonitions
> Affirmation: *I know*
>
> 5 Chakra: Throat
> Colour: Blue
> Location: Centre of neck
> Themes: Communication, Honesty, Expression
> Affirmation: *I express*
>
> 4 Chakra: Heart
> Colour: Green
> Location: Centre of chest
> Themes: Love, Self-love, Relationships, Compassion
> Affirmation: *I love*
>
> 3 Chakra: Solar Plexus
> Colour: Yellow
> Location: Abdomen
> Themes: Power, Ego, Self-esteem, Confidence, Purpose
> Affirmation: *I can*

2 Chakra: Sacral
  Colour: Orange
  Location: Below your belly button
  Themes: Energy, Life Force, Sexuality, Creativity, Emotions, Pleasure
  Affirmation: *I feel*

1 Chakra: Root
  Colour: Red
  Location: Base of spine
  Themes: Stability, Survival, Comfort, Foundation, Stress, Adrenaline, Safety
  Affirmation: *I am*

4. LIBERATION

The following prompts can help you to find more freedom in your life:

- In what ways are you keeping yourself small? Dimming your light? Where are you holding back? Withholding?
- What do you need to let go of?
- What resistances are coming up in your life? How can you surrender?
- How can you become bolder and braver? What keeps your fire lit?
- What are the facets to who you are as a multi-dimensional woman? E.g. describe yourself as a mother, the playful one, the sensual one, the mischievous one, etc.
- What needs to be said? Where do you hold your tongue? What are you afraid to say? What is your inner truth right now?
- In what ways are you acting in accordance with what you think you ought to? What are the 'musts' and 'shoulds'?
- What does it mean to be wild and untamed? How can you bring more flow into your life? Where can you tap more into your raw primal nature as a woman?
- What is your heart and soul's deepest calling right now?

- How can you embrace your sensitivity and emotions right now?
- Is there anything getting in the way of your most authentic self and expression right now?

WE ARE FAMILY

THE LEARNING
Family must look and act a certain way.

Families… yeah, they are complicated whether biological or not. Isn't the reason most of us end up seeing a psychologist and/or life coach because of family? They have such pivotal influence in who we are and why we are the way we are. From a young age we are bombarded with norms and ideologies of what family should look like. Happy and normal, of course. Everyone loves each other and gets along. Family gatherings with extended relatives are embraced. Pretty picture holidays. Loyal to the bone. However, there is no such thing as a 'perfect' family. We are conditioned to believe that family are our blood relatives. I was taught family meant two married adults (parents) living under the same roof as their children. The term family is a label with many definitions. Let it not limit us. It may be the blood that runs through our veins, or it could be the love and loyalty you feel in your heart. We all know the saying, 'Friends become family.'

Along with learning what we think family should look like, we also learn about how we think we need to behave. Something I see in many clients is the weight of expectations placed upon people by their family. Remember that your life is here for you. Your family is an important factor, but you were not born to follow their concept of an ideal career path or live the way they always wanted to. You're allowed to challenge their ideals and figure out what you want for yourself.

People pleasing starts as parent pleasing. Putting other people first becomes expensive. Your soul is on a budget which cannot afford stress, drama and negativity. It's like a bank account, you deposit money in, and they withdraw it. You don't get to enjoy the money you're working so hard for.

Children inherently desire strong connection with their parents. Parents cannot fulfill this desire all the time. You may have warm and fuzzy memories with your parents or maybe not… People pleasing starts with emotional inconsistency that conditions us to believe we have to do certain things and put other people first in order to earn their love. Instead of loving yourself, you strive to become someone that is loveable in other people's eyes. If you don't put yourself first who will?

Our upbringing influences the way we behave as adults, particularly when it comes to relationships. Something I have experienced myself and help my clients with is abandonment. Abandonment issues can stem from divorce, death, and so much more. If you have been abandoned, I feel you. The abandonment story is age old, no matter how hard you try or how deep you love, people will always leave. Life will rip you away from them. It crushes your heart and soul. It makes you tremble. It makes you question your worth and lovability. It makes you believe that maybe you're meant to be the lone wolf in this world, fighting for survival on a path that is less travelled and misunderstood. Abandonment has nothing to do with your love or worth. Abandonment is a story we tell ourselves to make sense of the pain we've endured. Abandonment is not a reflection of you. Take your power back from abandonment because even if you have been abandoned, you shouldn't abandon yourself.

Writing this chapter has led to me having very uncomfortable yet healing conversations with my biological family. When I got this book publishing deal, I told a few close friends, but I did not tell my family. I felt nervous because I knew that my family probably did not want me to write about them. Given the nature of this book, sharing personal stories is guaranteed. This means talking about the metaphorical elephants in the room and the metaphorical skeletons in the closet that every family has. I do this not to criticise or embarrass my family, I do this because I want to help you, beautiful soul reading this, and to be real about my life.

This is in conflict and tension with my Asian heritage. Stereotypically, Asians are unemotional. They're concerned with 'saving face'—it is about respect and reputation. The closest translations can be described as 'prestige,' 'pride,' and 'dignity.' Western societies tend to be more aware of and concerned by our individual reputation. Asian cultures believe it is more about how you are viewed by others. Your personal reputation impacts and influences your family's face too. Therefore, when you have problems, it's something to be dealt with privately. Yet, here I am, sharing them publicly in this book with you.

Accordingly, I acknowledge and understand why they would not want me to speak about personal matters however this book is not my family's story. This is my story and, of course, family is a huge influence in my life, whether they are present or not. By not telling my family, the internal blocks manifested physically. I found it very difficult to write this book initially, so I decided I needed to tell my family and ideally have their blessing. This journey started when I came back from Europe and met up with my mum for Yum Cha in the city. Of course, her motherly instincts had been activated because when I told her about the book, she said, 'I know, I had a feeling.'

I have a complex relationship with my mum. I love her very deeply. Upon reflecting on my life up until this point, it pains me to say that I have been harsh and critical in my judgement of her. I didn't try to understand her like I did my dad and everyone else in my life. I was hard on her, and I lacked empathy for a long time. Most of my love and attention went towards my dad before he passed and even more so after he passed. I was "daddy's little girl" after all. Through introspection I now understand that my mum triggers me because she is a mirror for the things within me that I see within myself that I resent. She is one of my greatest teachers in so many ways.

My mum used to do things that would embarrass me. My mum has never been one to go with the status quo. She rocks red or purple hair with shaved sides. She doesn't wear put together outfits, she wears clashing prints or outrageous fluoro tracksuits. She does whatever she wants and that triggered me. The child within me who wanted nothing more than to fit in as a minority. I wanted to look like Cinderella and Sleeping Beauty as a child, not Mulan. I didn't want to bring pâté sandwiches or fried rice to school for lunch. I forced her to make me 'normal' sandwiches that had ham or Vegemite in them. I wanted to look 'normal', but my hair was in that of a bowl cut and wore ugly skivvies that my mum had made me to keep me warm.

One day I snapped at her in the middle of a department store because she was doing something embarrassing. I said, *'Don't you care what other people think of you? You are being weird, and everyone is looking at us like you're a freak.'* I'll never forget her response. *'You want to know why I don't care? I fled Vietnam on a boat and came here with nothing. I'm happy, healthy and alive. So no, I really don't care what anyone else thinks because I am so grateful to be here in Australia and not dead in Vietnam.'* She shut me down hard and rightly so. From that moment on I accepted the fact that she would do what she wants. She wasn't hurting others, so I have no right to impose my projections onto her.

As I write this, I feel guilty for even doing so but this is my truth. My mum used to feel like the biggest burden—she's actually the biggest blessing in my life. I say burden because I'm an only child. Unfortunately, all of her direct kin have passed away: her mum, father and brother. Her ex-husband, my dad, is gone and she does not have a new life partner. Due to life and her choices, she doesn't have a large income or safety net. That has fallen to me. I resented her for asking me for money from a young age. I was no longer resentful when I realised how blessed I am to make such money with my mind when she would have to do physical labour as a cleaner. I was no longer resentful when it truly hit me that she is a badass super woman. She raised me as a single mum between long hours of employment to support me and against all odds managed to give me everything I wanted. I feel so blessed she is still alive and with me at this moment in time. I feel so grateful to have an abundant business which has allowed me to retire her early, so she now has all the time in the world for herself. It's true what they, as you get older, you really do appreciate your parents more because you understand life: bills to pay, a household to run, food to put on the table and a roof to cover your head.

At Yum Cha, I was nervous when I asked her about her life and experiences but I needed context for the chapter you're reading right now. Last time I asked her about her life would have been at least five-ten years ago. She had cried because I pushed while she was uncomfortable.

I was taken by surprise when my mum said that she could see before her a mature soul who was ready to hear the things she had kept from me. So, we talked. I gasped. I cried. I laughed. I empathised. It was truly soul-healing. I asked her how she felt about not owning a property anymore and not having a tonne of savings in the bank. From society's point of view and the masculine conditioning we've been raised with, this is seen as a failure. She said it didn't matter because she couldn't take any of it with her when she passed and money comes and goes like water. Truly an abundant feminine mindset. This is something I've had to work on to heal my relationship with money. My masculine mindset had previously condemned my mum but after engaging more with my feminine energy, I have come to admire her.

Up until that point, I had wanted to be the opposite of my mum. Now I know I want to be more like her! Everything I had to unlearn was right under my nose, the role model I was looking for was my mum.

The toughest topic I wanted to talk to my mum about was my dad. My dad cheated on my mum when I was a child. My mum was very kind when she spoke about him. She said he was a good man and only had positive things to say about him. She said that it was all in the past and she had forgiven him a long time ago because he's human and they were not the right match. She said the best thing about it all was that I gained a beautiful stepmum who loves me very much (she's right about that!). Honestly, my mum is so full of love and from the very beginning she told me to treat my stepmum like her. I now have two mums I can appreciate. I love that we all hang out together now too—my mum, stepmum, step-grandma and I.

My dad was a stoic man. He was a man of few words and emotions. He was incredibly intelligent and wise. He would do anything for his family. My dad was also hilarious and enjoyed dark humour like myself. On the last day I ever saw him in the hospice, he said to me, "Phi, why are you wearing make up? This isn't Sleepless in Seattle, I don't think you'll pick up any young men here." Whilst I would have loved to have more time with my dad, I am incredibly grateful for the in-depth conversations we had before his passing. They always happened in the car on a drive, that's how it was with my dad. I felt that my first boyfriend cheating on me was his karma. That's what my dad did to my mum, but it was on a whole other level given he was married and had a child (me!). I was moved when I saw him cry for the first time in my life and asked for my forgiveness. He made it clear that he didn't regret being with my stepmum at all (they were the loves of each other's life), but he did regret the way it happened and for breaking up our family. I forgave him. He wasn't perfect and didn't need to be. I loved him so much and I know he loved me so much too.

Through the journey of discussing this book with my family, I spoke to my cousins (on my dad's side) who are the core of my family, they're like my siblings. My dad's side of the family is large, he has five sisters and one brother. My mum comes from a smaller family, they are Chinese born Vietnamese. In fact, I have never met anyone from my mum's side. I spoke to my grandpa (her dad) once via a web call when I was younger but unfortunately, he passed away before I got the chance to meet him. This was the reason I wanted to go to Vietnam when I was younger. While my dad's family is in Australia, my mum's family remained in Vietnam. Vietnam is my ancestral homeland, but it isn't home for me. This used to be especially triggering when I had been told racist remarks to 'go back home'. Australia is my home. I was born in Australia and I consider myself more Australian than Vietnamese or Chinese. I've travelled the world multiple times, but I still have not been to Vietnam. I will one day and I am sure it will bring up a mixture of emotions.

I digress. I told my cousins about my conversation with my mum, including what she had said about the cheating and divorce. We all agreed cheating was morally wrong. One of my cousins shared that she talked to her mum (my aunt) about an incident involving a friend's mum cheating. My aunt would go on to say that cheating is very normal in Asian relationships and it's to be expected. We were all shocked but what unfolded next would explain why. My other cousin shared a shocking revelation about my grandpa, which provided me with clarity when it came to my dad's behaviour, though it did not excuse it.

I have never been close to my paternal grandparents. I couldn't speak Vietnamese and they couldn't speak English.

At the time of writing this, it is Father's Day and my grandpa (my dad's dad) passed away yesterday. I'm feeling a mixture of emotions. Yesterday, on the day of, I felt like I needed to show an outward display of emotion but I didn't. I've come to realise that there is no right or wrong way to feel. There is no feeling that you 'need' to or 'should' have. There is no 'normal' feeling. I am deeply saddened by his passing even though I was not close to him. He was the man that gave me my dad. I felt saddened because I know what it felt like to lose a dad. I felt sad for my grandma because she has been with my grandpa since she was sixteen years old. My grandpa passed away peacefully with family surrounding him at the age of ninety-two. He truly did live quite the life. Even after spending time in the army, and jail with my aunt for being against communism in Vietnam, he managed to survive and lived long enough to meet three of his great grandchildren. His funeral ended up being so beautiful and a tender release where my tears did flow.

The shocking revelation revealed about my grandpa and his children (my dad, aunts and uncle) grew up in an environment where cheating was the 'norm'. In fact, my grandpa had a mistress in Vietnam before he had to cut ties with her to come to Australia. My grandma even knew about it and would send her kids (my aunts) to shoo the mistress away from their home in her absence. When writing this, my cousin reminded me that the mistress did end up coming to visit Australia and had dinner with our whole family with my grandma present. Given all this, I now understand my dad more and have empathy for the situation he was in. Having context to his actions has been healing for me. Whilst I still don't think cheating is okay, I now have more compassion and understanding for it. At the end of the day, my stepmum was my dad's soulmate, and they were meant to be. Sure, it would've been ideal if it hadn't involved cheating but such is life.

Sometimes we forget our parents are human too. There are a lot of wounded children walking around in adult bodies, some of them go on to be parents as well. They are not perfect. They are adults just as we are now. They try to do their best, but they're flawed and bound to make mistakes. Having compassion and empathy for why someone behaves based on their experiences does not mean that you have to tolerate or condone their behaviour. Compassion does not take away from your values and boundaries.

Forgiveness is equally as important as compassion. To forgive is difficult. Forgiveness is not forgetting. Forgiveness does not take away from what your parents have done. Forgiveness is not necessarily a feeling but an attempt to resolve the resentment in our hearts so we can find peace with ourselves. Be discerning, you are the one who holds the power. You get to choose whether to forgive or not. Forgiveness is given for your sake, not for another's.

THE UNLEARNING
There's no such thing as a 'normal' family, all are different.

You don't just inherit your parent's traits and characteristics, you also inherit their beliefs, conditioning, values, attitudes, mindsets, perspectives and self-talk. By the same token, when you heal, you're healing your parents, your family, your ancestors and the generations to come. The greater the pain, the greater the capacity to heal. You're holding space for your collective family, humanity, to heal. You have the power to break patterns. You have the power to overcome misfortune. You are the revolution for your lineage. You are the soul born and living in this lifetime to awaken, here and now, with love and light. This journey is that of duality. You can be healing your lineage whilst you appreciate the teachings and lessons. You can love your parents, but you don't have to love their unhealthy habits and patterns.

Don't be afraid if you are the black sheep of the family—the one that is different and goes against tradition. In fact posthumously I was told my grandpa always thought of me as the dark horse of the family. I proudly own that label because I've never been one to follow traditions and who doesn't love an underdog? You don't have to continue the ways of the family that has come before you. Patterns of trauma resurface time and time again until someone decides to stop them.

From a spiritual perspective, every cell in your body carries the memories, stories, emotions, pains and triumphs of your family. This is oblivious to your conscious mind. You are here to break the chain and become the source of liberation. You are here to forge new ways of being. Forgive those who weren't able to do so like you are now. Forgive your mum who couldn't speak up because she wasn't able to do so without fear of being shamed or killed. Forgive your dad who repressed his emotions to focus on survival because emotions weren't socially acceptable. Forgive your mum for being overbearing because she had cold and distant parents. Forgive your dad for being absent because he wasn't mentally ready to be the parent you deserved.

You cannot change your upbringing, but you can step into the power you have now as an adult. Be the person you wanted and needed. Emotional wounds don't come about merely from what you experienced, they also form from what you lacked. Reparenting means giving yourself what you didn't receive as a child. The listener you always wanted. The protector you needed when you were left to fend for yourself. The validator to let you know feeling the way you did was understandable. The cheerleader that acknowledged and celebrated you. Self-compassion is key here.

To gain more perspective, ask yourself if you would talk to a child the way you speak to yourself. If you are struggling to have patience and compassion, imagine that you are talking to a younger version of yourself. Children do their best to navigate an adult world. Children deserve to be loved, supported and heard with patience, kindness and gentleness, right? This very child exists within you still.

Who is your inner child? The part of you that should have been able to freely express themselves and ask for what they wanted. The part of you that believes laughing and playing are important. The part of you that admires the innocence of being a child. The part of you that had to grow up quickly in order to survive. The part of you that wanted to cry but couldn't because she was told crying was a weakness. The part of you that wanted to be held when she was frightened. The part of you that strived for perfection and achievements in order to be loved and valued. The part of you that tried their best but wasn't good enough. The part of you that was let down when your parents forgot your birthday. The part of you that felt abandoned when there was no one to pick you up from school. The part of you that was blamed for everything that went wrong when really it had nothing to do with you and was not your fault. The part of you that finds it hard to trust because you've been let down so many times.

When we don't heal the wounds from our upbringing, we end up looking for our parent in a partner. This is where the 'mummy' and 'daddy' issues stem from. This refers to a complicated dynamic with a parent you experienced. No matter how amazing your parents were, from my experience as a life coach, everyone has 'mummy' and 'daddy' issues. I definitely had 'daddy issues' given my parents were divorced and my dad passed away when I was 'legally' an adult but still very much a young soul. My dad was very loving, but I still had 'daddy issues'. He was never cruel to me, but he was the stereotypical conditioned man who never showed his emotions. He showed love through his actions. This then played out in my dating life. I sought the qualities of a father in my partners. I sought out older, protective, secure and financially stable men. They happened to also always be emotionally distant just like my dad too. This further reinforces the trap of generalising men based on your father. The absence of my dad propelled me to seek validation and love in men. I wanted attention. I wanted to prove that I was worthy. The same things I wanted to prove to my dad.

It's sad that these issues have become jokes at the expense of painful wounds. I should also add that women can also have 'mummy issues', and men can have 'daddy issues.' It's not about gender but the roles that are played. To move past this, you must be aware of what you are doing. Be honest with your intentions. Reflect on the patterns you see in your relationships and if there are any similarities to experiences you had with your parents. We often recreate the scenarios that caused our wounds with our partners. For example, we might look to prove our worth to men by doing things for them such as cooking and cleaning. We might try to convince someone to be with us, so they won't abandon us. I came to realise that the qualities of a father or man I was looking for, existed within me. I didn't need a man. I could protect myself. I could validate my own emotions. I was strong without having or needing a man by my side.

This can also help to explain why we behave the way we do in relationships, particularly that of attachment theory. Attachment theory stems from the psychological development we receive in relation to the bond formed between humans, with that of the parent and child being pivotal. In theory, we are born with the need to form a close emotional bond with a caregiver, but this is not always given.

There are four attachment styles: secure, anxious, anxious-avoidant and avoidant. They are formed from how your caregiver responds to your needs. I used to be in the anxious category. It would manifest itself as the constant craving for closeness. My anxiety would be triggered when someone didn't reply to a text within a certain time frame. I worried when someone pulled away and sought reassurance. It was honestly exhausting. Pair this with dating someone avoidant and we get a hot and cold, push and pull dynamic. Not great for your mental health and nervous system. To work through this, I had to find security and safety within myself and not through another person. I had to learn to regulate and validate my own emotions. I had to learn to meet my own needs.

As a life coach, I tell all my clients we have so many invisible implicit rules that we follow with regards to family due to conditioning. I'm here to free you from them. You don't have to be like everyone else, it's okay to be different. Family members don't have to be exactly the same. You don't have to like or love everyone in your family. You are not obliged to have relationships with them or do anything for them. It's not your fault your parents couldn't give you love in the way you needed them to. You don't have to let their patterns, pain and trauma impact you. You are allowed to cut toxic family members from your life. 'Family is family' doesn't justify anything. Familial relationships aren't always straightforward, they can be complicated.

Something that I see often in clients is a need to understand why their parent is the way that they are. Whilst that can be useful in providing context, there comes a point where you realise you don't need to know in order to take back your power. You do this by acknowledging that you cannot do anything to change their behaviour and so it's best to focus your energy on yourself and being the best person that you can be. Part of this healing process involves letting go of the belief that they will be different now (when your parent has no desire to change or acknowledge their contribution to your upbringing) and letting in self-love and compassion.

Let's talk about unconditional love. Unconditional love does not mean unconditional tolerance and unconditional boundaries. It's time to unlearn this harmful conditioning that results in forming people pleasers.

Guilt is used as a weapon to manipulate and maintain control. Expand your guilt tolerance. Asserting boundaries when you are conditioned is difficult. That doesn't mean you're doing it wrong or it's the wrong thing to do. Oftentimes doing the right things feel harder. The easy things feel uncomfortable. The aim isn't to provide unconditional love. You can love someone to the moon, lifetimes beyond and still have boundaries. The aim is to find a love where you feel safe, comfortable and happy.

Accordingly, boundaries are an important tool in family relations. In fact, the family members that make you cringe or give you discomfort are probably the ones you need the most. Implementing boundaries need no apology, they are vital to your inner peace and mental wellness. When you honour your own needs, you know that it isn't possible to meet everyone's expectations of you. This can be particularly difficult as women who have been conditioned to gain a sense of self from doing things for others. The guilt of setting boundaries isn't yours to carry. Unlearn the need to feel as if you have to explain yourself. Family doesn't give anyone the right to hurt or disrespect you. If someone is unable to respect your boundaries, you cannot have a healthy relationship with them. This is vital because the price you pay for trying to do things for everyone else and be a certain person yourself is too costly.

Many of us lose and leak our power when it comes to family, but you get to be the beautiful soul that decides to step into her power and bring about sacred ancestral healing. If you didn't come from a happy and healthy family, you get to start a happy and healthy family. Imagine being an ancestor in another time and dimension watching you with great pride, love and relief. The work that you do to heal yourself will act as a ripple effect on your family. This can't necessarily be seen but it can be felt in the heart, soul and on a cellular level. You are the bridge between generations and worlds. You are restoring your family to the core of what family is: love. You get to be the one future generations will remember as the remarkable soul who was the turning point of change for the betterment of the family tree.

YOUR GREAT UNLEARNING

1. RECONNECTING WITH YOUR INNER CHILD

Here are some ways to reconnect with your inner child:

- Revisit childhood memories.
- Do things you liked to do when you were young.
- Spend time with children.
- Creating is a beautiful way to reconnect: finger painting, using your imagination, sensory play with play dough or slime.
- Journal as your inner child or younger self—give her a voice.
- Write a letter to a younger version of yourself.

- Go through photos of yourself as a child or look over keepsakes.
- Visit a place that reminds you of your childhood.
- Cook a meal that feels like home.

2. BOUNDARIES ASSESSMENT

The following questions will help show where you may need to set up boundaries with your family (and any relationships/areas of your life):

- What are the current boundaries you have in place for your family and do any of them need updating?
- Can you recognise some of the boundaries your family members have in place?
- As a result of having your boundaries in place, what is possible? How do you feel?
- What do you feel is a must do and have to do when it comes to your relationships?
- Where in your relationships do you feel most resentful?
- What values are important to you in family relationships?
- How do you best resolve conflict and tension in your family dynamic and relationships?
- What are your coping mechanisms when it comes to family?
- Why do you have the values and beliefs that you do?

3. THE IMPLICIT FAMILY RULES

This exercise will highlight your expectations of your family in alignment with your values and how you fulfil your own needs.

How you expect your family to behave?	Why do you expect this?	Why do you want this?	What value of yours does this represent?	How can you fulfil this desire or need by yourself?

Part 5

SPIRITUALITY

We live in a time where we are told to be logical and to think with our brain. Spirituality is seen as either woo woo witchy or deity worshipping. It's time to unlearn the old narratives and quantum leap into contemporary spirituality, which is rooted in the self.

SPIRITUALITY IS RELIGION?

THE LEARNING
Religion is God and a systematic approach to what you can and can't do.

Religion is a controversial topic. It's a strange one too. Many of us didn't choose to adopt the religious beliefs we have. Many of us are indoctrinated based on our family's belief systems. I write this chapter from the point of view of being raised Roman Catholic. I no longer identify with Catholicism but spirituality instead.

I became aquatinted with God from a young age. At first God was my hero. He seemed like an incredible guy. As they say, *'God is Good'*. Reading the Bible, it was evident how powerful God was! He created humans and the Earth. He had the power to grant miracles. I was taught not to question God. To do that would be contentious. As time went on, I became wary of God. Reading the Bible literally had me questioning why one would have to cut off a sinful body part for it would mean all humans would be a mixed bag of bits! We will sin, it's our nature.

I questioned religion and God more than ever when I was with my first boyfriend. We had been together for a year, and I had told him that I wanted to be married before we had sex. He was disappointed but never pressured me.

I then questioned myself. If I loved someone, why did I have to wait? Why was sex before marriage so sinful? I figured sex would be an expression and consummation of love. It was pure, it was innocent. Sex to the church was for the purpose of procreation. Without marriage, it was fornication. Even that word doesn't sound very pleasant.

I held guilt for being sensual or sexual for a long time. It would always lurk in the back of my mind. I felt dirty. It felt 'naughty' and 'bad' to touch myself or look at sexually explicit content. It felt wrong to receive pleasure or orgasm. So, I would do my best not to. I would be the typical giver not receiver. I was going to hell for feeling tingly!

It would leave me feeling tainted. Sex is seen as a weakness of the flesh. In the eyes of the church, women are either The Virgin Mary or a whore. The perfect and ideal mother or the slut. This upbringing bred shame. I know now of course that it's in our nature to be sensual and sexual. It's been a long, healing journey, given these beliefs were instilled upon me at a young age when I was malleable and susceptible.

Then came the judgement of religious organisations and structures. I have memories of being at Hillsong. It isn't catholic but contemporary Christian. I remember watching all the people crowded into a stadium mesmerised by the songs played and the words the pastors preached. It made me feel like I was part of something bigger. I have memories of being shamed at church because I didn't attend regularly and know every single word to Our Mother Mary.

I turned my back on religion. In fact, in my final years of high school I secretly changed my form from Catholic to Agnostic so I could use scripture class time to do my homework or read a book. That was until my dad found out. He was disappointed in me. I felt so bad. Through experiences like this, I came to believe that God is judgemental. He set the standards for what was good and bad. He was the gatekeeper who decided if you'd live eternally in the paradise that was heaven or descend to the fiery pits of hell with the devil. I felt pressured to be a good Catholic girl. Catholicism and the impossibly high standards felt out of date and irrelevant. Knowing Bible verses by heart, dressing with modesty, helping everyone before yourself, spending time with Christ in prayer and being pure felt tedious.

THE UNLEARNING
Being human is a spiritual practice and experience.

I never found God in church. I found God in my own spirituality. Through connecting to my soul and focusing on my personal development, I have a deeper connection with God than ever before because to me God is the universe, source, spirit and intelligence. God is no longer a judgemental white man in the sky. God is an all-encompassing force: love. God is everywhere, infinite and omnipresent. God is no longer something outside of you. God exists within you. God is no longer the almighty power at the top of the chain. God is a state of oneness, of unity. Religion shouldn't be about doing certain things and being perfect in order to enter a special club when you die. It shouldn't be about waiting to go to heaven. We are here to create heaven on earth. It shouldn't be about waiting for paradise. We are here to create and live in paradise.

Spirituality has been my medicine because it's so deeply personal. True spirituality isn't picture perfect enlightenment and transcendence. It's not up in the sky or in another dimension beyond that of which we live in now. It's being human. Being human is messy and complicated. It's an exquisite, pleasure-filled ride on a rollercoaster. Spirituality is grounded. It's grass roots. It's not about escaping your life to exist above it in the clouds. It isn't above being human, it's grounded in the fact that you *are* human. True spirituality isn't about thinking you're better than others or that you're more 'spiritual'—that's your ego in a sly disguise. Spirituality is recognising we all come from one source: the same energy. Divinity. Love. Everything is interconnected, from you to another human to a rock, tree or the sea. The difference is the channel.

Be aware that spirituality has been pushed as an all-encompassing label and identity—yoga, clean-eating, meditation, outer body experiences, plant medicine, rituals and the list goes on. The irony here is that spirituality become its own form of 'religion' with these structures and rules.

As you read this, know that your soul chose to have a human experience at this very time right now on Earth. So, be here and experience it in your body. That's not always easy. It's been said that our body is a temporary vehicle, a meat suit, for our soul and while this may be true, it doesn't take away from the body. The body is part of the spiritual experience and practice. It's about being in the present moment. That is done in your body!

Contrary to religion, following your desires is not sinful, it's the will of the universe. One of the most inspiring archetypes for me is Lilith, the original woman. She has been vilified and depicted as evil, demonic, sinful and ugly. She is far from that! She was Adam's first wife (yes, Adam [the first man] and Eve in the Garden of Eden). She has been eradicated from history because she was a badass woman. She didn't subscribe to the masculine narrative of society and its powers at large. Lilith refused to be subservient to Adam's sexual dominance. After all, they were created to be equal. She is the embodiment of female empowerment and independence. Reclaiming the Lilith within us is vital to our journey home, to wholeness.

We are in the time of the divine feminine. So many women, myself included, have thought they were exuding 'feminine' energy when really, it is masculine energy. Pushing. Forcing. Hustling. Controlling. It is how society engrains us to be successful. I noticed that whilst this masculine energy led me to quickly climb the corporate ladder, it also dimmed my dating life. There was no polarity. It felt like I needed to chase men instead of being chased, cherished, claimed and adored. As a society we are shifting and waking up. Men included. Men are tapping into their divine femininity and allowing themselves to soften, to feel and to express themselves. I've seen this firsthand in the amazing men I have the joy of coaching. As women, we should be proud to be women. Being a woman holds power. To be feminine is not weak. The feminine is strong. The feminine bleeds and survives. The feminine gives birth to new life.

The word 'whore' comes from the Hebrew 'hor', which means 'cave' and represents the darkness of the womb that we are all born from. The word whore is thrown around as a demeaning label for women. It's time we reclaim our power and bodies. Let's not be ashamed of our bodies. It's *your* body. It belongs to *you* and no one else. To be sensual and sexual is not sinful. It is in our natural wild nature. The untamed woman. *The woman who runs with wolves.* Let's not be ashamed of our periods but see the benefits and wisdom in our blood. Our body is a source of creation and life and has been twisted into something dirty or to profit from. To be a woman is to be multi-dimensional. You aren't just sensual or sexual. You're also smart. You're also caring. You're also beautiful.

A powerful goddess I have worked with is Isis. The Egyptian goddess of sensuality, reproduction, magic and wisdom. When working with divine feminine figures, I like to research and understand their journeys. I meditate and call upon them to channel their energy and healing. There's a reason society fears women. Our natural sensuality and sexual nature are so damn powerful.

Your touch is exquisite. Your desire is a turn on. Your beauty is ethereal. Men will wage wars and tear down cities over a woman. Men find it hard to focus around the presence of a magnetic and radiant woman. Pleasure is not evil, it is nourishing. It allows us to feel good in life. Pleasure isn't just sex either. Pleasure can be found in so many forms.

Realise that God/Universe/Source isn't found outside of you. It *is* you. You are royalty. You are divine. Act in accordance with this! You aren't at the mercy of the divine. You have free will. You are continually creating your life. Be devoted to yourself. You have the power. Don't fear it or run away from it. The physical world is simply a reflection of your inner world: your thoughts, beliefs and feelings. Take control of your path, don't leave it up to destiny or a deity. It all starts within you. It is all possible within you. Above all, let's not get caught up in being so spiritual that we become serious… life is also about having fun! Don't forget to play. Play is soul medicine and heart healing.

YOUR GREAT UNLEARNING

1. WORKING WITH THE DIVINE FEMININE

The divine feminine represents openness intuition, flow, expression and receptivity. We connect with her through the below:

- Create a sacred space such as an altar. Your altar may include flowers, candles, crystals and offerings (such as fruit, food and drinks) for certain goddesses you are working with.
- Track your period cycle and follow the moon cycle and how it may impact you.
- Research divine feminine figures throughout history and see who resonates. Some of my favourites are Lilith, Isis, Quan Yin, Green Tara, Mother Mary, Mary Magdalene, Hecate and Kali.
- Observe nature, it's seasons and patterns.
- Say a 'prayer' or 'invocation' to the divine feminine you'd like to connect with and ask for her assistance.
- The qualities of water are typically associated with the feminine, therefore you may access the divine feminine through it such as a swim in the ocean or a bath.
- Chant or recite mantras.
- Tarot/oracle card pulls.

2. RECONNECT WITH YOUR DIVINE FEMININE

Below are some ways to tap into your divine feminine energy:

- Be in flow.
- Kundalini Yoga.
- Cultivate nourishing rituals.
- Connect with your vagina. It could be through massage, using a wand or steam.

- Spend time with other women.
- Connect with your emotions and express them creatively such as through dance, song or art.
- Drop out of your mind and into your body.
- Play and pleasure.
- Sensuality.
- Spend time in nature. Walk barefoot on the earth, garden or swim.
- Honour your menstrual cycle. Give yourself space and rest. Try free bleeding on a towel or giving your blood back to the earth. Create your own 'red tent' where women used to gather during this time: a private, sacred sanctuary to retreat to.
- Live from your heart.

3. SPIRITUAL REFLECTION

The following prompts provide points of contemplation with regards to your spirituality.

- What does religion mean to you?
- What does spirituality mean to you?
- Do you resonate with God or another term?
- How can you honour the divine within you?
- Have you experienced the divine lately?
- What are you devoted to?
- How do you communicate with the divine?

TIME

THE LEARNING
*Time as we know it is what we see on the clock.
It's linear: past, present and future.*

Famous last words: There will be time.

I painfully reflect on my dad's life when it comes to time. It hurts my heart to know he saved all this money to one day go travelling around the world with my stepmum, yet he never got to. It hurts my heart that I thought I would have more time with him and so I let his instinctual judgement of my first boyfriend get in the way of our relationship. It hurts my heart that I chose to work instead of going on family holidays and spending time with him. I cry as I write this because even to this day, nine years later, it's still painful. Yet I know he is at peace with this. I am so grateful to be able to utilise my intuitive gifts to maintain a close connection with him beyond this physical world. Nevertheless, I often have a vision that the day I pass to the other side, my dad and I will go camping. We'll sit in our fold out chairs and watch the sun hit the water. I would do anything and give anything to have even a single minute with him.

When my dad died, so did a part of me. I completely changed. I became open in every facet of my life whether it was towards new things, people, places or experiences. When my dad died, I had a second chance at life. Through death I was reborn. I remember even telling my first ex-boyfriend that I was going backpacking solo around Europe, he was shocked. He had asked me to go on a trip to London when we finished high school and I had no interest in travel whatsoever back then (so funny given I've now travelled the world multiple times since that very trip).

As a society we are very concerned with time. We have timelines. We are obsessed with time management. We dread not having enough time. Time is too slow. Time is too fast. The supposed sweet spot and myth of the 'perfect timing'. Are we there yet? How long will this take? What's the wait time? What's the time? Real-time. It takes time. Time heals all. Be patient. How do I buy or get more time? It's not worth your time. Be on time. Past, present and future.

Most of us are so caught up in time, that we aren't *really* here. Time seems to slip through our fingers. When I was a teenager, time seemed to pass slowly. I wanted to grow up and become autonomous. Suddenly I was in my twenties and being thirty doesn't seem so 'old' anymore. Forties are the new thirties. We go from being told, 'I remember what it was like to be twenty-two' to being the one that says that. You go from drinking Vodka Cruisers to nursing a three-day hangover from hell after sharing a bottle of red wine. You go from being excited for a night out to the rush you get from a sparkling clean house. You go from avoiding kids like the plague to trying your best to conceive.

You'll feel like you're running out of time when you aren't consciously present in the moment. The present moment is eternity. It's the moments where you forget the time because you are so deeply involved in what's happening. It's those moments that make you forget to check your phone or the fact you even own one.

For me, there is nothing better than traveling. Especially when you are alone with no company to distract. Inhaling the crisp countryside air dotted with notes of freshly baked bread and bluebell woods in Abergavenny, Wales. The warm wind tumbling through my hair on the boat over to the majestic Benagil sea caves in the Algarve of Portugal. Gobbling down sticky morsels of kueh tapioca, washed down with steaming hot tieluohan tea in Singapore. Being amongst the tallest trees on Earth in Big Sur on the Californian coast.

In my daily life at home, being in the water helps me focus on the present. The silence being beneath the water, still, serene yet full of life. Floating stretched out like a star longing to return to the gulf of the galaxy someday. Water and I, we become one. Strong and soft.

Wild and free. My long strands of hair flow like a running river. My eyes, the sparkling sea and divine depths. My heart, beating to the rhythm of the rolling waves. My soul, the salt and swirl of the sea. My fingers, the turning tides and tumbling waves. My veins, rushing currents and vast horizons. My feet, dissolving into bubbles of foam and particles of ocean spray. It's in the sea, I find eternity.

But where are most people? The past or the future. I think we all have moments where we yearn and wish we could go back in time. Preferably with the wisdom and insight we have now. How fascinating it would be to visit past versions of yourself and those you love. To go back in time and tell your younger self that the heartbreak won't last forever and there's a reason why you didn't end up with that person. To go back in time and visit the ones we loved who are no longer here with us, to savour every moment with them and tell them how much we love them just one more time. To go back in time and tell your anxious self that everything will be okay, it all works out in the end. To go back in time and tell your depressed self that the sadness will not be forever and that better days are coming. Sure, visit memory lane but don't stay there. Memory lane is an endless graveyard. You'll go searching for answers in broken bones, rampant regrets and heavy hearts.

If you're not careful, the past will take you hostage. You'll carry it like a momento in your wallet and it will weigh you down. You'll linger in the mistakes of your mind. You'll watch as everyone else seems to have moved on except you. You'll torture yourself in the *'what ifs'*, *'could have beens'* and *'if onlys'*. You'll chase the feelings of the past. You'll try to recreate it here and now. You aren't who you used to be, you've inevitably changed. You don't have to be who you used to be. Know that you cannot hold onto the memories, they will fade. Life goes quickly and we cannot waste it reminiscing on what was.

I have a quote I saw on Instagram engrained in my mind, 'The past stays present until it's processed.' The life in front of you is way more important than the life behind you, keep moving forward. Think of the memories you will make and the people you will meet.

The future is seductive. It's funny how our minds behave as if they are fortune tellers. They apparently know with one hundred percent certainty, exactly what will happen… Don't fall into the trap of constantly looking to the future, it's an illusion. If you're in the illusion of the future, you may be holding out hope and waiting for the perfect moment. You'll get caught up in what happens tomorrow, or even the next hour or minute. You'll put your life on hold or miss it as it rushes by you. If you forget to be here in this present moment, you'll forget that at one point, this is exactly where you wanted to be. Right now, you're in the middle, the present moment. The beautiful bridge between past and future that you had been hoping for and looking forward to. Don't forget it's all about the journey, not the destination. Don't lose sight of that.

Here's the thing. There are feelings and experiences you're yet to have, beyond what your mind can comprehend. It gets better in ways that you can't even imagine yet. Open up to the present and all its possibilities. The present moment is the only true moment where anything can happen. You're not struggling with the past and your past. You're struggling with your mind because it's clinging onto memories and wondering what they mean. The past is dead and gone but you're desperately trying to resuscitate it. What you think, do, say and feel today will be your future thoughts, feelings, actions and results. The way to change the future is by what you are doing today. Time will continue on no matter what.

THE UNLEARNING
Time is an illusion and a human construct.

Spiritually, time is happening simultaneously, past, present and future. Time is infinite. It isn't linear or circular. It is shapeless. It just is. It's happening.

Our thoughts are a tool for our mind to direct itself in the direction of either the past, present or future. When you live in your head, you're trapped. You're busy planning life instead of living it. The truth is when you are truly in the present you aren't focused on thought. You become one with the moment. In this state there is a beautiful and profound peace with an energetic quality representing what it feels like to be truly alive. You feel connected with life itself and in turn everything and everyone around you.

I used to think that money was the most important currency. Money comes and goes; you can always make more. But time? No. Time cannot be refunded or exchanged. It doesn't matter if you're a billionaire. It doesn't matter if you're a celebrity. No one can buy more time. Perhaps money will give you access to a better quality of life and a longer life, but we all know that isn't a sure thing. That's the lottery of life. Accidents happen. Illnesses happen. Therefore, your presence is a present.

Buddhist practitioner Jack Kornfield says each morning you are born again but I like to say, each moment you are born again. Think of the value of a moment. Anything can happen in a moment, if you choose to change or let life change you. You can get on the plane. You can quit the job. You can tell that person you love them. You can say sorry. You can forgive that person. The potential of each moment is so potent and powerful.

It's also all about perspective. To someone, you're young and to another, you're old. There is comfort and privilege in getting older. You become wiser, you become more aware of what you want, and you know who you are. You've experienced pain and loss. You've taken things for granted and have a found a new way to approach life with less fear and regret. It's all relative anyway and, at the end of the day, it doesn't really matter what someone else thinks. What truly matters is what you do with your time, here and now in the present moment. Use your time wisely and intentionally with all your heart. And just maybe if you're one of the lucky ones, you'll get another shot, chance or opportunity in life—but it isn't guaranteed. So, what are you going to do with your time?

With regards to times in our life, it isn't a pick and mix. You have to take it all. The 'good' and the 'bad'. The highs and the lows. A dance between dualities. You cannot just have what you want without experiencing what you don't want as well. Duality is always at play.

To experience soul fulfilling love, you will also have to experience crushing heartbreak. To be rich with abundance, you will also have to experience scarcity. To become big, you will also have to feel small. To grow, you will also have to experience pain. To live your dream life, you will also have to experience the dark nights of the soul. To truly live, you will also have to know that death is nearby. For without duality, we wouldn't understand the value of a moment and experience. For without duality, we wouldn't understand the contrast of a moment compared to an experience.

Sometimes we wait for the things we want. The right opportunity to show up. The right person to show up. The right timing to show up. Here's the thing, life isn't about waiting. You don't have to wait to be in a relationship to feel love. You don't have to have lots of money to feel abundant. You don't have to be at the top of the career ladder to feel successful. You don't have to have it all to be grateful. Realise that the motivation underlying all our desires, is because we want to *feel* a certain way. Figure out that feeling and you can find a way to tap into it now because if you're waiting, you're not living. We never know the true value of a moment until it's gone…

I know you're sick of being in limbo, sick of not knowing, sick of feeling unsure and wondering what's next or waiting for a sign from the universe. Hear me out, even if you knew the details of every timeline, what meaning would life have? Life would cease to be the amazing miracle that it is. Life is full of infinite possibilities, unlimited potentialities, the joy and spark of wonder. To know exactly what will happen and when would make life so boring. What would inspire your growth? What would inspire you to seek different? What would life be? Isn't life so beautiful because of its secrets and mysteries? We cannot push, force or rush life.

At the end of the day, there is no better place than where you are right now. There are times we have to let down our guard and allow ourselves to fully surrender to the present moment. Sure, you can be frustrated by the timing, but you could also let the time in-between act as a catalyst for growth. After all, when we're born, we're in the present. There is no past, only what is unfolding right before your eyes. As we get older, we learn about dimensions of time beyond the present. We remember our past. We hope and plan for the future. We lose sight of our true selves until we return home into the here and now. We don't find our true self in the dreams we yearn for or the fantasy of tomorrow or the memory of yesterday.

Whatever the time it is, I hope you find inner peace. I hope you are kind and compassionate to yourself. I hope that you forgive yourself for the mistakes that you made. I hope you forgive yourself for doing what you needed to in order to survive. I hope you release yourself from the binds of replaying a situation or moment. I hope you release the shame and shadows that haunt your mind. I hope you're proud of yourself for being here right now and reading this. I hope you make the most of every moment and try to be the best you can. I hope you are here with your full consciousness. I hope you are here not half-heartedly but whole heartedly. Whilst you can't turn back time or change the past or start everything over, what you can do is begin *now*. Here in the present moment. Create a new ending… your ending.

YOUR GREAT UNLEARNING

1. HERE AND NOW

The following prompts are here to help you be grounding in the present moment and live life now:

- If you only had one year to live, what would you want to do?
- How could you incorporate aspects of the above into your daily life?
- What are you waiting for in life?
- Instead of waiting, how can you incorporate aspects of it right now into your life?

2. LET GO OF THE PAST

If you feel stuck, some rituals can help release you. Some examples:

- The full moon represents a time to let go. Every full moon make it a conscious practice to release the past in some form.
- Cleaning. Get rid of what no longer aligns with or serves your highest self.
- Write down all your past mistakes, regrets and what has a hold on you. Then dispose of it—you can rip it up or burn it as examples.
- Light a candle. Say out loud everything you would like to release and let go of. When you're done blow out the candle.
- Immerse yourself in water and really feel into 'washing' everything away.

3. RETURN TO THE PRESENT MOMENT

A list of things you can do to help you return to the present moment:

- Ask yourself, where am I? Past, present or future?
- Focus on your breathing, one breath at a time. Take deep breaths into your stomach.
- Pinch your thumbs.
- Focus on your surroundings—tune into your senses.
- Move slower.
- Be amongst nature.
- Meditate.
- Become aware of your body.
- Move your body.
- Yoga.
- Journal.
- Go for a walk.
- Do one thing at a time.
- Get off your phone.
- Bring your attention to the soles of your feet.

SPIRITUAL BREAKTHROUGHS

THE LEARNING
Spiritual breakthroughs are sudden epiphanies after dedicated practice and learning.

Many of us have preconceived notions of what spirituality looks like and who we have to be in order to be 'spiritual.' Spirituality isn't just 11:11 and morning matcha routines nor is it just meditating and being on a vegan diet. You are not less spiritual because you enjoy the finer things in life. You are not less spiritual because you sleep around. You are not less spiritual because you care about your appearance. Spirituality isn't a trend or religion. It's not a dichotomy, it's a duality.

Everyone involved in the mainstream spirituality is chasing a breakthrough. A quantum leap. Enlightenment. We want everything to happen quickly. We want everything to happen in a big life changing way. We want to rid ourselves of suffering. We want to heal and grow. We want the magic pill that will do exactly what we need it to do. We look for it in a person, a course, a process and a technique. No one can save you from your own work. No one can save you from your own healing. It's never anyone else's job but yours.

Often breakdowns lead to breakthroughs. That doesn't make it easy nor does it feel fair. That is life in itself. It's not 'good' or 'bad,' nor is it 'fair' or 'unfair' because it just is. What would life be without change? The same. Stagnant. Boring. It's only natural that when you evolve, your life will too. You'll experience the ebbs and flows, the highs and lows. When life falls apart, know that the future is coming… so enjoy the ride and know that one day you'll look back knowing that everything wasn't falling apart but falling *together*.

My first spiritual breakthrough happened on the floor after my dad died. I think it had been three weeks since I had seen anyone. I barely moved. I was depressed. I had no will to live. I remember my skin was pale, ghostly, almost translucent. I had withered away. After marinating alone in darkness, sick of myself, I finally gave way. The light had suddenly appeared through a shift in my thoughts, although deep down it always was there. What was I doing on the floor? Was I really going to do this for the rest of my life? Was I going to go out like this knowing that there are people out there literally dying to live. That light was a result of realising I had to stop being a victim of life and take back my power. Whilst I couldn't change what had happened, I could change the way I approached and lived life inspired by my dad. It was this experience that set in the motion the life that I now lead and live today.

Since then, the majority of my biggest breakthroughs have been through the support of my own coaches holding space for me. My own personal cheerleader who is willing to listen with love and caring intention. You can only go so far on your own. After all, I am a life coach myself and truly believe in the power of mentorship and an objective presence. As you've read throughout the book, I put up with being bullied by one particular boss over a span of years. I never received an apology from her, nor did I need to in order to find closure. In processing it all, I came to the realisation that *hurt people, hurt people.* Yet despite that, I was still deeply traumatised and upset. I *knew* spiritually I should forgive her and wanted to for myself, but I struggled too.

It is only recently that I've been able to do so when one of my coaches, Charlotte, offered a different perspective: 'What if you knew in a past life, her soul made a contract with yours to ensure your highest growth and expansion. In order to do that, she did what she did, from a place of so much love for you, that she was even willing to sacrifice your relationship to keep that promise in this lifetime…' Wow. I was speechless because I'd never thought about it that way.

My coach offered a reframe which enabled me to feel genuine gratitude and compassion for this boss despite everything. I have no desire to communicate with that boss ever again however I am thankful because dealing with her truly changed my life in multiple ways. The mental health battles I endured under her management were a driving force of my passion for mental health that led to me starting my Instagram page. This woke me up to my life's purpose, to help people and ultimately fulfil a lifelong dream, writing this very book.

Human design also reaffirmed to me that difficulties serve a greater purpose in life. Through it, you can find your life's purpose through what is known as your 'incarnation cross', composed of four major energetic themes you'll experience in your life. Further to that there are 'energetic channels' which serve as significant sub plots. I have the 'channel of struggle', which speaks for itself. The breakdowns which have turned to breakthroughs have given my life meaning because they are the foundation of this book you are reading. The pain you go through isn't for nothing, it can one day help others whether you work with people for a living or not.

What you can take out of this all, is that if you're seeking spiritual breakthroughs, you can expect a clearing to make space for new growth. When you ask the universe to go to the next level, don't be surprised if people leave your life and tell you that you've changed (like that's a bad thing! It's in your nature to evolve and transform, not to stay the same). When you ask the universe to go to the next level, don't be surprised when it feels like your heart is bursting open at the seams and your soul is shaking.

You'll experience the rise of emotions you've hidden or repressed, and they'll leave you trembling and questioning everything. During this time, you are collapsing old stories and stepping into your power. When you ask the universe to go to the next level, don't be surprised when it feels like life is too hard, almost unbearable at times. Your strength resides deep within you, even when it doesn't feel like it. The universe would never give you anything you couldn't handle. Life is tough but so are you.

THE UNLEARNING

Your biggest spiritual breakthroughs won't be found on a yoga mat or in meditation. You'll find them through the greatest spiritual practice of all: your life.

It's likely that your spiritual breakthroughs will involve healing. When it comes to healing, repeat after me: You cannot heal what is not revealed. You cannot heal if you do not feel. You cannot heal what is not revealed. The starting point for a spiritual breakthrough will always be awareness. If you don't know, how can you change it? (This applies to other people too!) Consciousness and intention are the keys to personal growth and self-development. It's not just about mental awareness either, it's also about emotional intelligence and embodiment. The body is the wisest inbuilt navigation system—the secret is to listen to the subtle whispers instead of the screaming and shouting when you aren't.

In fact, you have to be willing to feel it all. You have to be willing and open to being triggered and in turn awakened and *activated*. You have to be willing to be lonely, as your vibration rises and what is no longer an energetic match falls away. You have to be willing to take responsibility. You have to be willing to get out of your comfort zone, into the abyss of the uncertain and uncomfortable. It's not for the faint hearted, it's for those who are ready to fly.

After my dad died, I made a conscious decision to be brave and to live from my heart because I realised my mind caused me so much pain. As a result, one of the biggest spiritual breakthroughs I had was listening to my gut and following my heart. Whilst it led me to an incredible life better than I ever dreamed of, it wasn't easy—in fact, it often results in difficult decisions that appear illogical or even break your heart first to achieve the breakthrough.

Often a spiritual journey is downright ugly. It involves confronting the parts of yourself that you're ashamed and afraid of. It involves calling yourself out on your own bullshit. It involves having a puffy face from all the tears you've shed. It involves questioning yourself and your decisions. It involves making peace with a past you're not proud of and would rather forget. It involves doing the things you've been putting off. It involves knocking down the walls you built to protect yourself. It involves secrets that bubble up and resurface. It involves opening the skeleton-filled closet. It involves going headfirst into the dark. You will be stripped down, raw and vulnerable. But you wouldn't have it any other way.

At times, it will feel uncomfortable and unpredictable. Life has its own seasons, some mean growth like Spring or rest and integration like Winter. The next level isn't meant to be easy and paved with positivity. New level, new *devil*. You have to deal with things that others don't want to. You have to ask questions that others don't dare to. You have to pay attention to the niggling of your soul deep down that others ignore. It may feel like you're alone on a rocky road—but you're not. At the very least, know you have a whole team on the other side supporting you, your higher spiritual council.

Being in-between changes can be painful and make us feel strange. It feels like you're a butterfly in the cocoon aching to break free, yet you're not quite there. You know that you love who you are now and who you are becoming but you also process the fact that you needed to go through great pain and heartache to become this person. Who you are becoming also means letting go of things and people that used to mean so much to you. You'll never be the same, you've changed an extraordinary amount for the better but deep down there's a part of you that might mourn how you used to be. Change isn't comfortable. It's the duality of life, the dance between breaking down and breaking through.

We've established that the greatest growth and spiritual breakthroughs come from change. So why do you only want change if it's on your terms? That is not how change works. Change pushes you to expand. The circumstances of life and the universe will show you what is happening. Some doors are closed to redirect you. A door to another path will open and show you another way of doing things. Rejection is protection. You cannot control the pace of change. It just happens and is inevitable, so you might as well embrace it because you'll emerge stronger, wiser and smarter than before.

All in all, maybe it's the mishaps, mistakes and melancholy that lead to the most beautiful and unexpected spiritual breakthroughs. Growth isn't always about the gains. It's also about the losses. Like losing the weight of others' opinions, your appetite for ego, your old self, the past and your mistakes, pleasing others, relationships that have run their course, self-criticism, self-sabotage, and your fixed mindset. This is what *The Great Unlearning* is all about.

YOUR GREAT UNLEARNING

1. CONNECTING WITH YOUR HEART

Many people have asked me how to connect with their heart. Here are some ways:

- Approach it like learning a new language—it will take time and repeated practice.
- Put your hand on your heart. Feel the natural beat of your heart.
- Quiet your mind.
- Ask yourself, if no one was to judge me, if there were no rules, what would I want?
- Connect to the feeling of love and ask yourself, what would love do?
- Close your eyes and meditate. Bring your attention to your heart, you may want to visualise the colour green (heart chakra). Silently repeat the words, 'Heart, you are safe with me.' And, 'It is safe to open up, what do you want to tell me, heart?'
- Reflect and journal on what makes your heart beat faster and swoon.

2. EGO INTEGRATION

Write a list of what you think the worst qualities of humans are. Once you've done that, ask yourself how you exhibit the quality, because we all do. Our ego convinces us that we are different, when really, we are all one and from the same.

3. SPIRITUAL BREAKTHROUGH REFLECTION QUESTIONS

Take a moment to pause and reflect. What insights have you drawn from life?

- Am I consciously creating my life?
- What do I want to change in my life?
- Where in my life am I in victim mode?
- How can I step more into my power?
- What is in my control? What is not in my control?
- Where do I need to surrender more in my life?
- What excuses do I use?
- What is something I can do right now to move closer to my desires and dreams?
- How am I feeling right now? How is my heart and soul?
- How do I define my highest and best self?
- Who am I right now in this moment of time?

GOTTA SEE IT TO BELIEVE IT

THE LEARNING
You have to see it to believe it.

Let's talk about the F word. No not that one. I'm talking the spiritually scary and ego crushing… FAITH! We live in a world where facts are pitted against faith. We are a society that demands evidence and validity (though I don't think it's either science or spirit—I believe the two co-exist and do not cancel each other out). We long for logic, laws and materiality. Through this lens, manifestations and miracles seem to be wishful thinking on steroids. We have become the greatest sceptics but, hey, it was not that long ago we thought the world was flat and that we were the only existence of life in this universe.

Though I understand why we want concrete proof, I find the concept sad. This way of thinking has drained the magic and mystery out of life. Do you remember being a kid with a wild imagination? Anything was possible. Nothing was out of the question.

There is a whole dimension that operates beyond the visible eye. You may be doubtful, I used to be too until I experienced it firsthand. I believe that the universe sends us love letters. Have no fear because you can't miss messages from the universe. The messages will become louder until you cannot ignore them.

Whenever I talk about signs and synchronicity this expression never fails me: 'You can't make this shit up. Seriously.' I share the following stories to show you how I had my logical beliefs suspended and trusted in the magic of the universe. The universe is always communicating with us, but it doesn't use words. The universe speaks through energy, vibrations and signs. It transmits through intuition, soul and body.

When my dad was battling his aggressive cancer, I would see him meditate frequently. He would go on to tell me that he believed you could see past lives through meditation and that he'd receive messages from one of his deceased aunts in his dreams. This was before I had my spiritual awakening (cruelly and ironically through his death). This surprised me as I never knew my dad had this spiritual side to him, I considered him to be a stoic intellectual with Catholic values. I honestly thought his tumour had gotten to him and he was delusional.

In the aftermath of my dad's passing strange coincidences occurred. Whilst he no longer lay in the bed at his hospice, visiting the room after it happened, I felt a warm radiant energy around me. I knew it was him and from there I would come to associate birds, butterflies and frogs as signs from him. Funnily enough, I would indeed go onto glimpse one of my past lives where I was burnt alive on the stake. Knowing I had been a witch in a past life explains fears around being seen or tapping into my intuitive gifts initially. From that moment two years ago, when I was twenty-six, these gifts have come more to light. I received validation of my gifts when I would get messages for people I just met and somehow knew very intimate details of their life. I had always believed you had to be born 'psychic' but that's not true. Everyone is naturally intuitive for themselves at the very least. You can tap in at any stage in your life, including right now! All you need to be is open to your gifts and practice.

One of the greatest experiences I had was on the eighth anniversary of my dad's passing. I walked back home from the beach with my ex and stopped in my tracks. I couldn't believe what I saw: a framed print of the ocean. My ex didn't understand my commotion. I had a photo of that very print on my vision board when I was fourteen years old. Back then I didn't have the money to buy this limited-edition print. Now, here it was ready for the taking, it felt like a gift from him.

When my ex decided to leave Australia, I put out to the universe my desire for help and support in finding my next place. Oh, boy, did the universe deliver my manifestation! I enquired about four potential places but only one agent got back to me. He said I could view the property that morning. Before inspecting, I asked the universe to show me a sign if this place was to be mine. The location of my new home is on the beachfront of one of Australia's most busiest and iconic beaches. Parking is notoriously painful and gives me so much anxiety that I leave half an hour early to allow time to find a spot.

When I arrived, I got a park right outside. No problems at all. That was a miracle in itself. My phone stated I had arrived at 10:30am but mysteriously my car gifted to me by my stepmum and dad said it was 11:11am. Yes, the angel number for alignment! I should also mention the fact that this number was also on the ticket in line to finalise the official paperwork finalising the separation between my ex and I, given we were legally de facto for Visa purposes.

As soon as I walked in, I knew this place would be my home. Do you want to know what the icing on the cake was? One of my neighbours regularly parks their car in front of mine and the numberplate has 'DZU' in it. My dad's name was Dzung. The funny thing is, we don't have permanent car spots given where we live, however this very car without a doubt will always reappear with uncanny timing, such as on Father's Day or the day my grandpa passed away. Not only that, my home is on the street of an apartment I so badly wanted when I was younger but missed out due to a delayed promotion. Now here I am on this very street except it's better because my current home is closer to the beach (110 metres directly across the road!). Once I moved in, I had a new client and guess what her father's name was? Dzung (what are the chances!?). Truly, I feel like my home had chosen me.

Later in the month I did a human design reading for a beautiful soul named Donna. Donna found me through the explore page of Instagram and figured out that we had been neighbours in my old apartment complex! Although I never saw her while we lived in the same building, it was so surreal to be recognised in public. As soon as we jumped onto Zoom for the meeting, my jaw dropped.

Donna was living in my old apartment! How divine! I had found out that her apartment, number five, was getting sold and she saw that number four was available to rent. Funnily enough, my new home is number five. We connected the dots and realised my apartment was divinely available, thanks to the timing of my ex leaving the country, at the very moment Donna needed to find a new place to live. As you may recall from previous chapters, I was upset he didn't give me much notice but it worked out for the best for both Donna and I! Ultimately, we crossed paths due to break ups, her moving into my old apartment complex in the aftermath of one and me moving out because of one.

I believe the Universe orchestrates events like these and it feels like magic—it defies your beliefs by what you see and experience in reality. I am so proud that I have also been able to facilitate signs on behalf of the universe with clients. It could be mentioning a sign for them or being able to pick up certain things that they're going through that no one else knows. One of the wildest times was on a weekend away for my friend Juju's birthday. On the trip, we find out that my roommate's ex-boyfriend's mother had passed away. That evening, whilst going to the bathroom through my third eye, I could see a woman singing and twirling in front of me. She told me to tell my roommate that she's okay and already thriving on the other side (she passed away very ill). I passed on the message and found out her ex's mother was an entertainer and dancer for a living!

The reason I prefer to use the word faith is because 'trust' can feel icky and resistant. Faith feels like ease. Faith feels smooth. I mean we've all lost our way at some point. We ought to have faith that everything is happening for a reason. It may feel as if the universe just keeps testing you, over and over again. Maybe it feels like you keep flunking the tests. Maybe it feels like your time will never come. Maybe it feels like you've been pushed past your limits. We fall into this role of the victim. It feels like the universe is punishing us or making life hard for fun. Perhaps the universe is giving us an opportunity to show who we really are so we evolve beyond our comforts.

The difficulty in surrendering to faith is also a matter of fear. It creeps up in many different ways. Fear that you've been abandoned. Fear that hard work doesn't pay off. Fear that there isn't enough money, time, love and opportunity to go around. Fear is seductive, it makes us want to control everything. We believe that the more we can control, the safer we are. Fear isn't the way though… fear is '**f**alse **e**vidence **a**ppearing **r**eal.' Having faith and surrendering are the two solutions. Faith allows us to receive love and support from the universe. Faith knows we aren't alone in this adventure, we have a co-pilot in the form of the universe. It's not all on you. There is something beyond you, an infinite life force that supports you every step of the way.

THE UNLEARNING
You have to believe it, to see it.

Manifestations and miracles do exist. They don't operate in the world of logic; they operate in the world of energetic magic. We live in a world of potent possibilities. Just because you can't see it, doesn't mean it's not happening. It's coming, it's just around the corner. You don't need to wish or hope… it's already done. You are powerful, you are a co-creator with the universe. All you have to do is be an energetic match with what you desire. It all starts with you. Once you are in alignment, the universe conspires to make it happen.

So, what is faith? Faith is the evidence and existence of things not seen. Faith is trusting what you feel, not what you see. Faith is to believe in magic, not factual evidence. Faith is not understanding but knowing. Faith is the whispers of your soul, not mind chatter. Faith is the tug of your heart, not the demands of your mind. Faith is the force of your inner light, not your thought loops. Faith is surrendering to miracles, not logic. Faith is conscious and considered, not blind. Faith is a choice not everyone will understand but your heart and soul will. Faith is using our other 'senses' such gut feelings (they're guardian angels!) and your intuition. Even Einstein himself says, '*The most beautiful thing we can experience is the mysterious.*'

One of the most common questions I get asked is how do I know if it's my intuition or not? From my experience, the more illogical and irrational it is, the more likely it is to be your intuition. Intuition doesn't operate by human rules, nor is it restricted by logical thinking. Intuition is nuanced and subtle. It won't always scream at you; at times it may whisper. It's an underlying foundation beneath it all, a resonance of knowing. Intuition is a feeling. At times it is a word or an image. Why should you put your faith in your intuition? Well, you were born with it. Your intuition is the incredible GPS system built within you. Your intuition is always right. If you let the judgement and fears of others in, you will doubt yourself. No one, and I truly mean *no one*, knows you better than yourself. Not even a psychic or a coach. There is no need to second guess yourself, you've got to tap into your body and flex your faith. After all, natural instincts and intuition have led humans to evolve into what we are today. Your intuition is like a muscle, it can be honed. The more you use it, the more it will develop and strengthen.

Faith is also very much like fear. They both require trust and apply to the theory of believing in something you can't see. What you choose to opt into is your choice. To act in faith is to let go of the how and just allow. You don't need to understand the details of how it works. You trust electricity without knowing all the details. You just flick the switch and know it will work. So have faith. Have faith it will all work out. What's meant to be will be. Even if it looks or feels like it won't. Even when you think everything is going wrong. Even when you feel discouraged and want to give up.

Relying on faith can be overwhelming. At times you'll need a moment to take it all in. You can't mess it up. It's yours. All you have to do is believe in the process and continue your journey. It might take a day, maybe a year but what is meant for you will always find its way to you. The waiting, the gap, the in between, the changes, the transitions, the meantime... they all serve a necessary purpose. Even delays and detours are part of it. You will arrive at the perfect time, as the exact person you need to be, ready. Eventually everything will work out. It always does. Take a deep breath in and let go. Hold your power and vision. Everything will fall into place. You don't have to worry about anything. Have faith.

'What if nothing works out the way I want, Phi?' The universe doesn't want you to try harder, it wants you to have more faith. The universe is always here for you, working 24/7, 365 days a week. You were not born to suffer. A part of life is pain, yes. A part of life is going through the high highs, the low lows and everything in-between. Loss, heartbreak and disappointment are part of life. But suffering? No. Suffering is a mental narrative you create and opt into. You can choose to transmute this into power. Choose to see that while you're creating suffering, you can also create abundance. You can create liberation. You can create and choose joy. It's not the outside world that creates these feelings, it's you. You have the power. Your reality reflects your inner world.

There will be times where you feel lost and that's okay. The path isn't always clear. At times the path may be hidden or full of twists and turns. It's okay to change your mind. It's okay to be scared. What matters is that you know that whichever way you go, all will be okay. There's no such thing as a 'right' or 'wrong' decision, it's just a decision. The universe will adapt with whatever you choose. Think about how proud your future self will be of you for continuing the journey despite the pain, fear and confusion you experienced along the way. Sometimes all you need is perspective. Zoom out a little and see all the progress you've made and will continue to make.

Sometimes things end without explanation. They haunt you and leave you searching for answers and overanalysing everything instead. You may never find the closure you desire or deserve, no matter how hard you try. And that's okay. Nothing is taken from you without something being given back… something bigger and better than you could have ever imagined. Endings are beautiful. They open you up to greater growth, greater adventure and greater love. Endings make way for new beginnings, if you let them…

All the obstacles and challenges you face are gifts from the universe. They don't feel that way at the time, but they are. The universe will never give you anything you can't handle. In fact, the toughest challenges are reserved for the strongest of souls. Life itself is a gift that we are given, and the universe truly loves to spoil us. How does it feel to willingly allow the gifts that life presents you? How does it feel to embrace what you are given instead of complaining about what is missing? Are you the spoiled brat at the party or are you the grateful one? I mean, who doesn't enjoy gifts? Learn to receive things with open arms and the gifts will come flooding in.

The universe is so incredibly loving, it wants you to succeed and be your highest self. The universe wants you to be your highest self. The universe wants you to have everything you've ever dreamed about. The universe wants you to feel joy. In order to have it all, the universe has to challenge you. At times the universe will break your heart open so you can receive. At times you'll be pushed off the cliff to teach you that you can fly. No matter what, you'll always end up back on the path you're meant to be on. The universe is fighting for you to manifest and live out your highest destiny. The universe wants you to have every single thing you desire.

While the universe wants you to have it all, it wants you to have it as your best, most loving, highest and aligned self. The universe knows what it's doing. It has meticulously planned everything out and, yes, you still have free will. Life has been perfectly engineered. The plan is so detailed, all variances are accounted for.

The way I like to explain energetics and your relationship with the universe is through a dating analogy. How's your relationship with life and the universe going? Are you clingy and desperate? Are you always questioning things? Doubting things? Do you have a hard time relaxing and going with the flow? Are you being overbearing and suspicious? Are you guarded and have a hard time letting love in? Are you bringing up your baggage or are you having fun? Feel secure in yourself and everything that is happening. Make love every day. Commit through the good and bad. Be forgiving, understanding, patient, kind, loving and appreciative.

Isn't life such a beautifully wild adventure!? How the strings of fate and free will dance. Everything has led you to this moment, right here and now. The aphrodisiac of knowing anything is possible. What is unfolding behind the veil? Magic. Bliss. Your return and journey home, to your true nature, of heart and soul. Never forget, you are a child of the universe. Not just a child but you actually *are* the universe. Yep, just being you, you are the universe.

What I mean by 'universe' is you. You are the universe experiencing itself through a human body. You are the mountains and lakes. You are the sun and stars. You are the wind and the waves. You are the one calling the shots. How does it feel to surrender to your highest self? To know that nothing is by chance? Every single thing that happens and every single thing you do is part of a bigger picture. What you do has ripple effects. You are part of something bigger than you consciously know. In fact, your soul chose this very journey that you are having. This is your soul's curriculum in the school of life.

Everything happens for a reason. If my dad hadn't died, I would probably be a miserable lawyer right now and not a life coach. If I got the promotion in my corporate job, I would probably still be at my old company today. If I had continued the situationship I was in, I would have never been in a relationship with my ex who I met shortly after that. Everything will make sense when you eventually arrive at your destination. You just have to allow the process and have faith.

YOUR GREAT UNLEARNING

1. LOVE LETTERS FROM THE UNIVERSE

Here are some prompts that give me comfort that the Universe has my back. I like to read through them and reflect about how the below instances have been true.

I had to otherwise because you wouldn't have. - xo The Universe

I know it hurt but I did it for you. - xo The Universe

I did it because you deserve better. - xo The Universe

I promise it will all make sense one day. - xo The Universe

Trust me. - xo The Universe

I did it because I know you can handle it. - xo The Universe

Something better is on its way! - xo The Universe

I had to make you uncomfortable so you would move, change, learn, expand and grow. - xo The Universe

If it's meant to be, I will make it happen. You don't have to worry. - xo The Universe

I got this. - xo The Universe

I did it because I knew it was too hard for you to do on your own. - xo The Universe

---

2. INTUITIVE GIFTS

The media has conditioned us to believe that only certain special people are 'psychics' when in actual fact everyone is. Further to that, you've only got spiritual gifts if you can 'see' things (insert woman wielding crystal ball image). Seeing is one of many psychic gifts known as clairvoyance.

Here is a list of psychic senses and a simple practice you can do to strengthen it. Everyone has each sense however make note you may be drawn to one more than the other.

- Clairvoyance: to see images or even a moving sequence as if it were a movie in your third eye or mind. Strengthen your clairvoyance through visualisation practices.
- Clairaudience: to hear messages or sounds in your mind. It could be a voice that says "don't go there" as an example. Strengthen your clairaudience through becoming more attuned to sound such as meditation and really focusing on what you can hear surrounding you.
- Clairsentience: to feel. It could be through sensations as tingles or the strong pull of your gut. Strengthen your

clairsentience by developing a strong connection with your body and actually listening to your body even when you're tired.
- Claircognizance: to know. Strengthen your claircognizance by shuffling a deck of cards and tapping into which card you think will emerge. You can start by only guessing the colour at first, then the suit, numbers and so forth.
- Clairalience: to smell. For example, at times I know my dad is around because I'll randomly smell cigarettes even though no one is smoking around me. To strengthen your clairalience, when reading a magazine look at particular images and conjure the smell. An example is food magazines with fruits.
- Clairgustance: to taste without anything even in your mouth. What's weird is you might not always taste a food it could even be a place or thing such as a tree. To strengthen your clairgustance, consume a variety of flavours and textures to broaden your palate. This gives your gift more 'flavour' information to draw from. When you're eating try guess the ingredients, such as the spices in a curry.
- Clairtangency: to physically touch something and receive a message as a result. For example, you could hug a friend and receive a message for them. To strengthen your clairtangency is to get touchy-feely. Notice the sensations and vibrations when you touch different objects. I like to play with this creatively by imagining if I were a certain object what would I say? What's my backstory, what have I witnessed and experienced?

Please note when connecting with the other side, first ensure you are grounded such as visualising a cord dropping from your body to the centre of the Earth. Proceed to set up energetic protection (such as through a white bubble of light and calling in your guardian angels). It's also best to set the intention before doing anything, that you only will only connect with spirits that have your best interests at heart and have unconditional love for you. After any connection (even using tools such as tarot cards) it's best to energetically cleanse (such as imagining a waterfall of light washing over you or physically having a shower with said intention).

3. BELIEVE IT TO SEE IT

As established in this chapter you have to believe first to see the signs from the Universe.

- Start with the desire to receive. Have an open mind. Declare out loud and in your mind to the universe: I am open and ready to see the signs and receive the messages.
- Ask for the signs, make them specific so that when you see it, you know it to be truth. Literally say, 'I want a sign.' Make it unique, such as a purple frog. You can also specify an ideal timeline knowing that the universe does not operate on our timeline but its own.
- Be aware and attentive of what is going on around you. Look for synchronicities and repetition of numbers, a song, words, something you continually see such as an animal, insect, colour, etc. Seeing angel numbers is the most common sign: repetitive numbers such as 111, 222, 333, etc. You can even ask for certain signs in a geographic location. A sudden wave of feelings or something unexpected happening. Delays or breakthroughs.
- Take note of your dreams. They are the fertile soil the universe communicates with you through. I recommend keeping a dream journal and writing down a dream as soon as you wake up before you forget.
- Other people can also be messengers. They may say something you need to hear or mention something you've been thinking about.
- Tune into your body and turn up the sensitivity. Take notes on your feelings. Take notes on your bodily reactions.

LIFE, DEATH AND BEYOND

THE LEARNING
We are all afraid to die.

Have you realised that every single day you are inching closer to death? You know you're going to die, so when are you truly going to start living? Strong opening lines, I know. To be afraid of death means being afraid of living. If you live in fear, you're not truly living. You've bubbled wrapped yourself so nothing can get in, not even the good stuff. Where is the zest in your life? Where is the spark and fire? You might be living, you clearly are if you're reading this, but are you **alive**? Do you feel your heart beating? Do you feel the rise and fall of your chest? Do you feel the potential of every and any given moment? Do you feel the yearning to taste more of what life has to offer? So why is it that you're waiting to live? Why do you wait for ill health to give you a reason to truly be alive? Why do you wait on death to take you, as if it should happen at some 'old' age or when you get sick? … Why do you wait?

Have you ever taken a moment to think about what a privilege it is to simply be alive? Have you taken a moment to think about what a privilege it is to be healthy? The opportunity to live is so great, it's beyond winning the lottery ticket. You have no idea how many entities, angels and other aspects of the divine desire to experience life as a human! It truly is a privilege and you're one of the lucky ones. The chances of you being born are 1 in 400,000,000,000,000—1 in 400 trillion. The odds of winning the lottery are 1 in 300,000,000—1 in 300 million. You truly are a living breathing miracle. The odds of being born in this lifetime are slim, yet here you are. Smell the flowers. Dance in the rain. Make mistakes. Take the leap of faith.

Have your heart broken. Eat the burger. Feel the pain. Start your own business. Get on the plane. Quit the job. Kiss the stranger. Tell them you love them. Be excited over the little things. Spend the money. Go on the date. Feel the fear and do it anyway. Make your dreams happen. Follow your heart. Life is so damn precious and so are you.

Oftentimes we think we are truly living when life is perfect. It's as if everything is going to plan, just as we wanted it to. Here's the thing, we don't just live in the good moments. Want to know when you're really alive? You are truly living when you're in the depths of despair. When your soul is crushed and lit up in flames. When the cold creeps in and cracks your bones. When the tears don't stop streaming down your face. When your heart thumps as if it will jump out of your chest. When the anxiety paralyses every inch of your body. When your blood feels like it's curdling within. When the darkness within seems like it will take over. It's when we truly break, that we are cracked open for the light to come in. Love. Light. That is what it means to truly live. To be truly alive.

Some days in life will be harder than others and that's okay. Some days will feel heavier than others and that's okay. Some days you'll be convinced that the pain and suffering you feel will last forever. It won't. Better days are coming, beautiful soul. They always do. It may take time, but it's always worth the wait. The light will trickle in. Your heart will mend piece by piece. You'll remember why you loved life so much in the first place. Remember rainbows hide behind stormy clouds. Your tears will nurture the flowers that blossom in the seams of your soul. You may look back to this time and think life had buried you, when really, you've been planted to bloom. You'll look back in awe of your strength and beam with pride. You'll look back and realise you wouldn't change a thing, because everything unfolded the way it was meant to, for your highest self.

We can become distrustful and weary of life because of the hurt we endured in our journey. Your pain and wounds need not be ugly. Our pain should not stop us. Our pain shouldn't make us want to give up life. Pain can be a portal to a deeper and more conscious form of living. Live for the moments you cannot put into words. Live for the kisses that will take your breath away. Live for the people you are yet to meet who will change your life. Live for the conversations that touch your heart and soul. Live for the day you look in the mirror and fall in love. Live for the moment when you discover and understand why you are here right now. Live for the day all your wildest dreams come true. Live for all the endless possibilities in this lifetime. Live for today, here and now, even when times are tough, because there are so many reasons to keep going.

THE UNLEARNING

We should not fear death. We should fear not truly living and being alive.

The fear of death is misdirected. Your soul isn't scared of dying, for it has been reborn many times. Your soul is eternal, there is nothing to fear. Life has no meaning without death. Death invites us to be truly alive, to savour every breath, to inhale more deeply, to savour every bite, to tune into your tastebuds, to savour every hug, to love more deeply, appreciate every hand hold and to enjoy the thrill of it all. Isn't it surreal to think about how you will never have this exact moment ever again?

On your death bed, you won't wish you'd worked more hours. You will wish you spent less time working and more time with your loved ones. On your death bed, you won't wish you were thinner. You will wish you appreciated your body more for its strength and grace. On your death bed, you won't wish you were just like everyone else. You will wish you stayed true to yourself and stood out from the masses. What you should be afraid of is never truly living… to have an unlived life.

Don't let it be a death that makes you truly realise life is precious. There is no guarantee in life except that you will die. This is death's greatest gift to us. Knowing this is an opportunity to live. Don't live in fear, live in love. Live with appreciation and gratitude. Live as though life is a training ground, embracing all the insights and experiences that come your way. Live in awe of all life's beauty and mystery. Live with power, pleasure and radiance. Live with the courage to speak from your heart. Live with fullness.

All life is asking of you to do is try and do your best in any given moment. No matter what happens, you've got a good heart. Even when you make mistakes. Even when you try your best and don't succeed. Even when you snap because you are angry and frustrated with the world. Even when you're annoyed at yourself and others. Even when you're caught up in an anxious loop. Even when you fall asleep with tears in your eyes. Even when you feel like a burden to everyone. Even when you are caught up in the past. Even when you feel stuck in your head and feel like you're making everything about you. Even when you doubt yourself. Even when you have a critical self-voice that says otherwise. It can be easy to forget, so this is a gentle reminder: you are loveable, and you are loved. You are trying your best and I see you.

Even when it feels like life is a tangled chaotic mess, it's all going to work out, beautiful soul. Loose ends will be tied. Stagnant energy will unravel to reveal a beautiful symphony. You will end up exactly where you need to be, as exactly who you are, doing exactly what you're meant to be doing, doing what you are supposed to do. Everything will align in your favour, trust the process, trust the journey, trust the timing. You deserve the light you yearn for. Hold on, beautiful soul, the darkness is temporary. All is conspiring in your favour.

I hope there are days when you fall in love with being alive. One day you're going to feel alive again and it will be worth it. Your cheeks will hurt from smiling so much. Your stomach will ache from how much you laugh. Your shoulders will be free from the aches and burdens of the world. You'll be dizzy with euphoria from riding high on life. Your eyes will sparkle like you've seen the world for the first time. Love will course through your veins and fill your heart. Your name will go down a treat like warm whisky on the lips of your lover. These days are coming and how beautiful they will be.

One of the most hauntingly inspiring things I've read is a quote by Les Brown, *'The graveyard is the richest place on earth, because it is here that you will find all the hopes and dreams that were never fulfilled, the books that were never written, the songs that were never sung, the inventions that were never shared, the cures that were never discovered, all because someone was too afraid to take that first step, keep with the problem, or determined to carry out their dream.'* Live life with no regrets.

So, what does happen in death? It is but another chapter in our soulful existence and experience. We transcend into a world unseen, live in ascended energetic frequencies and revel in new dimensions. You remain timeless, there is no yesterday and no tomorrow. Pain and suffering are replaced with peace. You will be free and liberated, to soar. Your physical body transforms into the soft brown earth that gives sustenance to the trees and life to the flowers that will grow. You will become the fierce roar of the sea and eternal rhythmic waves. You will become slivers of moonlight and speckles of sunlight. When people look up at the sky, people will see the stars that you have become. Living the dream continues into a new realm. A bigger dream. You will be cocooned in love. You will be surrounded and reunited with loved ones. You will help those you love still on earth. All the pieces of the jigsaw puzzle will come together. Your evolution continues. For now, until that day, I hope you truly live and feel alive, beautiful soul.

YOUR GREAT UNLEARNING

1. WEEKLY LIFE CHECK IN

The following check in provides a strong foundation to ensure you are not just living but truly alive in a conscious and deliberate manner.

- What are you taking for granted?
- What are you grateful for?
- Are you using the time that you have wisely in alignment with your values?
- Are you being your truest and most authentic self?
- What is life asking of you?
- What made you smile this week?

- What do you love about life right now?
- Perspective check—is your perspective right now serving you?

2. PURPOSE & LEGACY

One of my favourite series of questioning I like to ask a client is, 'If you were on your deathbed, what would you like to be remembered for? What do you want your grandchildren's children to hear about you? If you were to write your own obituary for how you have lived up until this moment, what would it say?'

3. MEMENTO MORI
(TRANSLATION: REMEMBER YOU MUST DIE, DEATH IS INEVITABLE)

The following prompts provide points of reflection regarding death.

- If you died tomorrow, would you have any regrets? Would you be proud of all that you've done and experienced thus far?
- How would you live knowing your death was imminent?
- What do you think happens when you die?
- Are you scared to die? Why or why not?
- What are healthy thoughts about death and what are some that do not serve you?
- Are you living and loving to the best of your ability?
- Imagine you are on the brink of death watching the movie of your life. How does it play out ruled by fear? How does it play governed by love?
- What is the legacy you will leave behind? What will be written on your epitaph (tombstone)?
- How do you want your body treated when you pass?
- What rites and ceremonies do you want performed when you do pass?
- Do you have thoughts about your ideal way to pass? When? Where? How?
- How does your age impact your passing, whether it's right now, in ten years, in twenty years?

- Are you willing to die for a cause?
- How can you prepare yourself for death?
- How can you treasure life more and savour its sweetness?

THE END...OF THESE CHAPTERS

Twenty-nine chapters and twenty-nine years of life. Thank you for joining me on this wild ride. Writing this book has been so cathartic and healing for me and my ancestors on so many levels. This book is a love letter to my life and all it has been up until this point.

I am so grateful for you, the beautiful soul reading this. My heart is so full of love and appreciation. Thank you.

We are taught so many things, but some things are best unlearned and forgotten. It's never too late to unlearn nor is it too early. I feel the initiations that are taking place inside of you. The push and pull. The tension and tenacity. I know this journey can be tough at times, and you may feel like you won't make it to the end of the day. It is my hope you will make it through. How many times have we thought we could not do something only to do it successfully!

I hope you unlearn and remember who you really are: powerful, wild and free. A child of the universe made in the image and depth of divinity. You are a unique experience and dimension of the universe itself. A part of the collective, you are so loved and supported. Know that whatever you are currently unlearning does not constrict you or define you. There are so many roads for you to take to return home to who you really are. Give yourself the space and time you need to release all the old narratives you've accumulated in your life. They get so heavy. You can let go.

I hope you know that you are brave. Congratulations for doing the work. The work is not for the faint-hearted. To face yourself and your fears. To dive into the depths of your heart and soul. I hope you celebrate who you are in this very moment. I hope you celebrate who you will unbecome.

We all want to be the butterfly, not the caterpillar. Interestingly enough, did you know the average life span of a butterfly is two-four weeks? We are so focused on the transformation, the metamorphosis and end result. To be a butterfly is to continually transform and die, it is the cycle, and the cycle will continue. To give way to the new parts of your being. The rise and rebirth. There is no rush, everything unfolds in perfect timing as it should. Waves of uncertainty and pain shall pass. It's in these times we are called to anchor deeper into our heart and soul. To love. To have compassion and patience for when the tides turn in your favour, you will emerge in full bloom. Know that even after your death, inevitably there will be new life.

For this very reason, the symbol of the phoenix came through for the cover, journey and embodiment of this book. Your soul is forged in the depths of despair and fires of life. No matter how painful, you inevitably rise, time and time again. Even through the darkness, your light is a vision. May the flames around you burn away layers of learning that no longer serve you. May the ashes serve you as a reminder of your continual death and rebirth—your great unlearning. May you be bold in the pursuit of what sets your heart and soul on fire.

This story is mine and mine solely, who knows what will unfold next. Though I have a strong feeling this book will be one of many I will go onto write. I hope through your great unlearning you decide in this moment that you are the writer of your very own story. Trust the next chapter of your life, because you are the author. You have the power to change your life and self at any given moment always. If nobody else tells you, I am so proud of you. I hope you are proud of yourself too.

Love & Positivity,

Phi

ACKNOWLEDGEMENTS

I wouldn't be here without these people, my support network. Thank you for always being here for me and supporting me.

To my mum, Rita (Nguyet), for all your love and encouragement. I know you've sacrificed so much for me to have a good life and I am so grateful. I'm in awe of your strength and capacity for love. You mean the world to me.

To my other mum, Trang, thank you for all your love, support and guidance. I am so grateful and appreciative to have you in my life.

A huge thank you to my publisher, Natasha, at the kind press. Your encouragement, support and belief in me from the first moment we spoke means so much to me. Working with you has been a soulful partnership that feels aligned on an energetic and heart level.

To my higher spiritual council—ascended masters, spirit guides (past, present and future), loved ones on the other side, intergalactic beings, to those who love and support me unconditionally, thank you.

My friends who really are my family—Abi, Dani, Georgia, Sonia, Kevin, Sim, Niall, Brian, Vince, Julie (Juju), Ainslie, Alena, Meg, Mollie, Steph, Kate, Shirley, Elisa, Emma, Nat, Marina, Marlan, Tom, Daniel, Patrick, Yas, Japna, Mili, Ellie, Carrie, Ash and George.

To my family and cousins Jackie, Viv, Vicky, Andrew, Ann, Andrew (AP), Cheryl, Jarren and Marty. The next generation: Alyssa, Austin, Connor, Ethan and my future children.

To all the beautiful souls who've played a pivotal role in my wild ride of becoming a full-time life coach and published author—Tiff, Kristina, Charlotte, Paige, Tameera, Patti, Anita and Jordanna.

To everyone I've crossed paths with for making a profound impact on my life.

To the men I've dated and loved—thank you for making my heart stronger and wiser.

To my beautiful clients: past, present and future whether through 1:1 coaching or a human design reading, it's an honour to support you—my deepest love and gratitude.

To my Instagram community, all those who follow @thephidang—I see you. Thank you for supporting me whether it's a like, share, comment or message it truly makes my heart so full. I appreciate you so much.

KEEP ON UNLEARNING

Thank you for going on this journey with me. I invite you to go deeper and discover more offerings to continue the work as well as to inspire and motivate you to live your best life.

Work with Me

1:1 Coaching - www.phidang.com/work-with-phi-dang/
Book a human design reading - www.phidang.com/human-design/

Get on the list

Be the first to know about my teachings and latest news by signing up for my newsletter at www.phidang.com/newsletter

Stay in touch

 phidang.com
 @thephidang
 Grow Through It Podcast With Phi Dang
 hi@phidang.com

ABOUT THE AUTHOR

Phi Dang is the first-generation born Australian daughter of brave refugees who serendipitously met on a boat fleeing the Vietnam War. Her name is pronounced Fee, which means flying high in Vietnamese. This is aptly, given time again, she has risen from challenging life circumstances including the heartbreaking loss of her dad at the young age of twenty. In 2021, she became part of 'The Great Resignation' turning her passion for mental health into a side hustle whilst climbing the corporate career ladder. Within a year, Phi went full-time, hitting six figures and is now a highly sought-after Human Design Life Coach.

Phi has the unique ability to speak to your soul in a relatable way. As such her posts on Instagram are well known to reach millions organically. She helps women and men all over the world through her Soul R(e)volution approach of mindset, self-love, energy and purpose resulting in life-changing breakthroughs and transformations.

Through Phi's practical expert guidance and intuitive insights, she helps her clients in all areas of life: starting and scaling a business, career, love, confidence, grief, heartbreak, family, friendships, happiness and more. You can work with Phi through 1:1 coaching, group programs or a human design reading. She is based on one of Australia's most iconic beaches in Sydney, taking appointments in person and globally online.

www.ingramcontent.com/pod-product-compliance
Lightning Source LLC
Chambersburg PA
CBHW020315010526
44107CB00054B/1849